Gangrene and Glory

Gangrene and Glory

Medical Care during the American Civil War

Frank R. Freemon

Madison • Teaneck
Fairleigh Dickinson University Press
London: Associated University Presses

Associated University Presses
440 Forsgate Drive
Cranbury, NJ 08512

Associated University Presses
16 Barter Street
London WC1A 2AH, England

Associated University Presses
P.O. Box 338, Port Credit
Mississauga, Ontario
Canada L5G 4L8

The paper used in this publication meets the requirements
of the American National Standard for Permanence of Paper
for Printed Library Materials Z39.48-1984.

Library of Congress Cataloging-in-Publication Data

Freemon, Frank R., 1938–
      Gangrene and glory : medical care during the American Civil War /
Frank R. Freemon.
          p.   cm.
      Includes bibliographical references and index.
      ISBN 0-8386-3753-1 (alk paper)
      1. United States—History—Civil War, 1861–1865—Medical care.
2. Medicine, Military—United States—History—19th century.
I. Title.
      [DNLM: 1. Military Medicine—history.   2. War—history—United
States.   3. History of Medicine, 19th Cent.—United States.   E 621
F855g 1998]
E621.F84   1998
973.7'75—dc21
DNLM/DLC
for Library of Congress   97-42816
                                                                                            CIP

PRINTED IN THE UNITED STATES OF AMERICA

Contents

Prologue

THE CAPTURE OF AFRICANS AND THEIR SALE AS slaves had been outlawed throughout the Western world for many decades. The navies of the world patrolled the sea lanes looking for miscreants still involved in the slave trade. Even on the very eve of the great American Civil War, a United States naval vessel patrolling off the coast of the African continent came on and captured the ship *Nightingale* loading captured Africans near the mouth of the Congo River. The U.S. Navy placed a small crew aboard the *Nightingale* and it headed for Liberia to free the 931 Africans who were chained in its hold. The prize crew consisted of three officers (one of whom was ill), six marines, and twenty-five sailors, but no medical officer. In Liberia, 801 Africans were debarked; the fate of the missing 130 was not specified in the official report; they may have died and been thrown overboard. A terrible fever began among the crew even before the vessel arrived at Liberia. The official report of the commanding officer describes the mysterious epidemic:

The African ship fever made its appearance on board, and several of the prize crew, as well as Lieutenant Hays and myself, suffered from it. On the 3rd of May, 1861, John Edwards, landsman, departed this life. His remains were committed to the deep, decomposition following death so closely in this case that I deemed it advisable to throw overboard his bedding, etc., to remove their contagious influence. On the 7th of May, about 10 PM, we anchored near Monrovia, Liberia, and on the following day landed the recaptured Africans. The President of Liberia very kindly tendered to me any aid in his power, either official or personal, and by means of his prompt and efficient cooperation the landing was effected in so short a space of time.

After filling up with water and purifying the ship we sailed from Monrovia for New York, about 4 PM, Monday, May 13. Our crew had become so debilitated and sickly from the effects of the climate and from continued labors and exposures that it became very difficult to carry sail and manage a ship of this size (1,066 tons). At one time there were only 7 on duty, 3 in one watch and 4 in the other. On the 17th of May, Michael Redmond (marine) departed this life. His remains were committed to the deep. On the 20th of May, Henry Nagle (ordinary seaman) departed this life. His remains were duly committed to the deep. Both cases were malignant. Shortly after this the fever began to subside, and these are all the casualties which it is my painful duty to remand.

The remainder of the cruise was without important incidents. At 12:30 last night made Barnegat light, bearing W. by N., distant about 17 miles. At 2:30 received on board a New York pilot. At 10:30 came to off the quarantine ground and was boarded by the health officer and quarantined, where we remain.

Very respectfully, your obedient servant,
John Julius Guthrie, Lieutenant, U.S. Navy[1]

His duty to the U.S. Navy now complete, Guthrie resigned his naval officer's commission and went South.

Acknowledgements

THIS WORK IS BASED ON MY DOCTORAL DISSERTATION at the University of Illinois, Urbana. I thank my committee: O. Vernon Burton, Evan M. Melhado, and Daniel C. Littlefield. I have been working on this book for more than a decade and have incorporated papers from seminars led by these advisers: Frederick C Jaher of the University of Illinois for the section on nurses, William S. Peterson for the military analysis of why the North won, David Carlton of Vanderbilt University for the survey of Confederate medical administration, Wayne Cutler of the University of Tennessee for the review of Hammond's court martial, and Clark Spence of the University of Illinois for prewar U.S. Army medicine. Robert Johannsen advanced the idea of presenting history by withholding knowledge from the reader that was not available to participants. I thank the following individuals for reading over parts of the work: Edward B. Davis of Messiah College, Grantham, Pennsylvania; J. Patrick O'Leary of the Louisiana State University School of Medicine; and Robert H. Alford and John Tarpley of Vanderbilt University. Brandon Lunday took the excellent photographs and Ann Rees and Mary Margaret Peel drew the maps. I also thank Peter J. D'Onofrio, Alex Peck, William D. Sharpe, and Mary Teloh for encouragement at key moments during my study of Civil War medicine. The Department of Veterans Affairs provided sabbatical time to write this work, despite the fact that we did not see many Civil War veterans at our institution.

Most of all I thank my wife.

List of Tables

Introduction

Have you ever returned from a long trip to find that your freezer went haywire during your absence? As you stand on your front step, you notice just the whiff of a strange odor. When you open the door, you are frightened by the unpleasant smell of rotting meat. You make your way to the freezer, but each step is more difficult because of the growing assault upon your nostrils. You throw open the freezer and almost swoon because of the overwhelming stench. You quickly shut the freezer and stagger away, gagging.

If you had visited a Civil War hospital, you might have suffered a similarly unpleasant experience. But you could not stagger away, wondering who would clean up this mess. During the American Civil War, the rotting flesh was attached to real, living human beings. You had to suppress your nausea and press forward to visit the sick. If you were a doctor or nurse, you had to steel yourself to treat the unfortunate victim.

If this book fulfills its mission, the reader will see the same gore and smell the same putrefaction as the doctors in blue and gray saw and smelled. Take home this message: the American Civil War involved suffering. The degree of suffering overwhelms all military glory. The exhilaration of battle dissipates under the load of fever, diarrhea, maggots, blood, dysentery, blindness, pain, pus, and putrefaction.[1]

If the reader has a medical background, he or she can appreciate this work as a series of medical mysteries. How could the pus from a patient's wound transfer its virulence to a cut on the surgeon's finger? How does yellow fever spread from a ship in the harbor to afflict people on shore, when no person ever leaves the ship? What is this horrible new disease, never seen by any doctor in the area before, which takes a man from normal at breakfast, to feverish at noon, to prostrate with spots all over his body at supper, to dead by nightfall? What is causing the strange epidemics that afflict and paralyze armies? The text only gives information available to the doctors of the era, thereby attempting to avoid the most common defect of medical history: judging historical individuals by later standards. The author will not afflict the reader with modern medical concepts (don't peek at the endnotes). In this way, the present work adopts the method of Thomas Connelly, whose works on Confederate military leadership give to the reader only information known to the Confederate commander.[2]

The structure of this work intersperses narrative with a series of anecdotes. In this respect, the book is modeled after James Michener's *Tales of the South Pacific;* the author doubts, however, whether any Broadway mogul will be able to adapt this story into a musical stage play. Each chapter is written from a different viewpoint; things happen in parallel rather than in a linear fashion. Gettysburg is described from the viewpoint of the wounded soldier lying on the ground, looking at the sun through a haze of gunsmoke. He only knows the actions of his own regiment and where upon his body is the wound. That is all the information the reader possesses. The Vicksburg campaign, on the other hand, is written as if it were a scientific paper, analyzing the causes of illness, but using only contemporary medical knowledge. When Confederate activities are described, the Northern forces are the enemy, the invading

Yankee. When the perspective changes to the North, the opposing Confederates are the rebels. When this work refers to the first major battle of the War, chapters maintaining the Southern viewpoint call it the Battle of Manassas; chapters that see the War through Union eyes refer to the Battle of Bull Run. When the narrative relates events prior to August 1862, the terms First Manassas or First Bull Run are not used because no one knew there would be a Second.

Interspersed with these anecdotes and analyses are the events that encompass the growth, development, and trials of two similar but independent medical organizations. Both were designed to improve the health of the soldier and aid the wounded. Some aspects of the Confederate medical system, such as Chimborazo Hospital, represented the best in nineteenth-century medicine, but the later chapters describe the agonizing decline of the Confederate medical organization. Union medicine surpassed its Southern counterpart at several key points and may have helped the North win the War.

The author hopes to build upon the explanatory classics, *Doctors in Blue* and *Doctors in Gray*.[3] These works described Union and Confederate doctors, nurses, and hospitals as they existed during the American Civil War. History, however, is not an object, but a process; this work attempts to show how medical thought and institutions changed over the course of the War. Do not expect the chapter on the introduction of women nurses, for example, to say everything about this topic, as one would find in an explanatory history. Women nurses are not a separate entity, to be analyzed fully at one sitting and then discarded; rather, they will appear at many points in this book, trying to help the sick and the wounded. Although this book uses many quotations, all are from individuals who claim to have heard the exact words spoken; this work contains absolutely no fictional elements.[4]

On yet another level, this work can be read to study the reactions of individuals under stress. In the very first chapter the reader meets a series of obscure physicians serving in the U.S. Army. Their reports from scattered and isolated military posts are a mixture of confused bias against Indians and blacks with brilliant observations about health conditions. Some of these individuals the reader will never hear from again; others will reappear later in the book directing the medical fortunes of great armies. In war, you meet an interesting character, but in a just a moment that person is gone. You never know if you will meet again. The reader of this book will face the same uncertainty.

This is the story of imperfect human beings, struggling to save lives and support their respective causes, fighting the enemy, fighting their superiors, fighting against strange afflictions that defy understanding. Always ask yourself, Do the actions of the historical person make a difference to their armies, to their respective nations, to the way we live today? Around such mundane items as quarantine and quinine, great nations rise and fall. Healthy armies win, sick armies wither away, one nation disappears, and another survives the searing heat of fratricidal war to forge a steel Union.

Abbreviations

Abbreviations used in the tables and notes:

MSH *The Medical and Surgical History of the War of the Rebellion* was published by the Surgeon General's office, U.S. Army, from 1875 to 1885. The first three volumes, called the Medical Volume, were written by J. J. Woodward and Charles Smart. The last three, called the Surgical Volume, were written by George A. Otis and D. L. Huntington. This work has been reproduced with a full index by Broadfoot Publishing, Wilmington N.C., under the title *The Medical and Surgical History of the Civil War.*

OR *The War of the Rebellion: A Compilation of the Official Records of the Union and Confederate Armies* was published by the U.S. War Department beginning in 1888. This collection of reports and orders, gathered under the direction of Robert N. Scott and Henry M. Lazelle, officially fills 128 volumes in four series. Many of the volumes are broken into two or more parts so that the actual number of books approaches 200. If not otherwise indicated, the volume quoted is from the first series.

ORN *The Official Records of the Union and Confederate Navies in the War of the Rebellion* was published by the U.S. Navy Department from 1894 to 1922. These naval reports and orders were compiled in thirty volumes by Richard Ruch and Robert H. Woods.

Identification of regiments: During the Civil War, the dominant military organizational element was the regiment. Each regiment is referred to by number and state. Cavalry and artillery are specified; if no type of arm is indicated, the regiment is infantry. For example, the 6th Indiana is the 6th Indiana Infantry Regiment, U.S. Volunteers. The 4th United States is the 4th Infantry Regiment, U.S. Army (called the regular army). If the same state had regiments fight for both sides, then the side is in parentheses. The 1st South Carolina (Union) was formed of former slaves; in February 1864 it was redesignated the 33rd regiment, U.S.C.T. (U.S. Colored Troops).

SOURCE ABBREVIATIONS FOR ILLUSTRATIONS:

Holland: Mary A. Holland, *Our Army Nurses*, Boston: B. Wilkins and Co., 1897.

HW: *Harper's Weekly.*

Miller: Francis Miller, *Photographic History of the Civil War*, New York: Review of Books, 1911.

MSH: *Medical and Surgical History of the War of the Rebellion.*

NA: National Archives, Washington, DC

NLM: National Library of Medicine, Washington, DC

USAMHI: U.S. Army Military History Institute, Carlisle, PA

Gangrene and Glory

1

American Medicine in the 1850s

THE EXHAUSTED HORSEMAN RODE INTO THE ISO-lated post at Fort Buchanan, New Mexico Territory, with terrifying news. Cochise and six hundred braves had surrounded the fortified mail station at Apache Pass and threatened to massacre its defenders. The post surgeon, Dr. Bernard J. D. Irwin, was the only officer on hand to respond to this startling information. He dispersed messengers to the other small forts nearby with orders to concentrate the regiment. In the meantime, Dr. Irwin determined to take all available military force to reinforce the defenders of the mail station and cheer them with the news that relief was on the way. Leading fourteen volunteer soldiers and one civilian, he rode two hundred miles without rest, part of the way through a blinding snowstorm. This group fought their way into the isolated mail station; the reinforced garrison held out until the full regiment arrived and drove away the Indians.[1]

This is an unusual—almost a unique—incident, for doctors in the U.S. Army in the 1850s seldom led troops. They treated the minor illnesses of soldiers, bound the occasional wound, and made observations about the conditions around them. A medical career in the army involved many years at the entry rank of assistant surgeon, equal in pay to a lieutenant. Eventually, the assistant surgeon could undergo examination to rise to the rank of surgeon, sometimes called major surgeon because it was equal in pay to a major. The U.S. Navy had so few places for doctors that a third rank was formed, that of passed assistant surgeon. The doctor holding this rank was an assistant surgeon who had passed his examination for the rank of surgeon but had not yet been promoted; he had to wait for someone bearing the higher rank to die or to retire.[2]

Army physicians encountered different diseases depending on the part of the nation where they were stationed. Malaria occurred frequently in the military forts located along the coastal areas of the South, but was also prevalent in many other locations. In one year, Fort Buchanan in New Mexico Territory experienced 450 episodes of malaria in its garrison of 243 soldiers. The disease showed a marked seasonal variation, from a low of 3 new cases in May to highs of 95 in September and 139 in October (autumn was the sickly season). Dr. Irwin thought that the high rate of malaria was caused by the proximity of the fort to swamps and quagmires. He further noted that one group of fort residents had been entirely free from malaria because they were "protected from the influence of the marsh by a small knoll, which acted as a kind of screen to shelter them from the carrying influence of the southwest wind."[3]

The chief army doctor, Surgeon General Thomas Lawson, asked all U.S. Army doctors to report their experiences with the new drug quinine. He had read European medical reports concerning this agent, obtained from the bark of South American cinchona trees, suggesting that it might be able to ameliorate the symptoms of malaria. Their responses confirmed the value of quinine, saying that it often had to be given in high dosage, up to thirty grains per day. Assistant Surgeon David C. DeLeon thought that quinine was especially

Lafayette Guild in the late 1850s was an assistant surgeon in the U.S. Army, assigned to the quarantine station at the port of New York. NLM

valuable in the South. The constitution of Southerners was different from Northerners, he thought, and Southerners certainly required quinine when they contracted malaria. In his report to the surgeon general, Dr. De-Leon complained that too many doctors who practiced medicine in the South had attended medical schools in the North, a region with different climate and sicknesses than the South.

Military forts in port cities were likely to undergo the terror of yellow fever. This disease, often fatal, broke out suddenly after a ship bearing an infected sailor arrived at the port. In some ports, ships with feverish sailors were kept at a quarantine station, but U.S. Army doctor Lafayette Guild found that the disease could spread from the quarantine station to military posts and civilian establishments on the shore. Yellow fever appeared at New York harbor in 1856 and was closely observed by Dr. Guild, post surgeon on Governor's Island. By studying who was affected, Guild drew the conclusion that "morbific elements of the disease" were carried by the wind from ships at the quarantine station to the shore. He could not imagine what these causative elements were that could travel on the wind.

U.S. Army soldiers in the Far West sometimes developed scurvy. Soldiers subsisting on bread and hardtack, occasionally varied with fresh meat but without vegetables, developed listlessness and fatigue. They noted how easily their skin was bruised and how poorly the bruises healed. Full-blown scurvy could produce dangerous bleeding complications. If fresh vegetables could be obtained, all these symptoms were reversed in just a few days.

Contemporary medical knowledge recognized that scurvy was a disease produced by nutritional deficit. In the terminology developed by William Farr of Britain, and adapted by the U.S. Army, scurvy was a "dietetic disease." In the previous century, James Lind of the British Navy had prevented scurvy on long voyages by feeding sailors oranges or limes. Limes became so closely associated with the British Navy and merchant fleet that its sailors were called "limeys." But it was difficult to keep citrus fruits for long voyages, so naval authorities attempted to obtain an antiscorbutic principle that could be stored. Various citrus extracts did not prove as successful as fresh limes and oranges. By 1860 the entire concept relating citrus fruits to scurvy prevention had become muddled.

The scurvy epidemic at Fort Laramie, Kansas Territory, in 1858 provides an example of the problems physicians faced in supplying a nutritious diet. Assistant Surgeon Edward W. Johns was the doctor in charge of the post; he reported several cases of scurvy. He attributed this to many factors, including monotony, but the main cause was that the troops subsisted upon desiccated vegetables. Johns thought that "some of the components of vegetable food in its natural state are necessarily, from the course of preparation, lost."

Surgeon General Lawson referred this problem to the Commissary Department, the section of the army responsible for supplying food. The troops at Fort Laramie, he reported, in order to maintain their health, needed fresh, not desiccated vegetables. The laconic reply of the supply officers showed their disdain for medical opinion: "Attempts have on several occasions been made by this department to forward potatoes, fresh, to Fort Laramie from Fort Leavenworth, but the loss and decay has been so great as to make the expense for the benefit conferred, very heavy. On this occasion it was deemed the less necessary, as that post was liberally supplied with desiccated mixed vegetables, and desiccated potatoes." The Medical Department said that scurvy occurred because only desiccated vegetables were available; the Commissary Department replied that scurvy could not really be a problem because the supply of desiccated vegetables was quite liberal.[4]

U.S. Army doctors tried to develop a dietary additive that could be more easily stored in isolated posts and carried by troops on the move. Assistant Surgeon William A. Hammond was the post surgeon at Fort Riley, Kansas Territory, when he performed a series of dietary experiments, using himself as his experimental subject. His published dietary studies earned him in 1857 the annual research award of the American Medical Association. Exhausted from his army duties and his self-experimentation, Hammond received a period of rest and study in Philadelphia, where he worked with a leading medical scientist, Silas Weir Mitchell.[5]

In addition to their efforts to prevent or cure diseases such as malaria, yellow fever, and

Silas Weir Mitchell was a young physician practicing medicine and performing research in Philadelphia. William A. Hammond studied with Mitchell in 1857. From Anna Robeson Burr, *Weir Mitchell*, New York: Duffield, 1929.

scurvy, U.S. Army doctors on the frontier treated gunshot wounds. Treatment involved dressing, and a considerable difference of opinion existed concerning the best dressing for an open wound. If the wound were small and very recent, the doctor might attempt to close it with suture. Most wounds were treated without any attempt at closure, however, and healing was a long process involving the slow growth of granulation tissue. If the bullet had caused a limb fracture, this was splinted. Occasionally, amputation was required. All wounds developed inflammation and drainage of pus. Medical science was just beginning to understand the nature of infectious diseases; pus could be carried from one wound to another or even from a wound to the doctor.

Dr. Irwin, the army surgeon at Fort Buchanan, New Mexico Territory, encountered a dangerously infective wound after he had returned from his defense of Apache Pass. A civilian had received a gunshot wound in the shoulder during an altercation with Apaches. Over a period of days, the wound filled with pus and the patient developed fever and prostration. Irwin determined that the patient's only hope of survival was a difficult operation—removing the entire arm at the shoulder joint. During the operation, Irwin pricked his own finger with the scalpel just after cutting across a pus-filled cavity. Over the ensuing days, the finger became red, hot, and swollen. It grew to immense size and one of Dr. Irwin's colleague's cut along the length of his finger to allow the pus to escape. Irwin survived (although his patient did not), but his finger was so badly damaged that he no longer possessed the dexterity to perform difficult surgical operations.

Army doctors also encountered arrow wounds. If the arrowhead remained in the body, an abscess formed, suppuration progressed to pyemia, and the patient died. In order to remove the arrowhead, the surgeon pushed his finger into the wound along the arrow shaft. He then snaked a long forceps along his guiding finger and took a strong purchase upon the embedded point. One army doctor described how he had great difficulty locating the arrowhead, but "at last I succeeded in grasping it tightly and, bracing my knees against the patient's thorax, I applied all the traction I could muster. Suddenly, the arrowhead flew out of its seat, and I would

have fallen to the floor had the steward not caught me."[6]

In every U.S. Army fort, the medical doctor was the only individual with any scientific training. He made observations on the climatic conditions of the area. Climate had medical application because of its relationship to health. But he also made many observations without any direct medical interest. He sent botanical and zoological specimens to the Smithsonian Institution in Washington. A few frontier doctors became leading ornithologists.

Irwin's report on the climate and surroundings of Fort Buchanan, written in February 1859, is a model of careful analysis. He first described the location and terrain surrounding the fort, built just the previous year. He described the climate (highest temperature recorded, 107 degrees Fahrenheit), the type of trees, and the plants and the mammals of the area. He had personally seen seventy different species of birds; his report lists each. He described fish, reptiles, and insects that he encountered in the New Mexico Territory. He directed the reader of the report to "the collection made at this place by me for the Smithsonian Institution."

In their reports of the geology, climate, flora, and fauna of the Western forts, Army doctors invariably described the local inhabitants in most unflattering terms. Irwin described the Apaches near Fort Buchanan as "a cowardly, treacherous, thieving race of Indians." Dr. Joseph K. Barnes thought that the Osage Indians living near Fort Scott, Kansas Territory, were "notoriously intemperate, and will deprive themselves of the actual necessaries of life to procure whisky." He attributed this drunkenness to prolonged association with the whites. Roberts Bartholow was not impressed with the peaceful Indians of Utah. They were, he said, "very debased, having none of the refined sentiments attributed to Indian heroes in Hiawatha." He went on to hypothesize that the Indians had "served their purpose in the social economy of humanity" and were now about to disappear; their extinction was, he thought, "an immutable law of nature."

The negative comments about residents near military compounds were not restricted to Indians. Fort Brown, located at the southern tip of Texas, just across the Rio Grande from Matamoras, Mexico, had been built in

1848. By the middle of the 1850s a large population of Mexicans lived near the fort in an area called Brownsville. The post surgeon, Dr. Samuel P. Moore, spoke disparagingly of these residents. "The Mexicans are a miserable race of beings," he said, "existing in squalid wretchedness in their foul cabins, very ignorant and superstitious." Assistant Surgeon Jonathan Letterman, writing from Fort Meade, near Tampa, Florida, noted that the white residents near the fort had sallow skin, protuberant bellies, and premature senility. He attributed this appearance to endemic malaria and to the habit, said to be common among these poor people, of eating clay.

As the medical officers of the U.S. Army struggled with these ongoing problems of military medicine, momentous events were occurring back east. Representatives of the seceded states were meeting in Montgomery, Alabama, to form a new government, which they called the Confederate States of America. Whether or not this new government represented an independent nation or only a rebellious portion of the United States of America was a determination that could only be decided by force of arms. The lives of all the doctors of what would soon be called the Old Army would be changed by these actions in the new capital of the Confederacy.

American medicine, like the American nation itself, threatened to break apart. The sectional conflict that disturbed the populace also tore at medicine. Many Southern doctors were trained at Northern medical schools, particularly those in Philadelphia, but they worried that medicine was truly sectional. As Dr. De-Leon had pointed out in his official report on quinine, Southern medical problems were not the same as those of the North; a different climate produced different diseases and different responses to the same disease. Northern academic physicians showed no interest in understanding, or even in examining, the medical problems of the huge slave population of the South. Some Southern physicians thought that blacks might experience different disease processes than whites. Some doctors developed world reputations for their knowledge of races. Josiah Nott of Mobile, Alabama, was famous throughout the world for his idea that blacks and whites had separate origins; John L. Cabell of the University of Virginia was one of the most vigorous opponents of this idea.[7]

In addition to clashes along sectional lines, American medicine of the 1850s groaned under other strains. Two worldviews competed to organize ideas about what made people sick and how could they best be treated. The old view held that a sick person could be restored to health by correcting an imbalance in his system. The new worldview emphasized the entity that caused the illness; a disease was a thing that existed externally to the person, spreading from one individual to another. A disease could be treated by a specific remedy that did not change the response of the individual to other diseases. Quinine came to be called a specific treatment, or just a "specific," because people suffering from malaria recovered when they took it, while quinine had no effect on other forms of fever.

This intellectual transition, from individual sufferer to external disease, was a worldwide phenomenon, but American medicine was undergoing a social change unique to the American condition. In the early days of the republic, few men held the degree of doctor of medicine. Those few had been trained in the great universities of Europe, most notably at Edinburgh. Under the influence of Jacksonian ideology, the idea that medical practitioners formed a professional elite had almost disappeared. Many new medical schools sprang up throughout the United States, but their educational rigor sank. The worst became merely a system to transfer fees from student to professor in exchange for a medical degree. Even the best schools lowered their standards in order to compete for students.

By the 1850s the typical medical practitioner had attended one set of lectures for five or six months, perhaps less, and then the following year he heard these same lectures again. He might have worked with a practicing doctor, a remnant of the old medical tradition, but he might have had no apprenticeship at all. America had more doctors but their quality had declined.[8] The best American physicians felt that they could obtain a complete medical education only in Europe. The sectional conflict in the United States spread to the American medical students abroad; classes were disrupted by clashes between students from the northern and the southern American states.[9]

Therapeutics remained wedded to the old worldview. In the absence of pharmaceutical

Table 1

American Medical Schools in 1860

Medical School	Location	Faculty	Students
Maine Medical School	Brunswick, ME	7	50
New Hampshire Medical School	Hanover, NH	6	50
Castleton Medical College	Castleton, VT	7	104
Med Dept, Univ of Vermont	Burlington, VT	6	49
Vermont Medical College	Woodstock, VT	8	91
Med School, Harvard Univ	Boston, MA	6	104
Berkshire Medical School	Pittsfield, MA	5	103
Med Institute, Yale College	New Haven, CT	6	34
College of Physicians & Surgeons	New York, NY	6	219
Med Institute, Geneva College	Geneva, NY	9	16
Med Faculty, Univ of New York	New York, NY	9	300
Albany Medical College	Albany, NY	8	114
Med Dept, Univ of Penna	Philadelphia	9	453
Jefferson Med College	Philadelphia	7	514
Med Dept, Pennsylvania College	Philadelphia	7	140
Philadelphia College of Med	Philadelphia	7	75
Med School, Univ of Maryland	Baltimore, MD	6	100
Washington Medical College	Baltimore, MD	6	25
National Med College, Columbia	Washington, DC	8	17
Med Dept, Georgetown College	Washington, DC	6	32
Med School, Univ of Virginia	Charlottesville	5	99
Med Dept, Hampden Sidney College	Richmond, VA	7	90
Winchester Med College	Winchester, VA	5	–
Med Dept, Univ of S Carolina	Charleston, SC	8	158
Med College of Georgia	Augusta, GA	7	115
Med Dept, Univ of Louisiana	New Orleans, LA	8	222
Med Dept, Univ of Nashville	Nashville, TN	8	436
Med Dept, East Tenn Univ	Knoxville, TN	8	–
Med Dept, Transylvania Univ	Lexington, KY	–	–
Med Dept, Univ of Louisville	Louisville, KY	–	–
Med Dept, Western Reserve	Cleveland, OH	6	160
Medical College of Ohio	Cincinnati, OH	8	130
Western College of Homeopathy	Cleveland, OH	8	62
Starling Medical College	Columbus, OH	8	124
Rush Medical College	Chicago, IL	6	70
Med Dept, Univ of Michigan	Ann Arbor, MI	7	143
Med Dept, St. Louis Univ	St. Louis, MO	9	125
Med Dept, Missouri Univ	Columbia, MO	7	103
Med Dept, State Univ	Keokuk, Iowa	6	80
Med Dept, State Univ	Madison, WI	6	–

Source: The American Almanac and Repository of Useful Knowledge for the Year 1860 (Boston: Crosby, Nichols, 1860), 209. Courtesy of Roger A. Rose.

techniques to produce medications of reliable strength, physicians had to treat until something immediately visible happened. If the patient had a shaking chill, the physician removed blood from his arm until the shaking stopped. If the patient had not had a bowel movement after a small dose of a physick, a larger dose was given. Following the lead of Benjamin Rush, the dominant Philadelphia physician at the turn of the century, doctors administered huge doses of powerful therapies. If the removal of blood from the patient's arm did not stop the fever, then more blood was removed. If the patient remained ill after calomel had produced a full evacuation of the bowels, then more calomel was given.

Leaders of the next medical generation rejected this heroic brand of medicine. Many diseases were self-limited; they ran a characteristic course unaffected by any available therapy. Oliver Wendell Holmes was speaking for this new viewpoint when he claimed that if all the medications in America were thrown into the sea, it would be better for the Americans and worse for the fish. One heroic idea, the use of bleeding to restore balance and health, gradually declined and had almost disappeared in America by 1860.[10] But many physicians continued to use huge doses of powerful medications, especially the mercury compound calomel. The loose standards of medical education and licensing had produced too many doctors; competition for the available patients led the practitioner to do something, anything, to show his capabilities.

Traditional medicine competed with a wide variety of healing arts. Homeopathy promised results from minute doses of drugs; botanic practitioners administered natural products; electrotherapeutics used galvanism; hydrotherapists applied water. Mainstream physicians referred to those who used these special forms of healing as sect practitioners or single-idea men.

Because the medical schools were turning out as many students as would pay the fees, the practice of medicine was financially shaky. Many doctors moved to an area of the country thought to be unhealthy, hoping that their medical expertise would be in demand. Some doctors were unable to make a living and gave up the practice of medicine. A few of these became noted in other fields: a dentist developed the Maynard rifle; a Southern physician used his botanic knowledge to patent a form of writing paper made from the okra plant.[11]

Southern doctors had an advantage when setting up a medical practice. A doctor could contract to treat a plantation family and all the plantation slaves for a fixed annual fee. This annual income provided a base to allow the development of traditional, fee-for-service practice. "Our laboring class is different from yours of the North," wrote a leading Savannah doctor to a Philadelphia colleague. "The interest, if no other motive, causes the master to obtain medical aid for his slave, and instead of looking to the laborer for his remuneration, the physician looks to the employer. This is the true reason why physicians get into practice more readily at the South than at the North, and that here he stands some chance of making his bread while he has teeth to chew it." By laboring class, the doctor meant slaves and by employer, slave owner.[12]

This difficulty expressing the human relationships under the system of slavery symbolizes the growing sectionalism that divided the nation into the North and the South. The people of the Southern states wanted to form a separate nation; the people of the North believed that the United States was a single, unbreakable nation. The conflict represented by these varying concepts of nationhood could only be decided by force of arms.

American medicine divided as did the nation. Both civilian and military doctors were called to provide medical care for the great armies that formed in 1861. The military doctors who had been lowly assistant surgeons serving a few soldiers at isolated posts were suddenly thrust into the unaccustomed role of medical directors of vast armies. Doctors North and South prepared themselves for epidemics and for carnage.

Table 2

U.S. Army Doctors Who Went South

Name	U.S.Army rank	Date (1861)	
Anderson, William W.	assistant surgeon	resigned	20 April
Berrien, James H.	assistant surgeon	resigned	17 March
Brewer, Charles	assistant surgeon	resigned	7 May
Brodie, Robert L.	assistant surgeon	resigned	7 May
Carswell, William A.	assistant surgeon	resigned	25 March
Covey, Edward N.	assistant surgeon	resigned	1 June
Crowell, Nathaniel S.	assistant surgeon	resigned	17 May
DeLeon, David C.	major surgeon	resigned	19 Feb.
Fauntleroy, Archibald	assistant surgeon	resigned	9 May
Foard, Andrew J.	assistant surgeon	resigned	1 April
Gaenslen, John J.	assistant surgeon	resigned	17 August
Guild, Lafayette	assistant surgeon	dismissed	1 July
Haden, John M.	assistant surgeon	resigned	25 April
Herndon, James C.	assistant surgeon	dropped	27 Nov.
Johns, Edward W.	assistant surgeon	resigned	22 April
Langworth, Elisha P.	assistant surgeon	resigned	30 April
Madison, Thomas C.	major surgeon	resigned	17 August
Moore, Samuel P.	major surgeon	resigned	25 Feb.
Potts, Richard	assistant surgeon	resigned	7 May
Ramseur, David P.	assistant surgeon	dismissed	17 August
Smith, Charles H.	assistant surgeon	resigned	25 April
Wall, Asa	assistant surgeon	resigned	11 May
Williams, Thomas H.	assistant surgeon	resigned	1 June

These military medical officers left the United States Army
and later joined the Confederate States Army.

Source: Francis B. Heitman, <u>Historical Register and Dictionary of
the United States Army from its Organization, September 29, 1789 to
March 2, 1903</u> (Washington D.C.: Government Printing Office, 1903),
vol 2, 180-84.

2
Creating Confederate Medicine

AT THE EXACT MOMENT THAT DR. IRWIN WAS fighting Cochise at Apache Pass, the representatives of the seceded states were meeting in Montgomery, Alabama, to form a new government. The Provisional Congress of the Confederate States of America established the general military staff of the new nation on 26 February 1861. The new military organization contained a Medical Department, consisting of a surgeon general, four surgeons, and six assistant surgeons. The new regulations stipulated that the surgeon general would hold a rank equivalent to colonel and would be paid $250 per month. Each surgeon was paid $162 per month; each assistant surgeon received $110 per month. These regulations were identical to those of the old U.S. Army.

The kernel of the new medical department of the Confederacy consisted of military physicians with experience in the U.S. Army, an organization now called simply the Old Army. Some physicians, such as David C. DeLeon, joined the Confederate Army immediately, even taking all available U.S. Army medical supplies with them. Other U.S. Army physicians from the South chose to leave military life altogether. Samuel P. Moore entered private practice in Little Rock, Arkansas. Lafayette Guild was promoted to the rank of surgeon by the U.S. Army; this new rank required that he again take the oath of allegiance to the United States. He could not take the oath, so he was dropped from the army rolls on 1 July 1861. He also "went South" to join the new Provisional Army of the Confederate States.

The Confederacy made its first medical er-

ror on 6 March 1861. The Provisional Congress organized the new Confederate Army, using the regulations of the old U.S. Army as a guide. Unfortunately, the copyist let his eye wander and left out the medical officers. The U.S. regulations are given below; the Confederate regulations were exactly the same except that the words in italics were missing:

> Each regiment of infantry shall consist of one colonel, one lieutenant-colonel, one major, *one surgeon, one assistant surgeon,* and ten companies. Each company shall consist of one captain, one first lieutenant, two second lieutenants, four corporals, two musicians, and 90 privates.

According to official army regulations, no regiment would have any medical officers. The entire Confederate Army would contain only eleven doctors, all working in the surgeon general's office. Most authorities who raised regiments, however, conformed more to tradition than to regulations and included regimental doctors. Many young physicians entered the ranks as privates, hoping to defend their new nation with arms; they often found themselves pressed into service as regimental surgeons because the Confederacy needed their medical skills more than their military ones.[1]

The Confederate government, overwhelmed with the unprecedented task of creating itself, was slow to form the headquarters of the army medical department. In his report to President Jefferson Davis, submitted on 27 April 1861, Secretary of War Leroy Walker had to admit that "the medical department of the Regular Army has not yet been organized, chiefly from the fact that up to this time only a small proportion of its officers have been appointed." This report stimulated President Davis to appoint a surgeon general: David C. DeLeon.

Dr. DeLeon came from a prominent South Carolina family, members of the large Charleston Jewish community. He had received the best American medical education of his day at the University of Pennsylvania. Despite his education in Philadelphia, DeLeon had developed the conviction that doctors who practiced in the South should be educated in the South; the climate and the ethnic cultures of North and South were quite different, he thought.

DeLeon resigned his medical commission in the U.S. Army on 19 February but was not officially accepted into Confederate service until 16 March and was not appointed to the top medical post until 6 May. Even before his official appointment, however, DeLeon was considered to be in charge of Confederate medical affairs. With other officers, he rented a house in Montgomery and arranged for board; the nickname of this organization of top Confederate military officials was the Ranche.[2]

Dr. DeLeon began helping the Confederate medical service even before it was created. After submitting his resignation to the U.S. Army, but while still on duty at the military hospital in New Orleans, he wrote to Jefferson Davis, asking him what to do with all the medical supplies under his control. DeLeon and Davis looked upon the Confederacy as a continuation of part of the United States; therefore, a portion of the material possessions of the United States should be transferred to the Confederate States government. Davis directed DeLeon to send his military medical supplies to the large Confederate military force gathering around Fort Pickens, Florida.

Fort Pickens and Fort Sumter were Federal outposts located within the borders of the new country. If the Confederacy was to exercise sovereignty over its own territory, these forts should be transferred to the control of the new government. If the United States would not turn them over peacefully, then the Confederate States government would take these installations by military force. While DeLeon prepared to handle casualties from the storming of Fort Pickens, his plans were superseded by unexpected events at Fort Sumter. Lincoln announced that the fort in Charleston harbor would be resupplied. The Confederate government considered this an act of war, and began artillery bombardment of the U.S. bastion. The U.S. Army surgeon on duty in the fort, Dr. Samuel W. Crawford, became one of its most vigorous defenders. He was frequently seen above the ramparts, supervising the loading and firing of the huge cannon. He barely escaped injury when one of the cannon was dislodged from its parapet and crashed down into the center of the fort. Union soldiers were seriously injured when a cannon exploded during the formal surrender ceremony; they were taken to Charleston and treated by Southerners until they could be evacuated to the North.

The firing on Fort Sumter plunged the confused country into civil war. For America, this became *the* Civil War. When President Abraham Lincoln enlarged the U.S. (soon to be called the Union) Army to subdue the rebellion, other slave states seceded. The Confederate capital was moved from Montgomery to Richmond, Virginia. DeLeon transferred his medical supplies from the area of Fort Pickens to Richmond and began to organize the surgeon general's office.

DeLeon had a very small nucleus of military medical expertise to build upon. In addition to the twenty-three military surgeons who had resigned from the U.S. Army, the South acquired three doctors who had been surgeons of the U.S. Navy and three civilians with some military medical experience. Two Richmond physicians, St. George Peachy and E. J. Ethridge had medical experience from the Crimean War. John J. Chisholm, who held the chair of surgery at the Medical School of South Carolina, had in 1859 visited the hospitals in Milan, Italy, that held the wounded from the battles of Magenta and Solferino.

Everyone thought that the War would be short. The Confederate Congress only appropriated $350,000 for the medical service; this sum was supposed to provide for the activities of one year. DeLeon used this money to acquire several of the largest buildings in Richmond to be used as hospitals. The City Alms House on the north side of town was outfitted for medical use and christened Hospital Number 1. The Richmond Female Institute became Hospital Number 4. The large warehouse on the corner of Grace and 17th Streets, Seabrook's, became Hospital Number 9, and the United States Hotel became Hospital Number

The Richmond City Alms House was located at the end of Second Street on the northern outskirts of town. As one of the largest buildings in the city, it was converted into a hospital at the very start of the War, becoming Confederate Hospital Number 1. The doctor in charge was Charles Bell Gibson. The nursing staff were Catholic nuns from Baltimore; the chief nurse was Sister Valentine. USAMHI

10. These hospitals were expected to handle the wounded from the anticipated great battle that might determine the outcome of the War.

The Confederate Army concentrated around the small north Virginia town of Manassas. Separating these troops from the gathering Union forces was a small stream called Bull Run. The great battle occurred on Sunday, 21 July. Most people believed that this would be the only major battle of the War; independence or submission depended upon the outcome. DeLeon and his staff, along with the rest of the people of Richmond, awaited news of the result. Trains pulled into Richmond from the North, bearing unreliable and contradictory news. Finally, President Jefferson Davis returned from Manassas to announce that the South had, through the grace of God, won the decisive Battle of Manassas. But victory bore a heavy price; great generals such as Bee and Bartow had been killed.

Each subsequent train from Manassas carried a further payment for that victory. The first trains carried those individuals who had been mildly injured, or had been disabled by vigorous marching; they traveled sitting in passenger cars. Later trains carried the more seriously wounded lying in freight cars. All day on Monday and all that night trains kept coming into Richmond, jammed with groaning wounded. Each train seemed to carry more horribly wounded soldiers, those hardest to evacuate from the field of battle. No one knew if this train bore the final contingent of the seriously wounded, or if another train would soon arrive, bringing soldiers even more terribly mangled.

Some wounds had not been dressed. Pus oozed between layers of macerated detritus. Dressings that had been applied were dry; a hard crust irritated the open edges of the wound beneath. Some injured soldiers had been unceremoniously thrown into boxcars, where they lay unattended. No medical or nursing personnel accompanied the wounded during the rail evacuation; many received no sustenance during the long trip.

The hospitals that had been so carefully prepared by Dr. DeLeon were filled in just a few hours. Many beds were already occupied by individuals who had developed measles or other camp diseases while undergoing military training. The hospitals were full, but the trains bearing hundreds of wounded Confederates kept coming. The citizens of Richmond made up for the lack of medical preparation. They waited at the railroad station, searching for a wounded soldier or officer whom they knew. A private citizen would carry this individual to his or her home and care for him. Of course, the great majority of the wounded came from cities other than Richmond and from Confederate states other than Virginia. Many citizens took charge of one or several wounded soldiers whom they had never seen before; they cared for them in their homes as if they were members of the family. The citizens soaked the dressings and gently removed them. The family doctor, not a military doctor, redressed the wound and the family tried to nurse the patient back to health.

Many sick and wounded were transferred to other cities. The nearby university town of Charlottesville became a major medical center. Most of the buildings on the campus of the University of Virginia were fitted out as hospital wards and the medical faculty of the university became the nucleus of the staff of this new Confederate medical facility. The commander of the hospital was professor John L. Cabell, who retained his appointment on the university faculty, but at a decreased salary. In the first month of its existence, the hospital admitted 656 soldiers with measles and 300 with gunshot wounds. Eight of the soldiers stricken with measles died; 35 of the 300 wounded died of their wounds.[3]

The ordeal of a Confederate private illustrates what happened to a typical wounded soldier. On 21 July 1861 Private J. H. Wolf was shot while serving with the 4th Virginia Infantry Regiment at the Battle of Manassas. As he was marching forward, a bullet entered his right thigh. The bullet tore through his leg, shattering the femur; he immediately dropped to the ground. The assistant surgeon of the 4th

Virginia wrapped a dressing around his leg. The femur had been completely separated so that his right leg below the wound dangled uselessly. Hurrying to catch up to his advancing regiment, the doctor left Wolf lying alone on the battlefield. Passersby carried him to Manassas, where he waited all day for transportation to Richmond. He was placed upon the floor of a boxcar. The train moved very slowly southward, but the two ends of the crushed bone rubbed together every time the car swayed. Upon arrival in Richmond, Wolf was placed in a small hospital in the city. He was fed and his dressing changed.

In order to make room for more wounded expected from the battlefield, Wolf was carried back to the railroad station and shipped to Charlottesville. He was admitted to a ward that had been a classroom of the University of Virginia. Dr. Edward Warren examined Wolf; smelly pus oozed from the tissues through holes in the skin. Dr. Warren explained to Wolf that he had to amputate his leg above the site of the femur fracture. He informed the soldier that high femur amputations were usually fatal. Wolf was anesthetized with chloroform and his leg was amputated on 21 August 1861; he died the following day.[4]

Samuel Preston Moore read about the great events occurring in Virginia and thought that his years of medical training and military medical experience were being wasted in Little Rock. He traveled to Richmond and offered his services to the Confederate cause. President Jefferson Davis noted that he had been DeLeon's senior in the old U.S. Army. Both had held the rank of surgeon, but Moore had held that rank longer than DeLeon. Because of his seniority, President Davis appointed Moore to the position of surgeon general; DeLeon remained on duty with the Surgeon General's Office. There was a rumor, never corroborated, that President Davis was dissatisfied with DeLeon's leadership of the Confederate Medical Service.[5]

Moore determined to improve the medical conditions within the Confederate States military service. Using his experience with the old U.S. Army, he set up examining boards to evaluate the surgeons and assistant surgeons who had been appointed to regiments by state and local authorities. Those individuals with inadequate medical knowledge were given posts as hospital stewards with time to study

Table 3

Virginia Physicians in the Confederate States Army

Year	Number commissioned	Number discharged
1861	352	14
1862	198	44
1863	91	28
1864	58	25
1865	4	3

Note the large number of Virginia physicians who left
Confederate service in 1862. Some were dismissed after failure
before the medical examining boards set up by Surgeon General
Moore; others resigned rather than take the examination.

Source: Wyndham B. Blanton, Medicine in Virginia in the Nineteenth
Century (Richmond, Va.: Garrett and Massie, 1933), 393-420.

for a second examination. If they failed a second time, their commissions were revoked. More physicians were discharged from the Confederate army in 1862 than in any other year because of this winnowing process.

The initial $350,000 allotted to the Medical Service was rapidly expended. With additional appropriations from the Confederate Congress, Moore undertook a massive hospital building program. He attempted to assure a regular source of medical supplies by sending special agents to France and England to purchase drugs and surgical tools.

On 18 October 1861 Moore submitted an analysis of the problems of the Medical Department to the new secretary of war, Judah P. Benjamin. He admitted that the new military recruits had experienced a high incidence of measles and other camp diseases. He claimed that this epidemic was not the fault of medical officers, however, but of regimental commanders who had failed to observe proper hygienic regulations. Moore acknowledged that the evacuation of the wounded from Manassas had been poorly organized and that this disorganization had produced immense suffering. Up to six hundred soldiers had been crowded into a single train and some wounded were unattended while in transit for up to six days.

A special committee of the Confederate Congress investigated the failings of the Medical Department. Their report, submitted in January 1862, blamed inadequate preparations by the medical authorities for unneces-

sary suffering of the Manassas wounded. The report claimed that many physicians who had entered the Confederate service with state regiments were inadequate to the challenge of military medicine. The committee claimed that many regiments had no physicians at all, but did not comment upon the Congressional Act of 6 March, which had not required regimental surgeons. The congressional critique also railed at the lack of statistical medical reports from some regiments, although no reports can really be expected from officers who do not exist.

The committee claimed that no further legislation was needed, but that Surgeon General Moore should act under existing regulations to increase the availability of medical supplies and surgical instruments, to improve the transportation of the wounded, to improve the nutrition of the troops, and to establish a nursing corps. The committee also criticized the lodging of sick and wounded in private homes where they were lost to the supervision of military authorities.

In addition, the committee complained that it was too difficult for sick soldiers to obtain medical furloughs to recuperate at home. The regulations of the War Department required that each soldier who might benefit from such leave should first obtain the approval of his doctor and then travel to his regiment so that he could obtain the written approval of his regimental commanding officer. If the patient was in the hospital at Charlottesville but the

Samuel Preston Moore became the surgeon general of the Confederate States Army in the summer of 1861. After graduation from the medical school in his native Charleston, he spent twenty-six years with the U.S. Army. He accompanied the American expedition under Winfield Scott to Mexico City and had extensive experience in the West. Courtesy of the Valentine Museum, Richmond, Virginia.

The warehouse at the corner of 26th and Main in Richmond became Hospital Number 24, reserved for soldiers from North Carolina. It was later named the Moore Hospital for the surgeon general. USAMHI

regiment remained on duty near Manassas, the soldier's journey became an ordeal. The soldier had to be in reasonably good health before he could begin the excessively complex process to obtain a convalescent leave. The committee recommended relaxation of these almost impossible regulations. The congressmen claimed that they had personally observed that "a furlough and return to home and its associations caused speedy recovery and return to duty."

Many of the medical improvements recommended by the Confederate Congress were already in place before their report was ready.

Surgeon General Moore had already begun the examination of Confederate army physicians to weed out incompetents. He received supplemental funds from Congress; $100,000 had been voted on 21 August 1861; half was for new hospital construction and half to pay civilian surgeons who had helped take care of the unexpectedly large number of sick and wounded. Just two weeks later, Surgeon General Moore received an additional one million dollars to expend in any way he saw fit.

It was becoming obvious that this War was going to be a long one.

3

Lincoln Finds a Surgeon General

MANY WERE INJURED IN THE RIOT. ON 19 APRIL the 6th Massachusetts Infantry Regiment, while marching through Baltimore to reinforce the capital, was set upon by a pro-Southern mob. The injured were taken to the infirmary of the medical department of the University of Maryland, where they were treated by the civilian doctors on duty, Edward Warren and William A. Hammond. Hammond, who had ten years experience as a doctor with the U.S. Army, examined Private Sumner H. Needham. A rioter had struck Needham upon the head with a brick. Hammond determined that the unfortunate recruit had bled into his brain; he undertook the very risky operation of trephination, the drilling of a hole in the skull, in order to relieve the pressure caused by the hematoma. Needham did not improve following the operation and he died a few hours later.[1]

On 15 May 1861 the surgeon general of the U.S. Army, Thomas Lawson, died of natural causes at his home in Norfolk, Virginia. During his long tenure as chief of U.S. Army medicine, Colonel Lawson had accomplished many things. He had increased the collection of medical books for the Surgeon General's Office; he had obtained officer status for physicians; he had accompanied General Winfield Scott's expedition to Mexico City during the Mexican War. But Lawson proved most successful when he squeezed everything possible from the minuscule budgets allotted to the medical section of the peacetime army. "Finery and furbelows," he declared, "cannot he tolerated in field hospitals or other sick stations."[2] Lawson was respected for his long service to the

U.S. Army; the flag flew at half-mast for one day in all U.S. military posts and all officers of the army wore a badge of mourning for thirty days in his remembrance.

The next most senior medical officer, Clement A. Finley, succeeded him. Like Lawson, Finley had spent many years trying to manage with limited resources and did not fully grasp the magnitude of the problems facing the army after the South had fired on Fort Sumter. He reported with pride that for the fiscal year ending 30 June 1861 the Medical Bureau had actually spent less than it had been allocated.[3]

Just three weeks later, on 21 July 1861, the first major battle of the War found the medical service, like the rest of the United States Army, unprepared. The Battle of Bull Run shocked the North by showing that an armed mob does not make an army. The battle also demonstrated that a group of village practitioners, gathered together to help wounded soldiers, does not make a military medical organization.[4]

The physicians of the volunteer regiments had been appointed by state authorities and had no military experience. Some individuals who were officially regimental surgeons and assistant surgeons were not even doctors. Medical student William W. Keen was asked by his mentor John H. Brinton, a brigade surgeon, to act as assistant surgeon of the 5th Massachusetts, replacing a man named Smith who had been appointed by state authorities. Keen tried to decline the appointment; he argued that he was only a medical student who knew little about medicine and nothing about military medicine. "That is quite true," re-

After the Battle of Bull Run, the Union wounded came streaming down the main street of Centreville on their way to Washington. No water was available to quench their thirst; the wells were dry from the earlier passage of Union troops. USAMHI

plied Brinton, "but on the other hand, you know a great deal more than Smith." Keen was the surgeon for the 5th Massachusetts; during the entire battle, no one gave him any direction. He did the best he could treating the wounded of his regiment.

When the battle turned into a rout, there was no method to evacuate the wounded. Many who had been wounded in the arm walked the twenty miles to Washington. When the wounded fled down the dusty road through Centreville, they found no water available; the wells had been drained dry the previous day by advancing troops and Washington civilians. A few ambulances were available but these were under the control of the Quartermaster Corps; the ambulance drivers would not take orders from doctors. The ambulances that poured into Washington with the retreating army held drivers, officers, soldiers, even civilians, but very rarely carried a wounded man. Many doctors fled, abandoning all pretense at treating the wounded. Others stayed behind and were taken prisoner by the rebels.

The story of an individual patient illustrates the handling of the wounded at Bull Run. Colonel Noah L. Farnham commanded the 11th New York. This regiment consisted predominately of volunteers from the New York City Fire Department; they had been recruited by Elmer Ellsworth, a friend of President Lincoln. A partially spent musket ball struck Farnham on the left side of his head, about three inches above the ear; he was stunned and fell off his horse. He was carried by staff officers to Washington, where he was admitted to the E Street Infirmary under the care of Assistant Surgeon W. J. H. White of the regular army (not the new volunteer army). He was also examined by a leading civilian surgeon, Frank H. Hamilton, who thought that the ball had only grazed the head, taking off no more than hair. But Hamilton was worried because the colonel wished to be left alone and was easily irritated, potential symptoms of brain damage. The wound healed and the patient seemed normal until 10 August, when he developed confusion and fever. A few days later, the patient became paralyzed on the right side, then slipped into coma. He died on 14 August 1861. A postmortem examination disclosed an abscess within the brain under the wound site.[5]

A leading medical journal laid the blame for the medical disaster of this disastrous battle squarely on the shoulders of Surgeon General Finley. "The Battle of Bull Run took place under the immediate inspection of the official head of the Medical Bureau," said the *American Medical Times.* "It was planned weeks beforehand, and admitted the most ample medical provision; yet the nation has not and never will cease to thrill with horror at the mention of its name and the recollections of the terrible sufferings."[6]

Finley was blamed not only for his handling of the wounded, but also for the huge number of sick in the expanding Union Army. The proportion of new recruits who came down with measles, mumps, and diarrhea amazed both the military authorities and the civilian medical community. This high rate of illness was blamed on improperly trained and inadequately supervised military physicians. Measles and mumps were especially severe among new recruits from rural areas.

A movement arose among reformist elements of the civilian population to reorganize and invigorate the medical arm of the U.S. Army. Even before Bull Run, women in many large and small towns across the Northern states gathered to support their sons and husbands who were joining the army. The Ladies Aid Society of this or that location rapidly became amalgamated into a huge national society called the United States Sanitary Commission.

This organization was modeled after the British Sanitary Commission. In the first year of the Crimean War, the British experienced a very high mortality rate in their barracks and hospitals. A government commission was organized to examine this situation and began to clean up the military hospitals in the Crimea and the support hospitals in Turkey. A marked decrease in mortality occurred. The necessity of careful attention to sanitation was beginning to sink into the American consciousness through the writings of Florence Nightingale and British military physicians.

With the Crimean experience as the intellectual basis and the outpouring of support from women as the emotional stimulus, the United States Sanitary Commission began operation early in 1861. Its leaders were the Unitarian minister Henry W. Bellows and the architect Frederick Law Olmsted. The British Sanitary Commission was an official government agency; the new American organization remained under private control. It accepted no government funds but did receive permission from the secretary of war and Surgeon General Finley to inspect U.S. Army general hospitals and training camps.[7]

The Sanitary Commission pushed the U.S. Congress to reform the Medical Bureau. An act of 3 August 1861 added ten additional surgeons and twenty additional assistant surgeons to the regular army and allowed for a corps of medical cadets. The cadets were medical students who could dress wounds at general hospitals and drive ambulances or carry wounded from the field. Some medical cadets received course credit at their home medical schools for their military experiences. The cadets were to enlist for one year only and their number was not to exceed fifty. This law was not enough, however, and civilian reformers lobbied for further changes.

The leaders of the U.S. Sanitary Commission used their political connections to push for a new surgeon general. They felt that Clement A. Finley was too old and lacked the vigor for this important role. The list of candidates who might replace Finley included Charles S. Tripler, Robert C. Wood, and William A. Hammond.

Charles S. Tripler had been an army doctor since 1830. He was a graduate of the Columbia College of Physicians and Surgeons in New York. He knew personally many of the generals of both sides because as a young assistant surgeon he had been assigned to West Point and had taken classes with the cadets. He had accompanied Scott to Mexico City during the Mexican War. During the previous four years he had been assigned to an army post in Kentucky and had been associated with the Medical College of Ohio in Cincinnati. He and the professor of surgery of that college, Robert S. Blackmun, had delivered a series of lectures on military medicine. In 1861 they gathered these lectures into a small volume, *Handbook for the Military Surgeon*.[8] Despite his qualifications, the Sanitary Commission leaders did not favor Tripler. During Bull Run, Tripler observed the battle with several leading citizens, including some members of the U.S. Sanitary Commission. A wounded soldier fell near Tripler, who did not offer aid. This omission made the leaders feel that Tripler lacked the compassion to be surgeon general.

Robert C. Wood had been on the staff of the Surgeon General's Office for many years. He had collated reports for Thomas Lawson and was now performing the same duties for Finley. He acted as surgeon general when Finley was unavailable. It was Wood who convinced Secretary of War Simon Cameron to cooperate with the Sanitary Commission. Despite this, the leaders of the Sanitary Commission did not want Wood to become the new surgeon general. They thought that he was too closely identified with the existing medical hierarchy and the policies of the Surgeon General's Office.

William A. Hammond was well known in both military and medical circles. He was born in Annapolis, Maryland, in 1828 and was reared in Harrisburg, Pennsylvania. After graduation from the Medical Department of the University of the City of New York, he took additional medical training at the Pennsylvania Hospital in Philadelphia. Joining the army in 1849, Hammond spent nearly a decade in the West. His study with Silas Weir Mitchell in Philadelphia stimulated Hammond to give up his army career and enter academic medicine. He resigned from the army in 1860 in order to take a position on the faculty of the medical school of the University of Maryland in Baltimore. As just related, Hammond as a civilian had treated soldiers who had been injured in the Baltimore riot.[9]

Hammond rejoined the army in May 1861, but his lapse of service had cost him his seniority and his rank was only assistant surgeon. Because of his study of the great hospitals of Europe, he was sent on an inspection tour of military hospitals in western Maryland. His careful and detailed analysis came to the attention of the U.S. Sanitary Commission, which published portions of his report in a pamphlet.

From the point of view of the Sanitary Commission, Hammond possessed strong qualifications for surgeon general:

First, he was a regular army physician with eleven years of active military service. He knew enough of army routine to be effective but had not been so long in the army as to become inured to the proposition that bureaucratic efficiency was more important than outcome. Hammond's military experience should make him acceptable to the traditional army medical establishment.

Second, Hammond was known to the academic medical community through his nutrition research and his brief experience in medical school teaching. He should be able to draw civilian support into the war effort.

Third, he was an expert in hospital design and this war would certainly demand much hospital construction. Hammond criticized the design of the new military hospital at Hilton Head, South Carolina. This hospital, built by Surgeon General Finley, did not, Hammond thought, allow for adequate ventilation.[10]

Fourth, and most importantly, Hammond as a person appeared up to the demands of the position. He was open, self-confident, and projected an imposing physical presence with an aura of dignity and mission. Standing six feet two inches tall, he possessed a broad physique and military bearing, yet had the youthful enthusiasm of a man of thirty-four bounding upward in his multifaceted career.

One other subtle but important fact recommended Hammond. Traditional army practice promoted the next senior person to fill any vacancy. A considerable body of public opinion, however, favored selection of the best man for every military position, regardless of seniority. General George B. McClellan had been promoted to command all the Union armies over the heads of many other generals. Reverend Bellows compared the seniority system to the man who each day selected from a barrel the most spoiled apple; when the barrel was empty, he found that he had never tasted a good apple. The Medical Service had already experienced a change in leadership based upon the seniority system, from Lawson to Finley, but the leader so chosen seemed too lethargic for the demands of army medical command.

When Hammond had reentered the army after his period at the University of Maryland, he lost credit for his previous army service. Whether or not one favored Hammond as surgeon general, one had to admit that his training and experience justified for him a much higher rank than his entry level position as a very junior assistant surgeon. Every discussion of Hammond's qualifications contained an unspoken criticism of the seniority system.[11]

Early in April 1862 the Sanitary Commission redoubled its efforts to secure Hammond's appointment. The Medical Reform Bill passed Congress, and Finley, on extended leave, was prepared to resign. The Commission undertook a two-pronged lobbying attack. Dr. William H. Van Buren, the leading physician member of the Sanitary Commission, argued Hammond's case to Edwin M. Stanton, the new secretary of war, while Reverend Bellows intensified his lobbying efforts with President Lincoln.

Fig. 18.

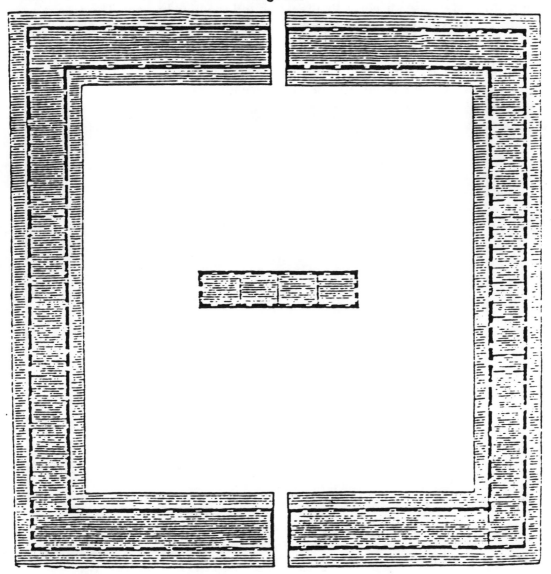

GENERAL HOSPITAL, HILTON HEAD, SOUTH CAROLINA.

SCALE $\frac{1}{1050}$.

The floor plan of the U.S. Army General Hospital at Hilton Head, South Carolina. Four corridors surrounded an open space. Wards were on the corners and along the upper and lower corridors. The dining room was located on the left while the building on the right held offices and an operating room. In the open central plaza were the kitchen and the laundry. The latrine consisted simply of the nearby beach; people used it during low tide and it was washed clean by high tide. Assistant Surgeon William Hammond criticized the plan of this hospital because a breeze blowing over the patients in one ward might carry sickness into the next ward. From William A. Hammond, *A Treatise on Hygiene, with Special Reference to the Military Service,* Philadelphia: J. B. Lippincott, 1863.

"I have called you into a bad case," the secretary of war said to Dr. Van Buren, meaning that he recognized that the medical bureau needed new leadership. Stanton, however, wanted to select his own surgeon general. He had no specific individual in mind, but did not like the way civilian reformers were forcing their own candidate upon him.

Reverend Bellows, president of the Sanitary Commission, took the case directly to President Lincoln. Bellows listed Hammond's virtues as the president was shaving on the morning of 17 April 1862. That same evening, he again buttonholed the president. Lincoln was signing a series of papers on his desk as Bellows regaled him with tales of how Hammond's appointment would energize the moribund medical bureau. The president remained silent until the reverend finally ran out of breath. Lincoln then quietly announced that he had decided to appoint Hammond. "Shouldn't wonder if he was surgeon general already."[12]

4

Maggots and Minié Balls

DURING THE WINTER OF 1861 TO 1862, BOTH THE Union and Confederate armies settled in and prepared for a very long war. Sharing the same medical and military backgrounds, the two nations built quite similar systems to handle their sick and wounded soldiers. The doctors, the enlisted personnel, the female nurses, and a various assortment of civilian volunteers made up the medical infrastructure of both great armies.

With certain exceptions, two physicians were assigned to each regiment. They bore the official rank of surgeon and assistant surgeon, even though they might or might not have any real experience with surgical operations. Each regiment had an additional individual assigned to medical functions, the hospital steward, an enlisted man equal in rank to a sergeant. Despite some confusion in the first year of the War, the hospital steward was not a servant for the doctors; he was part of the regiment and reported to the regimental commander, not directly to the doctor.

Sick call was held each day, usually in the morning. Any soldier who felt ill lined up to be evaluated by the assistant surgeon. The doctor listened to the soldier's symptoms and performed a brief examination. The artist Winslow Homer observed a doctor examining a young soldier by looking at his tongue. In the painting, the hospital steward records the doctor's diagnosis for the regimental report. Most complaints were trivial: headache, joint aches, constipation, loose bowels. Some soldiers suffered from significant chronic disabilities and were medically discharged from the army.

Sick call could be quite boring, both for the soldier-patients and for the medical personnel. One of the soldier's major symptoms concerned his bowels. One physician kept opium in one pocket and mercury compound in the other. Regardless of the soldier's main complaint, the doctor asked: "How are your bowels?" If they were too loose, he gave the opium; if the soldier was constipated, he received a pinch of the mercury compound.

Some soldiers developed illnesses that interfered with their abilities to carry out their usual military functions. Treatment was undertaken and the soldier was given limited duty. The illness producing this temporary disability was recorded by the hospital steward, as observed by Winslow Homer. The number of illnesses per month were calculated and a report was forwarded to the next highest physician in the chain of command, usually the brigade surgeon. Sick reports were collated and eventually made it to the medical director of the field army or the military department. These reports reached Washington or Richmond, where higher medical authorities could detect trends in illnesses. Both the Union and Confederate medical authorities used the British Farr system for the classification of disease.[1]

The physician carried a medical bag, often brought from home. At the beginning of the War the surgical tools in the doctor's bag were his personal property. The hospital steward carried a medical knapsack. In these were medicines and equipment supplied by the government. Each regimental knapsack was supposed to contain both chloroform and ether

In Winslow Homer's painting "Playing Old Soldier," a regimental assistant surgeon examines a young soldier during sick call while the hospital steward records the findings. The term "playing old soldier" refers to the feigning of symptoms to escape military duty. Courtesy of the Ellen Kelleran Gardner Fund, Museum of Fine Arts, Boston.

The band members of the 26th North Carolina carried the wounded off the battlefield. They posed for a picture in July of 1862 while the regiment was on leave in Salem. Julius Leinbach, the short man with the tuba second from the left, described how these musician-soldiers evacuated the wounded at Gettysburg. Courtesy of Moravian Music Foundation, Inc., Winston-Salem, N.C.

for use as anesthetics. The Confederacy rapidly ran out of ether, but chloroform remained, imported from England and made in pharmaceutical laboratories. Several types of opium were available to relieve pain and to slow the action of the bowels. Opium was carried in the knapsack in pills and in liquid form (laudanum). Paregoric and ipecac were official medications of the regimental knapsack, as was a bottle of brandy. Quinine pills and liquid quinine were both supposed to be present, but the Confederacy had difficulty supplying adequate amounts of this antimalarial medication. In addition to medications, each knapsack contained instruments that might be needed for treating wounds: tourniquets, bandages, lint, sponges, and candles.[2]

The most dangerous duty assigned to medical officers was the removal of the wounded under fire. The surgeon set up an area behind the battle lines where the wounded could be examined. Soldiers with minor wounds underwent dressing and returned immediately to

their place in the battle; soldiers with more severe wounds could be evacuated further to the rear. The assistant surgeon went forward just behind the troops to supervise the transport of those unable to walk. One Confederate assistant surgeon claimed that the surgeon of his regiment was a very informal person; medical work was shared in a spirit of egalitarian professional cordiality. However, when a battle threatened, the surgeon began to take on airs of military command. When the battle actually began, the surgeon demanded his rank; he took the safer job setting up the regimental examining area while the assistant surgeon was ordered up with the troops.[3]

The area where the surgeon examined the wounded was officially termed the regimental hospital. This is a deceptive term, because this so-called hospital was usually just a marked spot in a field. The surgeon tried to select a gully, an area protected by trees, or at least a depression in the meadow where medical personnel and the wounded were not likely to be

A group of Union hospital stewards relax in camp. Their status is indicated by the yellow caduceus on the sleeve. NA

struck by bullets or shells that passed over the battle line. Sometimes, the surgeon selected a site too close to the battle; cannonballs careened through the area, threatening the wounded and unnerving the doctors.

The people who carried the wounded to the regimental hospital were difficult to train and to supervise. At first, regimental musicians were designated to remove the wounded since they would not likely be needed to play instruments during battle. Actually this clash of duties did occur. Julius Leinbach, a musician with the 26th North Carolina, related how during the Battle of Gettysburg the division commander ordered his band to play in order to cheer up the troops although the doctors thought that the musicians should be engaged in removing the wounded.[4]

In general, however, musicians proved poor at removing wounded not because of this rare clash of duties but because of the common clash of attitudes and training. The musicians expected to play; they trained to play better. They did not like to practice their instruments only to remove wounded and, in the bitter world of combat, they liked even less to perform under fire that very action whose training they had avoided.

Each regiment in its own manner selected individuals to evacuate the wounded. This group of people was called the ambulance corps or, sometimes, the infirmary corps. Many of the soldiers of this group were those who were overwhelmed by the requirements of military life, a group of individuals referred to in later times as goldbricks or goofballs. One regimental physician referred to them as "Company Q."

More frequently, however, the soldiers of the ambulance corps were among the best of the regiment; they only lacked the "skill" of remorselessly killing an unknown enemy. The ability to aim a rifle at a human being, carefully squeeze the trigger, and kill a stranger is not possessed by everyone who volunteers to be a soldier. Company officers and sergeants observed troops in battle and noted those who were unable to fire their weapon at the enemy or who purposely missed; these soldiers were assigned to duty with the assistant surgeon.

The surgeon is operating at the left side of the picture in this artistic representation of a field hospital near the Antietam battleground. A soldier who has just lost his right leg is being placed in a wagon for evacuation. HW

Evacuating wounded required courage; sometimes the stretcher bearers would leave the protection of a stone wall to crawl out into the open to retrieve wounded. Depending upon the ferocity of the battle, the opposing line of rifles might or might not respect the activities of the stretcher bearers. Those soldiers selected for duty with the ambulance corps were those with great courage, but who hesitated to shoot the enemy.[5]

The wounded soldier was evacuated by the assistant surgeon and his litter bearers to the regimental hospital, where he was treated by the regimental surgeon. In general, the wounded came to the nearest aid station, regardless of regiment. In the earliest battles of the War, some wounded were turned away because they were from the wrong regiment. This practice was not so far-fetched as its seems; the medical knowledge of the day rec-

ognized that in civilian life the best physician to treat a patient was the doctor who had known him for many years, was familiar with his idiosyncracies, and could adjust treatment to the patient as well as to the disease. In ideal circumstances, a doctor would treat the soldiers from his own regiment with whom he was familiar. But in the confusion of battle, when one regiment might be torn to pieces and another not even engaged, the ideal virtues of civilian practice had to give way to military necessity.

At the regimental hospital, the mildly wounded were returned to duty after simple first aid, while seriously wounded soldiers were sent to the military general hospital. In the Old Army, the general hospital was at the nearest fort. Now, however, the general hospital was located at a supply depot, usually in the nearest major city. In these cities, the med-

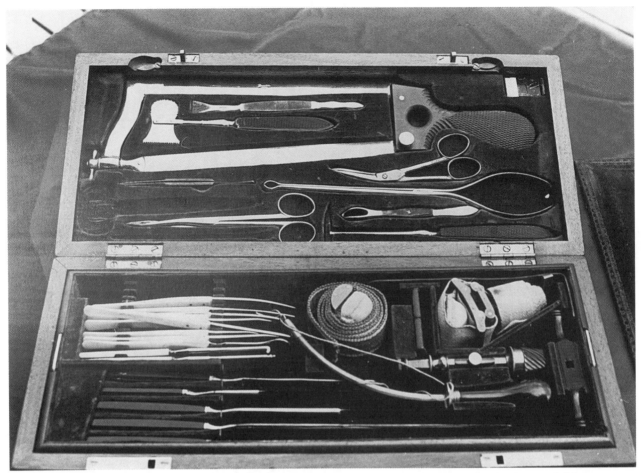

A surgeon's kit contains a selection of probes and tourniquets and an operating saw that looks much like a carpenter's saw. Courtesy of Gordon Dammann.

ical authorities took over a suitable building for the hospital, usually the largest building in town. As need dictated, other buildings were pressed into service: warehouses, alms houses, institutes of education, churches, hotels, and private homes.

After the Battle of Bull Run, Union wounded who could walk made their way to Washington. Some of the wounded officers actually checked into the Willard Hotel as ordinary hotel guests and sought medical help from civilian physicians. As already related, the trip from the Confederate regimental hospital to Richmond was not an easy one. The helpless wounded were exposed to the elements and suffered hunger as well as the discomfort of their undressed wounds. After Bull Run, or Manassas, both North and South determined that an intermediate medical station was needed between the regimental hospital at the battle line and the general hospital in the nearest city.

A system gradually came into being whereby a secondary hospital was formed, farther back from the battlefield, often in a barn. The wounded were examined at the regimental hospital, sent to this secondary hospital and only days later evacuated to the system of general military hospitals. This secondary hospital was initially formed at the brigade level, but even this proved too small an organization. Soon division hospitals concentrated the wounded from an entire division. This concentration of wounded allowed a concentration of medical resources. Surgeons of known ability were posted from their regiments to the division hospital; here the more complex operations were performed by the most skilled surgeons, regardless of regimental affiliation.

The surgery was brutal. Most soldiers of both armies had extensive experience with the butchery of farm animals: pigs, cows, chickens. These same soldiers observed the surgery performed on others, or upon themselves, and

This imaginative generic battle scene appeared in *Harper's Weekly*. The battle is raging on the hill above; in the foreground brutal surgery is taking place in the open. British military medical observers were amazed that soldiers waiting to undergo surgery watched operations on others. HW

In the 1850s this large building in Washington held three homes. John C. Breckinridge lived in the center and Stephen A. Douglas on the near corner. Like many large buildings in Washington during the War, it was converted for medical use, becoming the Douglas Hospital. USAMHI

could not help but note the similarity: "It was butchery, sheer butchery, pure butchery," is the comment of a hundred diaries. The surgery was performed in one large room in the house, or in the center of the barn, or in an open tent, or on a table under the open skies; but surgery always occurred with many people watching. Doctors watched to learn; officers watched with a strange and somewhat perverse fascination; all sorts of passersby stopped a moment to observe. The most pitiable class of observers were those who were waiting in line to lose their own limbs. A British military officer with Crimean combat experience described the surgery he saw with the Army of the Potomac; sixty army surgeons were "cutting and sawing more like devils and machines than human beings." He saw medical students fight over discarded limbs to be dissected for anatomical study. Military surgery had been difficult in the Crimea, he thought, but always the patients had been spared the spectacle.[6]

The patient was anesthetized with ether or chloroform. The blessed liquid was dripped upon a cloth or a pledget of cotton and held over the nose of the patient. When he went limp, the operation began. The surgeons were always in a hurry. They operated rapidly be-

cause many patients waited for surgery and the tradition of speed continued, despite the widespread use of anesthetics in civilian surgical practice. In the preanesthetic era prior to about 1848, nine-tenths of surgical skill was speed.[7] Many soldiers were only half asleep under the effect of the anesthetic. They felt no pain, but had a vague recollection of the surgery. General Stonewall Jackson remembered the sound of the saw cutting off his own arm.

The minié ball flattened when it encountered human flesh. It did not pass directly through the tissues as do modern bullets with metal jackets; rather, the deformed bullet tumbled, tearing a terrible swath through muscle and bone. Bones splintered and shattered into hundreds of spicules, sharp, bony sticks that were driven by the force of the bullet through muscle and skin. "The minie ball striking a bone does not permit much debate about amputation," concluded Union surgeon Theodore Dimon.[8]

Amputation was required above the level where the bullet shattered the bone. The surgeon made a deep cut in the tissues, down to the normal bone. The bone was scraped, then sawed straight through by a surgical tool that looked just like a carpenter's saw. The limb fell upon the ground and was thrown upon a pile. The stump was usually covered with skin and muscle tissue and sutured shut. If excessive pus formed in the stump over the next few days, the sutures burst, and a terrible smelly discharge poured forth. A second and higher amputation might be necessary.

After surgery was complete, the patient was taken to a place of rest. All available floor space was used in barns and houses. Boards were stretched across the pews of churches. When this space was full, patients were taken outside. Hopefully, tents could be erected to protect the patients from the elements. It seemed to many surgeons that the patients in tents healed more rapidly than patients in buildings; this was attributed to breezes blowing across the patients and their wounds, carrying away the smelly miasma that seemed to exude into the atmosphere above every sick person.

The patients were evacuated, usually by train, to the nearest general hospital with empty beds. These general military hospitals were often located in large cities and were staffed with military doctors, military nurses, and volunteers. Some civilian doctors helped at these hospitals, either as volunteers or as paid physicians; the latter were called acting assistant surgeons. A friendly rivalry developed between regimental surgeons and military doctors assigned to general hospitals. The latter were accused of soft living and perhaps a touch of cowardice. The hospital doctors countered with criticism of the hurried impromptu surgery that occurred in the field.

Private Milton E. Wallen was thrust into this system. He received surgical therapy from both the Northern and Southern medical departments. Wallen was forty-one when he enlisted at Albany, Kentucky, in the 1st Kentucky Cavalry (Union). He was captured by Confederate cavalry near the Cumberland River in

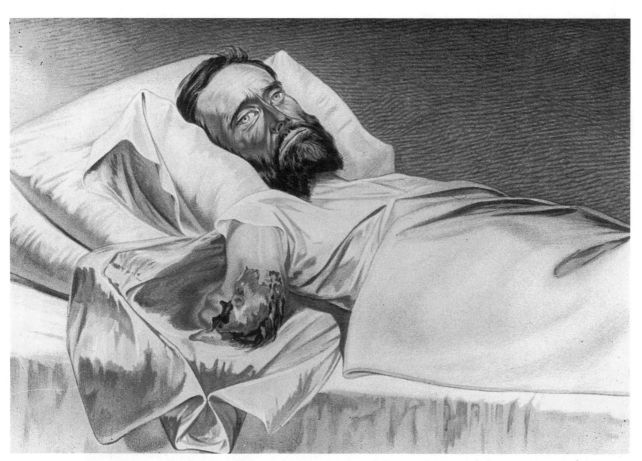

Milton E. Wallen of Albany, Kentucky underwent an amputation of the arm by a Confederate surgeon after a minié ball macerated his elbow. This sketch was made at the Naval School Hospital at Annapolis, Maryland, showing hospital gangrene in the amputation stump. MSH

Tennessee on 1 June 1863 and taken to Castle Thunder, Richmond. While trying to escape, he was shot in the right elbow; the minié ball shattered the lower portion of the humerus. A Confederate surgeon amputated his right arm above the elbow immediately after the injury. Since he was now without military value, the Confederates sent him to Union lines. Shot on 4 July, he reached Union medical care on 3 August, when he was admitted to the U.S. Army General Hospital at Annapolis, called the Naval School Hospital because it was on the grounds of the U.S. Naval Academy.

On 24 August hospital gangrene, a chronic problem at the Naval School Hospital, was noted by the physician in charge of the ward, Dr. B. A. Vanderkieft. The end of the stump was black and exuded the terrible odor of putrefaction, similar to spoiled meat. The flaps came loose and the cut end of the humerus was easily visible. A color sketch was made by the artistic hospital steward, a man named Stauch. Dr. Vanderkieft dressed the wound with charcoal and yeast, and the patient improved. He was sent home on furlough in October 1863, but did not return. He was officially listed as a deserter on 5 April 1864.[9]

Those soldiers who were too severely wounded to survive were put aside in a quiet place. They were made as comfortable as possible and there they waited to die. One Confederate soldier looked up a friend in the hospital to see what had happened to him in a battle several days earlier. He asked him how badly he was injured. The wounded man said nothing but pulled off the blanket covering his legs. "The lower part of his body was hanging to the upper part by a shred," described the visitor, "and all of his entrails were lying on the cot with him, the bile and other excrements exuding from them, and they were full of maggots."[10] He was just waiting to die.

5

The Introduction of Women Nurses

IN NINETEENTH-CENTURY AMERICA A SICK PERSON usually obtained nursing care from female relatives. The doctor visited the home, examined the patient, and made recommendations. If a surgical procedure was required, it was performed on the kitchen table. The dressing of wounds and the administration of medications were left to the care of the wife, mother, and grandmother. The only people treated in the hospital were persons unable to obtain

Before the War, the Marine Hospital at Vicksburg served as a place to hospitalize boatmen who were too ill to accompany their vessel on the Mississippi River and who had no family to care for them in their homes. The structure served as a Confederate and later a Union hospital. Miller

51

home care. The working poor were admitted
to the almshouse hospital maintained by the
city; the female relatives could not provide
care at home because they were also working.
Sailors and boatmen who were too sick to
travel when their vessel left port were treated
in marine hospitals.[1]

In the Old Army, soldiers were treated in the
small hospitals at every major military post.
Nursing functions were performed by male enlisted men who were recovering from an illness or injury and who were not yet able to
return to their full military duties. This system continued during the early years of the
Civil War. These enlisted personnel fed the sick
at the regimental hospitals, changed dressings, and did other tasks associated with
nursing.

Before the Civil War, women could work in
civilian hospitals associated with almshouses
only in the position of ward matron. A woman
was in charge of one ward of about forty beds;
she kept the ward clean and the patients fed.
She was responsible for dietary therapy as
prescribed by the doctor. At the start of the
War, army authorities, North and South, offered positions as hospital ward matrons to
women.

Women in the United States, and in the new
Confederate States of America, wanted to aid
the war effort of their respective nations. For
many women, their efforts centered on helping the sick and the wounded. Women's clubs
and societies sprang up in every city and state.
In the North, but not in the South, many of
these societies merged into large organizations, such as the Christian Commission or the
Western Sanitary Commission. The largest
private health organization was the United
States Sanitary Commission, which was devoted to improving the health and morale of
the Union Army. Katherine Wormeley observed how women provided the rank-and-file
workers for the sanitary organizations that
nurtured the Union military forces; she called
the Sanitary Commission "the artery that con-
ducts the people's love to the people's army."
Female representatives of these organizations
were soon in every hospital.

All these individuals were called "nurse"
and applied that term to themselves: convalescent soldiers, visiting women, unpaid volunteers, matrons, and female volunteers from
private organizations. One group of women

who rapidly took their place as nurses were
Catholic nuns. Some orders had nursing experience, but even nuns who had been teachers were readily accepted as nurses. Some
nursing functions were performed by visitors,
particularly women visitors. They fed soldiers
too weak to feed themselves and wrote letters
home for those unable to write. Some of these
visitors, particularly those from the upper
class, started as hospital visitors but later obtained an official position with a private relief
organization. Lower-class women flowed into
nursing from lowly paid hospital positions
such as laundress. Occasionally a man became
a volunteer nurse; Walt Whitman is an
example.[2]

Most medical authorities accepted nuns but
opposed other women in the role of nurses.
Walter F. Atlee, a leading Philadelphia physician, admitted that Florence Nightingale had
significantly aided the British Army in the Crimean War. In America, however, he foresaw
"serious objections to the employment of female nurses for soldiers." The military and the
medical authorities worried that women
would faint at the sight of the misery of sickness and the gore of tissue damage. A usually
unstated fear involved exposure of young
women to the naked male body.[3]

At the insistence of Dorothea Dix, who had
met Florence Nightingale and had visited
Crimean hospitals, the Union organized an official Women's Nursing Bureau. This government agency attempted to organize the
numerous unpaid nursing volunteers and,
after much effort, obtained a regular salary
for these women. The official orders of 23 April
1861 that established the Women's Nursing
Bureau, however, read as though the military
authorities were ambivalent about female
nurses:

> The free services [this program costs the govern-
> ment nothing] of Miss D. L. Dix are accepted by
> the War Department and that she will give at all
> times all necessary aid [aid only, no authority]
> in organizing military hospitals for the cure of
> sick and wounded soldiers, aiding the chief sur-
> geon [aiding only] by supplying nurses and sub-
> stantial means for the comfort and relief of the
> suffering; also that she is fully authorized to re-
> ceive, control, and disburse special supplies be-
> stowed by individuals or associations for the
> comfort of their friends or the citizen soldiers
> from all parts of the limited states [the govern-

Dorothea Dix initiated and headed the Women's Nursing Bureau of the Union army. She rejected nursing volunteers who were too young and comely. USAMHI

ment authorizes Miss Dix to disburse private contributions over which it has no control]; as also, under action of the Acting Surgeon-General [passing the buck to him], to draw from the army stores.

Nurses from Dorothea Dix's new organization were sent out to the hospitals supporting the field armies. Their arrival at the huge new Union base at Cairo, Illinois, exasperated the physician in charge, Dr. John H. Brinton. "Just at this period," he wrote later,

the craze spread among our good people that the women of the country could make themselves very useful by acting as nurses for the sick and wounded. So out they came, these patriotic women of the North. The Secretary of War, the generals commanding departments, divisions, or military posts, were besieged by them. By strained construction of certain paragraphs in the army regulations [just quoted], and of acts of Congress, positions, paid positions, were devised for them.

Brinton described how these women volunteers arrived at military bases such as Cairo. "On the arrival of certain trains they would stalk into the office of district commanders, and establish themselves solemnly against the walls, entrenched behind their bags and parcels. They defied all military law. There they were, and there they would stay, until some accommodation might be found for them." These obstinate persons were eventually sent to the helpless doctor in charge of a hospital. "To him at last these wretched females would come," Brinton continued. "They did not wish much, not they, simply a room, a bed, a looking glass, someone to get their meals and do little things for them, and they would nurse the sick boys of our gallant Union Army." Brinton was not opposed to all women, but only those who used scarce resources without service; he was pleased when he received fifteen nuns to nurse his sick and wounded, especially when the Mother Superior informed him that all fifteen would occupy only one room.[4]

In the South, local women's organizations assisted the soldiers of their communities. For example, the Ladies Aid Society of Montgomery sent Opie Hopkins to Richmond with delicacies and clothing for local soldiers hospitalized in that city. This organization became the Ladies Aid Society of Alabama and provided aid to the Alabama division of the giant

Chimborazo Hospital. Augusta Jane Evans of Mobile wrote to Confederate General P. G. T. Beauregard to say that in this trying time the "women's sphere of influence" should expand until "the centre is everywhere, the circumference nowhere." A poem, "Ladies to the Hospital," circulated in many Southern newspapers in 1861:

Up and down through the wards where the fever
Stalks noisome and gaunt and impure;
You must go with your steadfast endeavor
To comfort, to counsel, to cure!

One of the characteristics of the women volunteers that most irritated the doctors was their inability to understand the military chain of command. "They defied all military law," Brinton had complained. From the doctor's point of view, he had the authority and responsibility for everything that happened in the hospital. This hierarchial authority flowed from the president, through the secretary of war, through the surgeon general, to the medical director of the district or the field army, to the hospital director, and then to the doctor in charge of the patients on the ward.

The women had no concept of their place in this hierarchy. When one female nurse was having trouble with her male orderly, she bypassed several levels of authority to complain to Surgeon General Hammond. When he suggested she should go through channels, she asked: "Who is *your* superior?" She then went directly to Secretary of War Stanton, who, more politically adept than Hammond, ordered the arrest of the malefactor.[5]

The nurse with the greatest disdain for military authority was Mary A. Bickerdyke, known throughout the Union army as Mother Bickerdyke. Without warning or hesitation, she strode into a hospital and pronounced it indescribably filthy. Without stopping to check with anyone, she immediately began a thorough cleaning. She scrubbed the walls and floor, stripped all coverings from the beds for a complete laundering, and even washed the patients. Convalescents who had been unable to perform any work and hospital stewards who had considered themselves above manual labor were swept up in the whirlwind and, under her draconian guidance, were working like beavers when the amazed doctor-in-charge arrived. When the doctor asked Mother Bickerdyke where she obtained the au-

Amanda M. Colburn was accepted by Miss Dix as a nurse for the Women's Nursing Bureau. Miss Dix criticized her choice of clothes, but Colburn served as a nurse throughout the War. Holland

Catholic nuns were highly valued for their nursing abilities; they did not join the Women's Nursing Bureau. Sister Mary Joseph of the Order of the Sisters of Mercy served the Union in Beaufort, South Carolina. NA

Mary A. Bickerdyke left her two children with friends in Galesburg, Illinois as she carried church donations to Union soldiers. She worked largely on her own, but her energies were focused by the U.S. Sanitary Commission. Her whirlwind cleanups and simple clothes earned her the sobriquet of the calico cyclone. This sketch shows her confronting a surgeon in Memphis. From Linus P. Brockett, *Battlefield and Hospital*, Philadelphia: Hubbard Brothers, 1888.

thority to order these soldiers around, she answered simply: "From the Lord God Almighty."[6] The sudden appearance and whirling action of Mother Bickerdyke earned her the name of the calico cyclone.

When Dr. B. J. D. Irwin was in charge of all the Union military hospitals in Memphis, a complex containing over five thousand beds, his greatest headache was Mother Bickerdyke. She might appear in any one of his hospitals at any time. He had successfully opposed Cochise at the mail station at Apache Pass, but he was blown over by the calico cyclone. With time, however, these two people came to respect each other. Irwin, like other physicians, was amazed that Bickerdyke could accomplish so much. In turn, Mother Bickerdyke came to understand that Irwin was working hard to supply "her boys" with the medical care that they needed.

While the male doctors thought that women

were intruding into their domain and using scarce resources, the women nursing volunteers were also dissatisfied with the doctors. They echoed the complaints of the soldiers who thought that many doctors were incompetent and uncaring. They even accused the doctors of performing amputations just in order to develop surgical skills that would be of value later in civilian practice. Actually, many of the doctors in the army medical service were barely competent. Many were forced by circumstances to perform operations for which they were totally unprepared.

A certain story was frequently told, although it is probably apocryphal, that illustrates the low opinion of doctors held by some of their patients. A dying soldier with almost his last gasp asked his doctor to lean over his bed so that he could whisper in his ear. Summoning all his waning strength, the soldier punched the doctor in the face, then collapsed back upon the bed, and, with a look of infinite contentment, expired.[7] Although most of the women volunteers were from a higher social class than the enlisted soldiers, they expressed the same complaints about the doctors: incompetence, indifference, and, in some cases, drunkenness.

One concept that helps explain why male doctors and female nurses clashed so often was the belief common in nineteenth-century America, that men and women inhabited separate spheres of activity. The commercial and business fields, as well as the world of politics, were male activities. The central section of every major urban area consisted of warehouses, taverns, commercial enterprises, barber shops, and other male organizations.[8] Women had their own activities involving home, church, women's clubs, women's reform groups, and circles of female relatives and very close friends. The typical day for the people of the spheres involved the husband leaving home for his all-male place of commercial activity while his wife stayed behind to supply the physical nurturing and spiritual backbone for the family. The wife's interests overflowed the home to support the spiritual values of the community.[9]

The male doctors thought that the hospital was in the male sphere. The ward was part of the military hospital; the doctor had both the legal and moral authority to care for the patients. Why, they thought, did the nurses have so much trouble following simple orders? On the other hand, the female nurses thought that the hospital ward belonged to the female sphere. Sick soldiers were treated in the ward in the same manner that sick civilians were treated in the home. The home was part of the female sphere. Women nursing their sick relatives at home took the doctor's advice as they saw fit; hence, the female nurses could not understand why the doctors became so incensed when their advice was not followed.

The male doctors and their female associates clashed often, especially in the first year or two of the War. The biggest fights appeared to involve small aspects of treatment, but they really concerned authority. A sick soldier expressed his desire for eggs; of all the things the poor, prostrate, emaciated victim most wanted was the taste of eggs. The doctor informed him that eggs were difficult to digest and his bowel was weak from diarrhea; eggs were forbidden. The female nurse assumed that the doctor's order was simply a suggestion; she felt that the soldier's heartfelt desire overruled the hypothetical effect of eggs on the gastrointestinal system. The doctor became enraged to the point of apoplexy when he saw the soldier hungrily devouring the eggs provided by the nurse. The argument seemed to center over balancing the effect of the eggs on the bowel and on the psyche, but its real meaning concerned who controlled the sick person's diet. This argument ended in a compromise: the soldier would not eat eggs (thereby sparing his bowel), but could feel with his hands uncooked eggs (thereby experiencing the promise of consuming his favorite food after his recovery).[10]

Over the course of the War, the relationship of the male doctors and their female associates changed. Each grudgingly accepted the idea that the other hoped to be of service and might perhaps, on occasion, actually help the sick and wounded. Doctors saw that many women worked very hard for the recovery of their charges. An editorial in a leading medical journal in 1862 praised female nurses, claiming that "nursing is as absolutely the peculiar province of women as any branch of midwifery. The qualities of a good nurse are vigilance, discretion, and gentleness; and these are her special qualities."

In the South, women proved themselves in the crowded hospitals of Richmond. Sally Tompkins cared for wounded soldiers at the home of Judge John Robertson in Richmond, using her own and donated funds. When all hospitals were placed under military control, Jefferson Davis gave her a commission in the Confederate Army to allow her to remain in charge of this excellent hospital.[11] Phoebe Pember, a matron of one section of the huge Chimborazo hospital, kept the alcohol supply locked away from potential drunkards.[12] Samuel H. Stout, the physician in charge of the general hospitals of the Army of the Tennessee, at first opposed female nurses, but changed his mind when he saw their value in treating the Confederate casualties after the Battle of Shiloh. Confederate hospital women again proved their value when they aided in the sudden evacuation of the hospitals from Chattanooga to Atlanta. In the South as well as the North,

Clara Barton was 40 years old, working as a copyist in the U.S. Patent Office, when the War began. She nursed some of the injured soldiers housed in the Patent Office and began a career as an independent nurse. She gathered donated supplies and distributed them to sick and wounded Union troops along the Carolina coast and at the support hospitals of the Army of the Potomac. Miller

An artist records Christian Commission nurses helping the wounded immediately after a battle. The vast majority of women served in general hospitals rather than on the battlefield. HW

the clashes between the male doctor and the female nurse decreased because each became aware of the value of the other.

The gender problem was not simply nurses versus doctors. Doctors had difficulty getting the enlisted men to perform nursing duties. They were always amazed at how Mother Bickerdyke could force convalescents to scrub floors when the doctor could not get these same men to even take out the garbage. And occasionally a female doctor tried to enter the male sphere of military medicine. Many women doctors helped train female nurses or helped treat runaway slaves, but Dr. Mary Walker insisted upon becoming an official military officer.

She showed up at a Washington hospital, dressed in the uniform of an assistant surgeon, complete with pants; she had made the uniform herself. The doctor in charge of the hospi-

tal used her as a volunteer, but she insisted upon her official status as a military doctor. Hearing that medical personnel were scarce in Chattanooga, she went there. General Rosecrans noted that one particular regiment needed an assistant surgeon, but the medical director of the Army of the Cumberland would not accept her. She nevertheless acted as an assistant surgeon while in Chattanooga, still wearing her homemade uniform. After several months, she received in the mail, without explanation or accompanying information, an official U.S. government check. After several unsuccessful attempts to determine the source of the check, she divided the amount by four; this was the monthly salary of an assistant surgeon. She had received four months back pay for the duties she had performed; this is how she discovered that she was officially in the U.S. Army.[13]

6

Union Hospital Ships along the Western Rivers

WEST OF THE APPALACHIAN MOUNTAIN CHAIN, RIVers formed the natural conduits for armies to move toward their objectives and for the detritus of war to flow back from the battlefield. The cities along the great rivers became supply and hospital centers.

The first great battle in the Western theater occurred on 10 August 1861 near Wilson's Creek in the southwestern corner of Missouri. The wounded were hauled overland in wagons to the nearest railhead at Rolla, then shipped in rail cars to the hospitals in St. Louis. The jostling train ride was so painful that the soldiers improvised a system of placing poles in boxcars and hanging stretchers from the poles. This system threatened to collapse with every creak of the railroad cars, frightening the wounded and their accompanying medical personnel.[1]

The city of Cairo, Illinois, at the junction of the Ohio and Mississippi Rivers became a major base for Union military activities in the Western theater. Most of the city buildings were taken over for use as warehouses or hospitals. John H. Brinton was selected to command this hospital center. His disdain for female nurses was noted in the previous chapter. At the start of the War, this young Philadelphia surgeon had scored so well on the military entry examination that he had been appointed a brigade surgeon, a doctor not assigned to any specific regiment. When he arrived in Illinois, he found that a large number of the new soldiers were seriously ill with mumps or measles. All the hospitals in Cairo were soon filled and Brinton commandeered warehouses in nearby Mound City, Illinois.

The Union wounded from the Battle of Belmont crowded into these newly adapted hospital buildings. Brinton personally supervised the evacuation of the wounded from Belmont, Missouri, by boat up the Mississippi River.[2]

The Confederates planned to prevent penetration of their nation's rivers with a series of well-defended forts: Fort Donelson on the Cumberland, Fort Henry on the Tennessee, Island Number 10 on the upper Mississippi, and two forts below New Orleans. Combined forces of the U.S. Navy and Army pushed past all these defensive positions in spring 1862. Three of the largest cities of the Confederacy surrendered rather than suffer naval bombardment from the Northern river flotillas. Nashville, Memphis, and New Orleans became major Union bases and hospital centers.

In the first months of the War, the medical evacuation of the Union army by riverboat was confused. The civilian captains of these vessels looked upon the sick and wounded as just another type of cargo; they refused to depart until the vessel was fully loaded. Very sick soldiers waited aboard without treatment and sometimes even without food until enough sick were available to fill the vessel. On other occasions, the sick and wounded were taken part of the way to the hospital center, but had to wait at an intermediate port while other cargo was handled. On the worst occasions, a line officer would insist that the ship, half loaded with wounded and half loaded with ammunition, must return to the battlefield to deliver the important cargo of ammunition. The sick and wounded were held at the intermediate port until other transportation became available or, in the worst possible scenario, they remained on the cargo vessel to return to the battlefield.

The Quartermaster Department was in official charge of all transportation. The medical director of an army who wanted to transfer patients by riverboat to the northern hospital centers had to apply to the local quartermaster. That individual, inundated by many transportation requests from colonels and generals, often overlooked the request of the surgeon, whose rank was equivalent to major.

To relieve this problem, riverboats were dedicated to the transport of sick and wounded soldiers. The first vessel leased by military authorities for that purpose was the steamer *City of Memphis*. She was refitted to hold 750 beds, and from 7 to 18 February the steamer acted as a floating hospital, moored near Fort Henry on the Tennessee River. The ship carried wounded from the Battle of Fort Donelson to Paducah and Mound City. Another vessel, the *Louisiana*, was leased for medical use in March 1862.[3]

When the leasing of hospital vessels proved successful, the military authorities decided to purchase a steamer that could be completely refitted as a hospital boat. The steamer *D. A. January* had been built in 1857 to carry river passengers. The U.S. Army purchased this sidewheeler, 230 feet long and 65 feet across amidships, in April 1862 and sent it to St. Louis where its interior was completely revamped. The steamer had 160 interior beds in three wards; additional sick and wounded soldiers were housed on deck under awnings. A fan powered by steam circulated air through the ship. The cabin deck contained an operating room and quarters for the staff. Water, cooled by passage through an ice chest, was carried by pipes throughout the ship and was available at several points by faucet. These improvements were paid for by the Western Sanitary Commission.

The medical commanding officer of the *D. A. January* was Alexander Henry Hoff. Born in Philadelphia, he graduated from Jefferson Medical College in 1843, where his preceptor was John K. Mitchell, the father of Silas Weir Mitchell. As the surgeon of the 3rd New York, Hoff had a lantern shot out of his hand as he searched for wounded at night. When the *D. A. January* was purchased by the army, Hoff was placed in charge of all medical activities aboard.[4]

The U.S. Navy also had a problem with sick and wounded sailors. They were generally kept aboard their own ships. Most of the sick, especially patients with fever, were kept on deck under canvas. But when the ship cleared for action, the sick and wounded were unceremoniously hustled below, where they became an impediment. Ninian Pickney, the short and feisty senior naval physician for the river fleet, determined to remove disabled sailors from their vessels so that these warships could engage the enemy unencumbered. At first sailors were treated at army hospitals, but some of the patients thought that they received treatment only after all the army soldiers had been treated. The U.S. Navy set up its own hospital in a small building in Mound City, but soon felt the need for a special ship that could carry their sick and wounded sailors.

The *Red Rover* was built at Cape Giradeau, Missouri, in 1857 for civilian trade. In November 1861 it was purchased in New Orleans by the Confederate government. This Confederate naval vessel was commanded by Lt. John Julius Guthrie of the Confederate Navy. During his last service with the Old U.S. Navy, this officer had helped to capture a slave vessel; when he commanded the prize ship during its transit from Africa to New York, the crew endured a terrifying epidemic. Guthrie's first Confederate command, the C.S.S. *Red Rover*, traveled up the Mississippi to the huge rebel bastion at Island Number 10. There it was used as a floating barracks for troops of the garrison. During the bombardment of the island, a shell passed all the way through the ship. When Island Number 10 surrendered to Union forces, the Confederate naval vessel became the property of the U.S. Navy.

The captured *Red Rover* proceeded to St. Louis for repairs. While it was there, the Western Sanitary Commission offered to purchase bedding and equipment to outfit the vessel as a hospital ship. It had bathrooms, a laundry, an operating room, and nine water closets. It carried three hundred tons of ice for cooling. Special arrangements included an elevator to carry patients between decks and gauze blinds on the portholes to keep cinders and smoke from the patients.[5]

The *Red Rover* was ready for medical use in June 1862. Sick sailors from U.S. naval ships all up and down the Mississippi, Ohio, Cumberland, and Tennessee Rivers were transferred to it. It's chief doctor was George H.

A drawing of the U.S.S. *Red Rover*, the first U.S. naval hospital ship. A single cannon is present on the forecastle for active defense. HW

Bixby of Boston. Nursing was provided by the Sisters of the Holy Cross. Although fitted out as a hospital ship, the *Red Rover* was partially armored and had a single thirty-two-pound gun mounted forward. During the clash between the Mississippi River flotilla and the C.S.S. *Arkansas*, the *Red Rover* was present, but its cannon was not discharged. On 29 August 1862 the *Red Rover* caught fire from accidental causes. The fire was extinguished by the actions of its crew and the nearby U.S.S. *Benton*. During the first two and one half years of the war, the *Red Rover* transported 1,697 patients; 157 of these died on board.[6]

After Memphis was taken by the Union, the U.S. Army took over most of the downtown buildings for use as army hospitals. The navy was assigned the Commercial Hotel, which

A photograph of the *Red Rover* is less artistic than the drawing. The cannon, never used, is gone. Drying laundry is strewn across the forecastle. Boats coming alongside may be transferring sick or wounded soldiers. USAMHI

she turned into a hospital named for Ninian Pickney.

The civilian organizations concerned with health operated their own vessels, leased from private owners. The Western Sanitary Commission was formed by some of the outstanding citizens of St. Louis. The U.S. Sanitary Commission offered to absorb the St. Louis organization into its national structure, but the smaller commission wanted to maintain its independence, fearing that the national organization would overemphasize the eastern theater of the War. The Western Sanitary Commission agreed to limit its activities to the Mississippi River and areas west of that river, leaving the Tennessee Valley to the western branch of the U.S. Sanitary Commission, with its headquarters in Chicago. The two commissions worked together well, although they both competed for money from the same donors. Both commissions outfitted vessels to carry sick and wounded. The army staffed the vessels with its own doctors, but the nurses were generally employees of the parent Sanitary Commission.[7]

The *City of Alton* was leased by the Western Sanitary Commission. The chief nurse aboard was a very small woman who walked with a limp. At the start of the War, Emily Elizabeth Parsons was thirty-six years old, an invalid living with her parents. While her women friends rushed off to try to be of some vague help to the Northern cause, she at her own expense trained in nursing. One of her teachers was Elizabeth Blackwell, the first woman to receive a medical degree in the United States. After one full year of training, Parsons asked her father's permission to head west to become a nurse on the large hospital ship *City of Alton*. Her father, who had thought she would spend her entire life as an invalid dependent upon the family, was amazed at her determination. The diminutive Parsons was made chief of nurses on the vessel and directed the nursing aboard without rest.[8]

Control of steamboats by these four different organizations might have caused considerable confusion. The leaders of the U.S. Army, the U.S. Navy, the U.S. Sanitary Commission, and the Western Sanitary Commission made

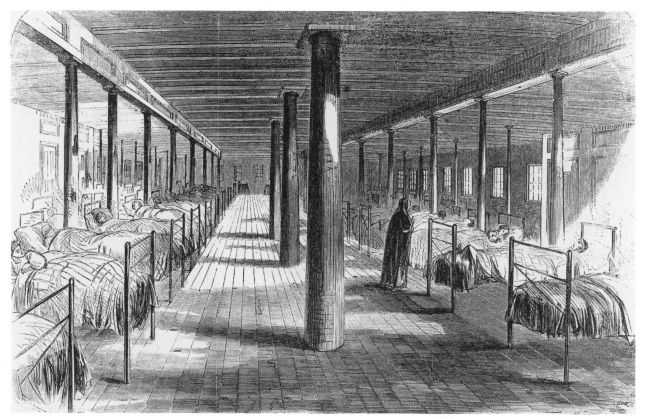

Below the decks of the *Red Rover* were large wards; nursing services were provided by the Sisters of the Holy Cross. HW

Ships crowd along the Tennessee River after the battle of Shiloh. At the far right is the *Tycoon,* a vessel leased by the Cincinnati branch of the U.S. Sanitary Commission and outfitted as a hospital transport. The night before, Federal gunboats in the center of the river dueled with Confederate artillery ashore; the shells passed over these ships. USAMHI

no effort at all to coordinate the movements of their hospital boats.[9] But at the lowest level, at the point where the sick were carried on board a vessel, there was little friction. The next available hospital steamer went to the place where the sick and wounded were accumulating and carried them to the place further north where facilities for their convalescence were available.

This system had just begun to function when the Confederates attacked the Northern forces gathered near Shiloh Church. The Federals fell back to the Tennessee River, where hospital boats and supply vessels were lined up on the shore. Frightened soldiers slid down the river bank and tried to get onto the hospital steamers. The doctors and boat captains placed guards on the gangplanks to assure that only wounded could come aboard. The boats rapidly filled with severely wounded soldiers; on some boats, doctors and nurses had great difficulty moving about without stepping on anyone. Federal gunboats cruising up and down the river fired at the rebels on the shore. Confederate cannon fired back. As the doctors and

nurses on the moored hospital vessels tried to treat the wounded, artillery shells passed overhead. They found themselves in the middle of a night artillery duel.

During that night, Union reinforcements arrived on the eastern shore and were ferried across the Tennessee River. The next morning, the Federals counterattacked and pushed the Confederates back. Bernard J. D. Irwin and John Brinton, physicians in charge of different sections of the Union Army medical support, organized hospitals on the battlefield. They placed the wounded in the tents left the previous day by retreating Union soldiers.[10]

The wounded from Shiloh were gathered at a small dock called Pittsburg Landing. The *D. A. January* crammed 431 wounded soldiers aboard and steamed for St. Louis. Disgorging these wounded into the St. Louis hospital complex, the hospital ship returned to Pittsburg Landing for another load of sick and wounded. These 284 patients were carried to Keokuk, Iowa. The vessel made a total of six trips to Pittsburg Landing, slowly dispersing the wounded from the horrible Battle of Shi-

Table 4

Schedule of the <u>D. A. January</u> for the Year 1862

Embarkation		Debarkation		Number Sick & Wounded
Date	Place	Date	Place	
11 April	Pittsburg Landing	14 April	St. Louis	431
18 April	Pittsburg Landing	23 April	Keokuk	284
2 May	Pittsburg Landing	4 May	New Albany	300
10 May	Pittsburg Landing	14 May	Jeff. Barracks	284
9 June	Pittsburg Landing	12 June	Jeff. Barracks	375
19 June	Pittsburg Landing	23 June	Keokuk	459
6 July	Paducah	8 July	Louisville	287
17 July	Helena	21 July	Jeff. Barracks	317
25 July	Paducah	27 July	Jeff. Barracks	298
4 Aug	Paducah	6 Aug	St. Louis	144
20 Aug	Helena	23 Aug	Mound City	160
23 Aug	Paducah	23 Aug	Mound City	30
	refurbished at St. Louis			
29 Sept	Helena	3 Oct	St. Louis	386
7 Oct	Helena	10 Oct	Columbus	273
12 Oct	Columbus, KY	15 Oct	St. Louis	372
21 Oct	Columbus	23 Oct	Mound City	88
30 Oct	Columbus	4 Nov	Keokuk	378
18 Nov	Columbus	21 Nov	St. Louis	410
28 Nov	Columbus	30 Nov	Jeff. Barracks	435
9 Dec	Helena	16 Dec	St. Louis	440

Throughout 1862 the hospital steamer <u>D. A. January</u> traveled the western river system carrying sick and wounded from Shiloh, Kentucky, and Arkansas to Illinois, Missouri, and Iowa.

Source: <u>MSH</u>, Surgical Volume, Pt. 3, 979-80.

loh to hospitals along the Mississippi and Ohio Rivers from Cincinnati to Jefferson Barracks, the old army post near St. Louis.

The commander of the Confederate troops at Shiloh, Major General Albert Sydney Johnston, was killed in action. While riding his horse near the front of his troops, he was hit by several minié balls. Two struck him near his right hip and one grazed his left lower leg. He did not think he was seriously injured and did not even dismount. He urged his troops forward, but began to feel light-headed. He then noted that blood was welling up out of his right boot. He was helped from his horse and the boot was removed. Blood gushed from behind his right knee. He had with him a tourniquet supplied by the medical director of his army, Dr. David W. Yandell. This was applied, but did not stem the bleeding.[11]

When Dr. Yandell arrived, Johnston was dead, lying in a huge pool of blood, sur- rounded by horrified staff officers. Yandell ex- amined the body. A minié ball had ripped a gash in the popliteal artery and the general had bled to death. Johnston had been wounded in the same leg in 1837 during a duel. The round ball had remained lodged within his hip and his right leg remained numb for the remainder of his life. Perhaps the defective sensation in his leg was the reason that the Confederate commander did not real- ize he had been wounded; if he had recognized the wound before the blood bubbled up out of his boot, he might have sought medical aid. Dr. Yandell thought that if he been present, he would have recognized the seriousness of the bleeding and ligated the popliteal artery, thereby saving his life. If Johnston had super- vised the Confederate attack that night and their subsequent defense the next day, the Bat- tle of Shiloh might have ended as a Confeder- ate victory.[12]

7

The Beginnings of the Letterman System

WILLIAM ALEXANDER HAMMOND BECAME SUR-
geon general of the Army of the United States
just as the great Peninsula Campaign was beginning. The Army of the Potomac, under General George B. McClellan, was transported
from the Washington area to the peninsula
formed by the York and James Rivers. McClellan planned to drive up this peninsula from
Fort Monroe, still under Union control, to
threaten Richmond. The Confederate army
would be forced to defend the capital of their
upstart nation and could be destroyed. Since
the U.S. Navy controlled the oceans and the
wide York and James Rivers, McClellan could
supply his huge force from vessels. But delivering the correct supplies to the correct location proved much more difficult in practice
than in planning.

The medical director of the Army of the Potomac was Charles A. Tripler, a well known
doctor of the Old Army who had written a
manual on military medicine. His communiqués to the Surgeon General's Office exuded
confidence in March, before the army left
Washington, but experience in the field led to
unexpected difficulties.

15 March 1862
To: Surgeon-General Finley, U.S. Army.
I have the honor to request that field supplies
for 140,000 men may be put up by the medical
purveyor immediately, to be transported with
Major General McClellan's army wherever it
may be ordered. I have appointed Assistant Surgeon Bartholow medical purveyor for this Army.

14 April 1862
To: Surgeon R. C. Wood, Acting Surgeon
General.
I learned this morning by telegraph that a portion of the supplies ordered from New York a
month ago has reached Fort Monroe. Their arrival is most timely as our field supplies are almost exhausted.

18 May 1862
To: The Surgeon General, Washington D.C.
The supplies that left Washington on the 11th
have not yet reached here. I suggest that medical
supplies be sent in charge of a special agent. . . .
Medical supplies have been found stored under
other supplies in the hold of vessels, and de-
tained there for weeks in this river.

19 May 1862
To: Brigadier General W. A. Hammond, Surgeon General, U.S. Army.
I stated that unless certain supplies for which
I had telegraphed that day reached me in 5 days,
this army would be in peril. It is now 10 days
later and they are not here. . . . The army is
marching today and a battle may occur at any
time. We are not prepared for it.

20 May 1862
To Surgeon General W. A. Hammond.
We are this instant receiving the cooking uten-
sils and furniture and the liquors sent by Dr.
Lamb. On the invoice with the letter are 100
ounces of quinine. I do not know how much of
this has been ordered. A requisition for 2,000
ounces was forwarded last week.

The medical director of the Army of the Potomac at the start of the Peninsula campaign was Charles A. Tripler. He fought with the U.S. Sanitary Commission over the control of hospital steamers. NLM

29 May 1862

To: Brigadier General W. A. Hammond, Surgeon General.

A considerable supply of stimulants has come to hand (some of it, however, in bad order), but no quinine has yet arrived. We are desperately in want of this article.[1]

These telegrams illustrate Tripler's problems as he attempted to provide medical support to the Army of the Potomac during the Peninsula campaign. Each request is addressed to a different individual because of the change in command of the Medical Service: to Finley, to the acting surgeon general, to the Surgeon General's Office, finally to Hammond. The tone of these communiqués changes from confidence to concern to exasperation to panic. Tripler begs for supplies, particularly quinine.

Supplies came to the Army of the Potomac on cargo ships. The sick and the wounded were evacuated by hospital vessels. One of the first officers injured and evacuated by vessel was Lt. Col. James C. Strong, the second-in-command of the 38th New York. While the regiment was advancing near Williamsburg, Virginia, Strong was hit in the right thigh. The ball struck the bone where the femur articulates with the pelvis and exited through the right buttock. The officer fell immediately and was unable to walk. He was carried to the regimental hospital, where he was examined by the regimental surgeon, Dr. A. J. Berry. Dr. Berry debrided the wound, removing small pieces of bone and some of Strong's clothing, which had been carried into the wound by the bullet. Fortunately, the rebels were using old round balls, not the new minié ball. The bone was damaged, but not splintered, as one would expect with a deformed and tumbling minié ball. Strong was taken to a landing on the York River near Williamsburg and trans-

During the first few weeks of the Peninsula campaign, sick and wounded soldiers were sent to the hospitals at Fort Monroe, on the eastern tip of the peninsula. This eyewitness sketch shows the morass of supplies, boxes, loafers, officers, women (probably Sanitary Commission nurses), and wounded. Several men have their arms in slings. Railroad flatcars covered by awnings carry sick and wounded soldiers; one of the cars is pulled by a single horse. HW

ferred by boat to the military hospital at Fort Monroe, located at the tip of the peninsula. Five days later, a Sanitary Commission hospital ship carried him to New York, where he traveled by rail to his home in Buffalo. Pus poured out of the wound for the next ten weeks.

Union forces continued to advance up the peninsula. They established a major base at White House Landing on the Pamunkey River, a branch of the York. A railroad connected White House Landing and Richmond; McClellan proposed to push his army along this line and into the city. Military supplies, including huge offensive guns that McClellan hoped to use to bombard the Confederate capital, moved west along this rail line. But the Confederates fought the advancing Union forces; wounded passed down this same railroad in the opposite direction.

On 1 May 1862 Confederate forces under the command of General Joseph Johnston attacked the Federals viciously near the village of Seven Pines. The Union medical authorities set up a field hospital in a group of buildings called Savage's Station. This area, soon known more simply as Savage Station, overflowed with an unprecedented number of seriously wounded. They were evacuated as rapidly as possible, carried on railroad flatcars, sometimes with awnings to protect against the sun. They arrived at White House Landing and were carried to vessels on the Pamunkey.

On 21 June Dr. William H. Page wrote a letter to a leading medical journal about his experiences at Savage Station. He had treated both Federal and rebel soldiers. Wounds among Union soldiers were caused by the round musket ball; surgical intervention usually recovered the ball. He assisted a South Carolina surgeon operating upon thirty wounded rebels. All had been wounded by the conical minié ball used by Federal rifles; only one of these bullets was recovered. Dr. Page thought that the conical bullet created much more severe wounds than the round rebel musket ball. The doctor concluded his medical report with his military predictions. He thought that the Union army would soon take Richmond, the war would be over, and the huge mass of wounded that he had seen at Savage Station "is something not likely to occur again in our time."[2]

With much difficulty, the wounded soldiers at Savage Station were evacuated by rail to White House Landing for sea transport to the North. Hospital vessels were unable to embark the wounded as fast as they arrived and makeshift hospitals had to be organized. After all available buildings were utilized for shelter, many additional wounded were housed in tents along the river.

The white house that gave White House Landing its name was the finest structure for many miles around. The house had been the home of the Custis family, the family of Martha Washington. General McClellan vowed to protect this famous landmark because of its historical importance. The buildings, shaded by huge old oaks, looked tempting to the hundreds of sick and wounded lying in the hot sun. But this house could not be used as a hospital; armed guards kept empty the building and its grounds.

The wounded accumulated at White House Landing because many of the hospital vessels had already left for Northern cities carrying sick soldiers. The U.S. Sanitary Commission controlled all hospital vessels. Frederick Law Olmsted, one of the major leaders of the commission, personally directed these hospital transports. Tripler claimed that Olmsted, who meant well but lacked all military experience, sent vessels North that were not fully loaded and contained only mildly sick soldiers who should have stayed with their military units. Tripler was embarrassed when soldiers who had been sick when embarked were perfectly well when the ships docked at Philadelphia or New York. On the other hand, Olmsted felt that Tripler's requests regarding ship movements were contradictory and impossible.[3]

Disease began to debilitate the Army of the Potomac. Quinine was in very short supply and malaria became a serious problem. Physicians even noted a few soldiers with signs of scurvy; this meant that the army was not receiving an adequate amount of nutritional food, such as fresh vegetables. Supplying this huge military organization proved more difficult than had been envisioned. Sometimes the supplies that were needed were found in the deepest hold of the transporting vessel; only after tons of unnecessary material were unloaded could the needed material be found.

Faced with heavy combat losses and a sick army, General McClellan concluded that the Union Army was too debilitated to take Rich-

Convalescent soldiers are leaving the peninsula aboard a hospital transport on the James River. The transports were controlled by the U.S. Sanitary Commission and Tripler worried that this organization evacuated many mildly ill soldiers who still possessed military value for the Union forces. Many of the convalescents in this picture appear able to shoulder a weapon. **Miller**

The wounded were taken on flat cars from Savage Station to White House Landing on the Pamunkey. USAMHI

The white house that gave White House Landing its name was not used as a hospital; in fact, armed guards prevented sick and wounded soldiers from lying in the shade of these large oaks. The house held historic value as the site where George Washington courted the widow Martha Custis. **USAMHI**

mond. He ordered the Army of the Potomac to retreat to Harrison's Landing on the James River. White House Landing on the Pamunkey would be abandoned. The beautiful dwelling that had been the home of Martha Washington remained unused throughout the period of Union occupation. The retreating troops chopped down all the trees on the property to allow ships in the river unobstructed lanes of fire upon any potential advancing rebels. Just before departure, the house was put to the torch. The War was changing from a polite duel between professionals to a vicious struggle for the survival of a way of life.[4]

Physicians were asked to volunteer to stay behind with the three thousand seriously wounded Union soldiers at Savage Station. Dr. Page was one of the few to remain; he was a civilian, appointed by the governor of Massachusetts to look after soldiers from that state, so he thought that he would not be taken prisoner. Union troops evacuated Savage Station, but due to confused orders, they retreated only a few hundred yards. When the Confederates arrived, they were met with three thousand

Federal wounded, a few Federal doctors, and incoming Federal artillery fire. Soon the shelling ceased as the Federals retreated further. The Confederates attempted to evacuate the wounded to Richmond, but most of the Union soldiers were so badly injured that they were unable to walk; those who could walk had retreated with their able-bodied comrades. Dr. Page convinced the Confederates to leave the wounded where they were.[5]

The rebels provided some food and medical supplies, but not much. Savage Station became a festering hole where all wounds became infected and everyone was always ravenously hungry. In subsequent battles, the Confederate Army transported wounded Union soldiers to this place. James Winchell was a private with Berdan's Sharpshooters. He suffered a splintering wound of the upper arm on 27 June 1862 at the Battle of Gaines' Mill. He was carried to Savage Station, where he begged Union surgeons to examine the wound that the rebels had dressed. He was told that they would get to him "as soon as we get through with a few bad cases." When his dressing was finally removed days later, the wound was infested with maggots. Dr. Elisha M. White of the 20th Massachusetts informed him that amputation was necessary, but that the Union doctors had long since run out of anesthetics. Winchell was wide awake throughout the amputation.

For the next two weeks, Winchell tried to survive. He was always thirsty, but before he could swallow the collected rain water, he had to spit out the dead flies. When he was finally able to walk, he staggered into Richmond. Passersby noted his condition and, even though he was in Union uniform, arranged wagon transport. Winchell was finally transferred to the Union steamer *Daniel Webster*, which the rebels allowed to dock.[6] The same steamer carried Dr. Page back to the United States.

Early in July 1862 Hammond removed Trip-

ler from his position as chief doctor of the Army of the Potomac. Tripler was an old surgeon of the Old Army and could not adapt to the wide range of abilities of the doctors serving with the volunteer forces. He complained of their pet remedies and damned them as sect practitioners: homeopaths, hydropaths, herb doctors, single-idea men.

As the new medical director of the Army of the Potomac, Hammond appointed a friend from the Old Army, Jonathan Letterman. Letterman was a graduate of Jefferson Medical College; when he was a student, the dean was George McClellan. The dean's son was George B. McClellan, now the commander of the Army of the Potomac. General McClellan, Letterman, and Hammond had all served together in the successful Western Virginia campaign in 1861. Letterman's vigor and com-

The Union wounded who could not be evacuated were concentrated at Savage Station, where they remained for several weeks. Miller

In July, Jonathan Letterman replaced Tripler as the medical director of the Army of the Potomac. He began to introduce a series of changes that would be called the Letterman System. He is photographed sitting in front of his tent. USAMHI

petence as well as their previous relations gave General McClellan enough confidence to permit major changes in the medical organization of the Army of the Potomac.

Letterman attempted to shift control of ambulances from the Quartermaster to the Medical Department. The Quartermaster Department used ambulances to haul supplies to the battle line and then, when empty, to stand by to serve as ambulances to evacuate wounded. In the confusion of battle, excited officers would take command of the wagons and order them to move ammunition or supplies to another portion of the battlefield. The wagons were often unavailable to serve as ambulances when needed. Letterman induced General McClellan to assign all the ambulance wagons to the Medical Service; they could not be used for other purposes even if they stood empty.[7]

Letterman's second great innovation was standardization. Prior to Letterman's improvements, each army doctor carried his own medical bag brought from civilian life that contained his personal assortment of tools and drugs. Each regimental medical supply wagon contained additional drugs and supplies in the amount and location determined by the regimental surgeon and hospital steward. Letterman introduced a standard supply wagon for each regiment and a standard medical kit for each doctor. If one doctor ran out of chloroform, he could obtain additional supplies from any kit or any regimental supply wagon; he knew the exact location of chloroform because it was the same in every wagon and in every kit.

Letterman's third great change involved a restructuring of the medical command system. Previously, any doctor with the rank of surgeon could direct the activities of any doctor with the rank of assistant surgeon, regardless of their actual expertise. An assistant surgeon who had been a professor of surgery at the leading medical school just a year before might find himself pushed aside by a career army officer with much less surgical skill. Letterman eliminated the small regimental hospital in order to consolidate doctors from several regiments. At the brigade or division hospital, surgeons were appointed from various regiments to perform needed operations; the appointment was based upon their skill and experience in their entire careers, mili-

tary and civilian, and had no relation to their military rank.

The Letterman system slowly transformed the care of the wounded in the Army of the Potomac. McClellan ordered ambulances transferred from the quartermasters on 2 August 1862, the standardization of the medical supply system on 4 October 1862, and the shift from regimental to division hospitals on 30 October 1862. The special order issued on 2 August 1862 made it crystal clear to everyone that the medical branch controlled the ambulance corps in the Army of the Potomac. "The officer in charge of the [ambulance] train will at once remove everything not legitimate," the order read,

and if there not be room for it in the baggage wagons of the regiment he will leave it on the road. Any attempt by a superior officer to prevent him from doing his duty in this or any other instance will be promptly reported to the Medical Director of the Army Corps who will lay the matter before the commander of the Corps itself. The latter will at the earliest possible moment place the officer offending in arrest for trial for disobedience of orders.

All of these orders issued by George B. McClellan, the commanding officer of the Army of the Potomac, were actually written by Letterman.[8]

Letterman demonstrated vigor, readiness, and unwavering attention to the mission of the medical component of the Army of the Potomac: maintenance of the health of the army and the rapid and skillful treatment of the wounded. Rather than suffer a shortage of medical supplies at one point, Letterman determined upon an oversupply at many points. "Lost supplies can be replaced," he said in a phrase that could be the motto of the Union Medical Department, "but lives lost are gone forever."[9]

Letterman's changes came too late to influence the Peninsula campaign. McClellan's sick and exhausted army was evacuated from the Harrison's Landing by boat. The Confederate army, now under the command of Robert E. Lee, moved northward. They engaged Union forces at the site of the Battle of Bull Run.[10] This Second Bull Run was a stunning defeat for the Union; the Federal wounded remained on the field after the battle. Surgeon General Hammond was almost hysterical as he rode

Letterman was present when one of the most familiar photographs of the Civil War was taken. He is standing with his hands on his belt between General George B. McClellan on his right and President Abraham Lincoln on his left. NA

through Washington, begging for volunteer physicians to help aid the wounded. He could not obtain enough wagons to transport the great number of wounded just the few miles from the battlefield to the hospitals in Washington. In the major force engaged at Second Bull Run, the Army of Virginia, the Quartermaster Department still controlled the ambulances. Hammond was exasperated when he wrote a very venomous letter to Edwin M. Stanton, the Secretary of War.

"Up to this date," wrote Hammond, "600 wounded still remain on the battlefield, in consequence of an insufficiency of ambulances and the want of a proper system for regulating their removal in the Army of Virginia. Many have died of starvation; many more will die in consequence of exhaustion, and all have endured torments which might have been avoided."[11] A subordinate who accuses his superior of starving his own troops to death balances on the border between courage and recklessness.

8

Confederate Medicine Organizing

THE PENINSULA CAMPAIGN ALSO TESTED CONFEDerate medicine. As the Union forces gathered in Washington prior to their naval movement to the peninsula between the James and York Rivers, the Confederate commander, General Joseph E. Johnston, expected a direct attack across the Potomac on his army in northern Virginia. He notified Surgeon General Samuel P. Moore that he was clearing from his regiments all those who were ill; 9,000 sick soldiers required hospitalization in Richmond. Moore quickly surveyed the existing hospitals and found that only 2,500 beds were available. Barracks had been built on Chimborazo Hill to the east of Richmond for use as winter quarters for Johnston's army. Since that army was in northern Virginia, Moore was able to acquire these barracks for use as a hospital. He built additional small wooden buildings to create the gigantic Chimborazo Hospital. Tobacco factories in Richmond were empty because tobacco was no longer being shipped abroad. The tobacco factory workers provided much of the labor for the construction of the new hospital. Wood for the Chimborazo pavilion buildings came from unused tobacco crates.

The surgeon general appointed Dr. James Brown McCaw to direct this huge new hospital. Born in Richmond, McCaw graduated in 1844 from the medical faculty of the University of the City of New York. He had studied surgery by apprenticeship to the leading New York surgeon, Dr. Valentine Mott. McCaw practiced medicine and surgery in Richmond, where he edited the *Virginia Medical and Surgical Journal* until it ceased publication at the beginning of the War. In addition to being a practicing physician and an editor, McCaw had been professor of chemistry at the Medical College of Virginia.

Administratively, Chimborazo Hospital was a separate army post. McCaw was commandant of the post as well as surgeon-in-charge of the hospital. This meant that he supervised a line officer with thirty soldiers as guards; Dr. McCaw became thereby one of the few medical officers to command combat troops. Dr. McCaw had studied the utopian communities of the early nineteenth century as a hobby and based his administration of Chimborazo upon what he had learned. McCaw received no extra funds from the Confederacy, only the money that the patients would have required for their rations if they had been with their regiments. The hospital owned its own livestock, about two hundred cows and five hundred goats, and grazed them on nearby farmland donated by the landowner. A boat named the *Chimborazo* traveled up the James River as far as Lynchburg to obtain food for the patients.[1]

The hospital was divided into five sections. These divisions separated soldiers by states and were often called hospitals; for example, the Second Division was called the Georgia Hospital and was under the command of noted Georgia physician Henry F. Campbell. Each division consisted of about thirty wooden pavilions, referred to as wards. Each was one story, one hundred feet long by thirty feet wide, containing two rows of beds. At times, the capacity of the hospital was increased by the use of large tents. The view from the eleva-

Chimborazo Hospital was a huge complex of wooden pavilions located on Chimborazo Hill on the east side of Richmond. NA

tion of Chimborazo Hospital was spectacular: the tall ships of the harbor to the south, the spires of the city to the west, and lush farmland to the east. A very small cemetery, the Oakwood Cemetery, was located nearby.[2]

But even this huge new hospital did not provide enough beds. The Confederate medical authorities decided to build another hospital complex in the rural area just west of Richmond. Wooden pavilions were constructed to house another four to five thousand sick and wounded. This complex was named Winder Hospital (pronounced Wine-der) after the career army officer who commanded the local Richmond troops.

The young doctor chosen to head the new Winder Hospital was Alexander G. Lane. Lane had graduated from the medical faculty of Tulane University in New Orleans in 1858. He had served as surgeon of the 18th Mississippi and was in charge of the Union wounded after the Battle of Ball's Bluff in northern Virginia. When the Winder Hospital was organized in April 1862, Lane was placed in charge. At age 27 he commanded eight hundred hospital attendants and was responsible for the care of up to five thousand patients at any one time. The hospital was organized into six divisions, each with one surgeon and six assistant sur-

geons. Each division had its own dispensary, laundry, and kitchen. The hospital contained a bakery and sixteen acres of food plots, tended by convalescents. The hospital ran its own dairy, producing three hundred gallons of milk each day.

A ravine ran through the center of the hospital grounds. Garbage and human waste were dumped into this ravine and every other day, two ten-thousand-gallon tanks were discharged, carrying these wastes into the Kanawha River. Mrs. Snowden of Charleston was in charge of the alcohol supply; she purchased imported liquors with her own money. The chief matron of the first division was Miss Emily Mason, daughter of Senator Mason, whose capture by the Union navy while on an English ship led to the *Trent* affair, a diplomatic crisis with Great Britain. Each morning except Sunday, the six division heads met with Lane; the seven men inspected one of the divisions, selected at random. Lane and his division heads taught a continuing medical education course for the assistant surgeons.[3]

Surgeon General Moore organized the hospital system in Virginia. While Richmond was the hospital center, other important general hospitals were located in Charlottesville, Lynchburg, and Petersburg. Moore developed

Table 5

Chimborazo Hospital Administration

Chief surgeon and post commandant: James B. McCaw
Commissary officer: John H. Claiborne
Quartermaster: A. S. Buford

Division	State troops	Chief surgeon
First	Virginia	P. F. Browne
Second	Georgia	S. E. Habersham
Third	North Carolina	E. Harvie Smith
Fourth	Alabama	S. N. Davis
Fifth	South Carolina	E. M. Seabrook

Source: E. E. Hume, "Chimborazo Hospital, Confederate States Army, America's Largest Military Hosital," <u>Virginia Medical Monthly</u> 61 (1934): 189-95.

an evacuation system to prevent another disaster like the one that followed Manassas. Two forward hospitals were set up at key railroad junctions. The rail system funneled patients from northeastern Virginia through Fredericksburg and Hanover Junction to Richmond and from northwestern Virginia through Gordonsville to Charlottesville and Lynchburg. A rail line ran between Gordonsville and Hanover Junction, and it was at those two locations that major forwarding hospitals were organized. The map on p. 000, illustrating Grant's campaign in Virginia, also shows this Confederate rail evacuation system.

The hospital in Gordonsville was formed from the medical facilities at Manassas that were broken up following Johnston's retreat in spring 1862. The Exchange Hotel, located near the railroad station, was taken over and renamed the Gordonsville Receiving and Distributing Hospital, the R and D. When sick and wounded soldiers filled the Exchange Hotel building, many other buildings in town were commandeered by medical authorities.

One of the major physicians at the Gordonsville R and D in 1863 was Edward A. Craighill.[4] He had graduated from the medical school of the University of Pennsylvania in 1861 at age twenty. He enlisted as a private, but Hunter Holmes McGuire, whom he had known when both studied medicine in Philadelphia, appointed him a hospital steward. Thomas H. Williams, medical director of Johnston's army, arranged for Craighill to take the medical examination to become a Confed-

erate surgeon. At Gordonsville, Craighill set up a separate hospital in the woods for patients with smallpox. The doctor changed his clothes on the way to and from this pest hospital, fearing that he might carry the disease back to the patients at the Exchange Hotel building. A slave known as Old Joe thought he had already had smallpox and volunteered to work there. Unfortunately, he developed smallpox and died.[5]

Hanover Junction was the site of another medical distribution center. Wounded from battles near Fredericksburg were carried to Hanover Junction and then forwarded to Richmond. Some patients were sent via the alternate route through Gordonsville to Charlottesville, and later on to Lynchburg. When the Army of Northern Virginia undertook incursions into the North, the hospital at Hanover Junction was not fully utilized. The doctors and facilities from that city moved to Winchester to set up a support hospital.

The hospital director at Charlottesville was John L. Cabell (rhymes with rabble), who had been on the medical faculty of the University of Virginia. He was famous for a book that argued that the black and white races were both descended from Adam and were closely related. Cabell wrote his book to oppose the racial theories of Josiah Nott of Mobile. Cabell was, however, more than a theoretician; he undertook some serious operations, including trephination. The buildings of the University of Virginia were taken over for medical use and were referred to collectively as the Midway Hospital. During peak periods, the wounded were housed in many other buildings in the city.

Cabell's problems with higher authority are exemplified in the exchange of remonstrances that became known as the Monticello affair. Cabell reported that some sick and wounded were housed in the Monticello Hospital. The Confederate military authorities notified Cabell that Thomas Jefferson's estate was too important as a Southern historical monument to be used as a hospital; patients should be immediately removed. Cabell replied that the Monticello Hospital was located in the Monticello Hotel, located in downtown Charlottesville; it was named after but not otherwise related to Jefferson's plantation.[6]

From Charlottesville, many sick and wounded were sent on to the major hospital center in Lynchburg. At that city, the sick and wounded were examined at the train depot; some were placed in the Wayside Hospital and later sent further South. Those requiring special nursing were sent to the Ladies Hospital at 6th and Main; this hospital was supported by volunteer women from Lynchburg. Those needing surgery were sent to the special surgical center located in the Odd Fellow's Building at 12th and Church Streets. Those with smallpox were sent to the pest house, located in a private dwelling immediately adjacent to the city cemetery. The remainder were distributed to the city hospital system, which included virtually all public buildings and a number of private homes. The surgeon-in-charge was William Otway Owen, who had graduated from the medical school of New York University.[7]

As the Confederate troops returned from their incursion into Maryland, they brought with them the seeds of smallpox. Actually, no one knew where the terrible outbreak originated; people assumed it came from the North because that was the site of origin of just about every evil thing that afflicted the Confederacy. The smallpox epidemic did not produce a large number of ill soldiers, but the high mortality of the disease frightened everyone who had not been properly vaccinated.

All soldiers in the Confederate army should

Table 6

Smallpox in the Confederate Military Hospitals of Virginia

Year	Month	Cases	Deaths
1862	October	12	1
	November	161	30
	December	424	145
1863	January	438	221
	February	187	137
	March	133	57
	April	192	162
	May	66	39
	June	110	24
	July	43	30
	August	8	4
	September	0	0
	October	13	2
	November	100	13
	December	403	114
1864	January	223	141

A smallpox epidemic began in the Confederate army in late fall 1862. Another followed at the same time in 1863.

Source: William A. Carrington, "Report of Eruptive Fevers Treated in General Hospitals, Department of Virginia, from October 1, 1862, to January 31st, 1864," Confederate States Medical and Surgical Journal 1 (1864): 37–38.

have been vaccinated. This official policy had been promulgated several times, most notably in March 1862. The medical authorities were slow to vaccinate everyone and the soldiers filled the medical gap by vaccinating themselves. "So great was the dread of smallpox," reported Confederate surgeon James Bolton, "that the men became impatient of the slow process of vaccination by medical officers with carefully selected virus."[8]

This difficulty was not due to the blockade; vaccine had never been imported. Rather, a doctor kept vaccine available by successful transmission from one person to another. A few days after a person was vaccinated pustules formed at the vaccination site; this represented the successful "take" of the vaccine. Material from the pustules was injected into the arm of the next person, or several people. Thus, the vaccine was transferred from one person to another directly. Soldiers began to help themselves to the apparently successful scar of a fellow soldier and pass the material without medical supervision.

An unusual and bothersome phenomenon occurred in a large number of soldiers. The site of vaccination became red, swollen, and painful. Sloughing of the skin could occur, and some soldiers even experienced systemic symptoms such as fever and malaise. None of the army physicians had ever seen this phenomenon. Old private doctors in Richmond were queried, but they also were baffled. It was termed spurious vaccination; no one knew if the soldier so vaccinated was immune to smallpox. This new disease became widespread throughout the South, from Virginia to Arkansas, and occurred when doctors as well as soldiers performed the vaccination.

No one could determine the cause of spurious vaccination. Some thought that the troops were suffering dietary deficiencies that somehow altered their reaction to the smallpox vaccine. Perhaps some strains of the vaccine material had been adulterated by contaminants. The two Georgia brigades of McLaws' Division of the Army of Northern Virginia suffered a severe outbreak of spurious vaccination. So many soldiers were ill with fever that for a time in early spring 1862 the brigades were unfit for service. Medical Director Lafayette Guild traced the outbreak to a single soldier. He had returned from leave in Atlanta with a new vaccination on his arm. The "take"

from his arm was spread throughout his regiment, and then, from soldier to soldier, to both Georgia brigades in the division. The soldier admitted that he had obtained vaccine material for his own vaccination from a prostitute in Atlanta. Guild worried that the entire division had acquired syphilis because of improper vaccination.[9]

An important medical event occurred during Stonewall Jackson's Valley Campaign. The medical director of Jackson's army was Hunter Holmes McGuire. Unlike most of the other leaders of Confederate military medicine, he had not served in the Old U.S. Army. He was born in Winchester, Virginia, in 1835, and studied medicine by apprenticeship under his father. McGuire attended and graduated from the small medical school in Winchester; his father was the dean. He practiced medicine in Winchester and became professor of surgery at his father's school. He thought that to be a leader in the profession of medicine, he needed to obtain more training.

Even though he already held the degree of doctor of medicine, he entered the medical school at Jefferson Medical College in Philadelphia. He was enrolled in that school in 1859, when the town became politically excited by John Brown's raid on Harpers Ferry. McGuire was appalled when the people of Philadelphia, and many of his fellow students from the North, treated crazy John Brown as a hero. He could not understand why they did not abhor the idea of a bloody slave uprising. McGuire led the Southern students out on strike; eventually they transferred as a group to the Medical College of Virginia in Richmond. The secession of the Southern medical students presaged the secession of the Southern states.[10]

Because of his extensive medical training, McGuire was appointed the senior surgeon in the brigade commanded by Thomas J. Jackson. McGuire's older brother was Jackson's secretary. Jackson was wounded in his finger at the Battle of Manassas. When he waved his arm above his head to signal his troops to move forward, a minié ball struck the middle finger of his left hand, breaking it. After the battle, Jackson sought medical aid; the regimental surgeon told him that the finger had to be amputated at once. Jackson merely walked away, got on his horse, and rode off to find McGuire. McGuire splinted the finger with two sticks and it healed. Jackson received his appellation Stonewall at Manassas; he also gained a strong trust in the judgment of Hunter Holmes McGuire. When Jackson was promoted to command a separate Confederate army in the Valley Campaign, he selected McGuire as the medical director of that force.

After the Battle of Winchester, 25 May 1862, McGuire inspected the field hospitals. The Union prisoners who had been wounded were being cared for by seven Union physicians. These doctors had stayed behind, knowing that they would be taken prisoner. They expected to be incarcerated in Libby Prison in Richmond until they could be exchanged for Confederate officers in Union hands, just like other prisoners. McGuire had another idea.

McGuire suggested to Stonewall Jackson that physicians should be treated as noncombatants and released. His argument was seconded by Dr. Daniel Conrad, who was a naval surgeon, but, because no Confederate ship could be found for him, had volunteered to act as surgeon of the Third Virginia. McGuire and Conrad convinced Jackson to release the seven Union doctors on the condition that these former prisoners would try to obtain the release of seven Confederate doctors and would also try to convince Union military authorities to treat physicians as noncombatants.[11]

The principle spread rapidly throughout both armies; physicians and chaplains were noncombatants and could succor the wounded without fearing capture. The United States officially changed its Laws of War on 24 April 1863 so that all Confederate physicians and chaplains "if they fall into the hands of the American Army are *not* considered prisoners of war unless the commander has reasons to retain them." The Union legal scholar Francis Lieber drew up these new rules and they were referred to as the Lieber Code. The new rules did not prevent a personal tragedy; at almost the same moment that Lieber was drafting the new code, his son Oscar, who had favored the Southern cause and joined the Confederate army, lay dying at Chimborazo.[12]

The Peninsula campaign strained Confederate medical resources as well as the Northern medical system. It was fortunate for the Southerners that the major battles of the campaign were fought on the very doorstep of their capital city and major hospital center. Despite the fact that the huge Chimborazo and Winder Hospitals had only recently been completed, the number of Confederate wounded soon swamped the Richmond hospital system. James McCaw, the director of Chimborazo Hospital, ordered the ambulance drivers not to bring any additional wounded to his

Table 7:

Union Doctors Released at the Winchester Accord

Doctor	Rank	Unit
James Burd Peale	brigade surgeon	regular army
Jarvis J. Jonson	surgeon	27th Indiana
Francis Leland	surgeon	2nd Massachusetts
Philip Adolphus	assistant surgeon	regular army
Lincoln R. Stone	surgeon	2nd Massachusetts
Josiah F. Day, Jr.	surgeon	10th Maine
Evelyn L. Bissel	surgeon	5th Connecticut

These seven doctors stayed behind to treat the Union wounded after the Battle of Winchester, 25 May 1862. They expected to spend many months as prisoners of war. Stonewall Jackson, urged by his medical director, Hunter Holmes McGuire, released them. He only required that they try to obtain the release of seven Confederate doctors and that they work for the principle that medical officers of both sides caring for the wounded would not be subject to capture.

Source: Samuel E. Lewis, <u>Southern Historical Society Papers</u> 30 (1902): 226-36.

THE CAMPAIGN IN MARYLAND.—SKETCHED BY MR. A. R. WAUD.—[SEE PAGE 568.]

Confederate and Union doctors mingled freely on the Antietam battlefield taking care of their respective wounded. This drawing by an eyewitness shows the doctors of the opposing sides shaking hands near the Dunker Church. HW

crowded institution. They brought them anyway, because they had nowhere else to go. Each wounded soldier was placed upon the ground between two beds filled with other soldiers. The battles raged within a mile of the Chimborazo grounds; the groaning patients could easily hear the boom of cannons and could sometimes make out the clackety sound of continuous musket fire.

The commanding general of the Confederate forces, General Joseph E. Johnston, was wounded. He was replaced by Robert E. Lee. The replacement of one commanding general by another was a new phenomenon; no one knew if the staff officers should stay or be replaced by the staff of the new general. Lafayette Guild was Lee's medical director; he replaced Thomas H. Williams, Johnston's medical director, in the middle of the Seven Days Battles. Guild, a native of Tuscaloosa,

Alabama, had graduated from the Jefferson Medical College in Philadelphia in 1848 and joined the U.S. Army. No military experience during his twelve years of service with the Old Army prepared him for the shock of inheriting the medical duties of the Army of Northern Virginia at the very height of a major battle. He was, he complained, "assigned suddenly and unexpectedly to the onerous and responsible duties of medical director of this large army, without instructions of any kind and without knowledge of the previous orders and assignments of medical officers of an army already engaged in action."[13]

Somehow Guild muddled through this difficult situation. After the battle, he took control of the medical facilities of the Army of Northern Virginia. When Lee's army headed North into Maryland, Guild accompanied it, setting up support and distribution hospitals.

9

Northern Medicine Organized

ON 14 APRIL 1862 WILLIAM A. HAMMOND, WITH great vigor and determination, began his tenure as chief of the Medical Bureau of the United States Army. Armed with the legislative mandate of the Medical Reform Law, which had just been signed by President Lincoln, Hammond threw himself into the challenge of organizing and rejuvenating the antiquated medical services of the Union Army. He set up procedures for the evaluation of the volunteer physicians, began the inspection system envisioned by the law, tightened supervision of hospital construction, appointed carefully chosen subordinates, and improved the system for tabulating medical information.[1]

Hammond devoted much of his energy toward improving his department's reputation with both the medical and the general public. Complaints about army medicine took two forms. Some critics, especially politicians and newspaper editors, claimed that the Medical Bureau inadequately supervised its poorly trained medical officers. One medical officer admitted that "inefficiency, gross carelessness, and dissipation are intimately associated in the mind of the Northern public with the medical officers of the army."[2] Other critics, generally from the civilian medical community, accused the army authorities of restricting the actions of their eminent physicians. "Red tape, official routine, dull and insensible formalism are the curse of our government," complained the *American Medical Times*, claiming that the wounded were without blankets because an administrator "could not unwind the red-tape which bound his official legs."[3]

These two forms of criticism seem contradictory, either too little or too much supervision. A less confident surgeon general might have sided with one group of critics to oppose the other, but Hammond countered both simultaneously. He appointed examining boards to approve new medical officers and to discharge those found incompetent. Yet at the same time he authorized the new medical director of the Army of the Potomac to purchase supplies from any source, regardless of traditional procedure, and to hire additional doctors and nurses "on the spot" without the need to check with higher authority.[4] The *American Medical Times* reproduced the Surgeon General's correspondence in their medical journal as an answer to its own editorial of just three weeks earlier that had complained about excessive red tape.[5]

In his efforts to improve the reputation of the medical bureau, Hammond always responded directly and forcefully to any criticism that he considered unjustified. When Senator John C. Ten Eyck of New Jersey complained on the floor of Congress that hospital patients sometimes went without food or beds, Hammond wrote to the *New York Times* to explain hospital inspection procedures that guaranteed that such scandals could not occur. He challenged Ten Eyck to identify the specific hospital, but the senator did not reply.[6]

The new surgeon general responded somewhat brusquely even when he received a request from the president. Lincoln wrote to Hammond that a delegation of Baltimore citizens claimed that soldiers discharged from

William A. Hammond appears confident as he becomes the surgeon general of the Union army. USAMHI

hospitals in their city wandered about with no place to go; Hammond replied the same day that the citizens were incorrect. Lincoln asked Hammond if he could set aside a ward of wounded soldiers so that a certain Dr. Forsha could demonstrate a new healing medication. Hammond replied immediately that he was quite familiar with Dr. Forsha, who was nothing but "an ignorant quack."[7]

While organizing the Surgeon General's Office, Hammond came across crates and memorabilia dating from the early days of the Republic. In one box, he was startled to find, properly labelled and preserved in alcohol, an arm amputated during the Mexican War. Amputations in that earlier war had been infrequent enough to generate uneasiness about what to do with such a specimen. Should Hammond now discard this arm, as was being done so frequently with freshly amputated limbs? He decided upon organizing and displaying medical and surgical material by founding an Army Medical Museum. Hammond did not intend this museum for the general public, but as an educational endeavor to improve medical and surgical care following the War.[8]

Hammond appointed John H. Brinton, brigade surgeon in the Army of the Tennessee, to be the first curator of the Army Medical Museum. Brinton had been in charge of the hospitals in Cairo, Illinois; he had evacuated the wounded from the Battle of Belmont, Missouri; he had, with Dr. Irwin, set up a tent hospital on the battlefield at Shiloh. He now transferred to the Surgeon General's Office in Washington, but traveled throughout the country, visiting field armies, looking for specimens of medical interest: broken bones, unusual bullet wounds, casts of amputation stumps, organs from autopsies. The museum needed a large supply of alcohol to preserve these specimens. During the course of police operations, the Washington military police frequently confiscated alcohol, which included some of the finest brandies and liquors; they turned this alcohol over to the Army medical services. Brinton took bottles of brandy on his trips to the field; he had no difficulty obtaining cooperation from field medical officers. As Brinton accumulated specimens, the museum enlarged from one desk to a separate building, a former schoolhouse on H Street between 13th and 14th. Brinton thought that the museum

might provide important information for future generations of physicians. "Even dry bones may live," became his motto.[9]

As medical reports and disease statistics poured into his office, Hammond envisioned a permanent record of all these medical experiences. He was familiar with the historical publication that had come out of the Crimean War, the *Medical and Surgical History of British Forces in Turkey and the Crimea.*[10] On 9 June 1862 Hammond issued a letter to all medical officers announcing his intention to publish a series of volumes to record the medical lessons of the present great civil conflict. The reasons for this work, Hammond stated, were both historical and educational, "to establish landmarks which will serve to guide us in the future."[11]

Hammond placed a young career army officer in charge of collating these statistics. Joseph Janvier Woodward had been born in Philadelphia in 1833 and had graduated from the medical faculty of the University of Pennsylvania in 1853. He served in the Army of the Potomac from Bull Run to May 1862, when he joined the Surgeon General's Office. He used official medical statistics to produce a major work on the afflictions of the training camps, particularly measles. He also wrote a book on the duties of the hospital steward. Hammond appointed a committee of career army doctors to evaluate this work; they found it "written in strict accordance with the regulations of the army and the customs of the service" and Hammond, therefore, made it an official manual of the medical department.[12]

It is likely that Hammond had met both Brinton and Woodward before the War when he worked with Silas Weir Mitchell. Hammond, like all career army medical officers, wanted to perfect his surgical abilities. During that year, Brinton lectured in surgery at the University of Pennsylvania and Woodward ran the surgical clinic at Jefferson. When Hammond became surgeon general, he found that both these young surgeons were in the army and summoned them to the Surgeon General's Office. Woodward transferred to the regular army, but Brinton remained with the volunteer forces.

Another doctor who joined the Surgeon General's Office at this time was Joseph K. Barnes. Born in Philadelphia in 1817, he had studied medicine by apprenticeship under U.S. Navy

Litter bearers practiced carrying wounded soldiers from the battlefield and placing them into ambulances. Letterman drilled the ambulance corps with careful attention to detail. He ordered that litter bearers should start off in unison: "the front man steps off with his left foot, and the rear man with his right." Miller

physician Thomas Harris. After graduation from the medical faculty of the University of Pennsylvania in 1838, he joined the U.S. Army and served in the Seminole and Mexican Wars. He accompanied Winfield Scott's expedition to Mexico City and was with the troops that stormed Chapultepec. Barnes was the surgeon at Fort Riley, Kansas Territory, before Hammond took that post. While Hammond was chief surgeon at Fort Riley, Barnes was not far away as chief surgeon at Fort Scott, Kansas Territory. Barnes served in Missouri during the first year of the war, but was called to Washington soon after Hammond became the surgeon general. Barnes was appointed a medical inspector; he soon became chief medical inspector with the rank of colonel.

Hammond called on Jonathan Letterman, a friend from the Old Army, when he became surgeon general. Letterman's relief of Tripler as the medical director of the Army of the Potomac has already been related. Hammond

supported the medical changes in that army that came to be called the Letterman system. He tried with mixed success to spread the Letterman system of the Army of the Potomac to the other commands of the Union army.

One of the major aspects of the Letterman system was medical control over ambulances. Because the quartermaster had official custody of the ambulances, they were frequently used for purposes other than evacuating the wounded. A civilian led the effort for a better ambulance service. Henry I. Bowditch, a respected Boston physician, helped in the effort to move control of the ambulance corps from the quartermaster to the surgeon general. Visiting Washington during Second Bull Run, he had heard Hammond riding through the city, crying for all doctors to ride out to Manassas to help the wounded. He had made the trip, under flag of truce, and was appalled at the disorganization of the ambulance column; many drivers were drunk. He wrote articles and gave speeches about this experience. Partly from the activities of this influential civilian physician, and partly because of the success of the Letterman system in the Army of the Potomac, medical control of ambulances spread to other commands. This change was ordered in Grant's Army of the Tennessee on 30 March 1863. The law of 11 March 1864 codified the Letterman system for the entire U.S. Army.[13]

Despite this improvement in the evacuation of the wounded, Dr. Bowditch suffered a personal tragedy. His son Nathaniel, a lieutenant of the 2nd Massachusetts Cavalry, died two days after being wounded. He was carried from the battlefield by a passerby from another regiment. The elder Bowditch believed that his son might have lived had he received expeditious therapy. Bowditch continued to press for a policy for the entire Union army similar to the Letterman system in the Army of the Potomac.[14]

The system of supply was a major problem that afflicted the Union army. The difficulty did not lie in purchasing supplies, but in delivering them at the time and place they were needed. Some items, such as medications, originated with the medical bureau; others, such as tents, were obtained from other army sources. Food came from the commissary department. The quartermaster delivered all supplies from their point of origin to the place needed. If supplies ordered were not received, bureaucratic wrangling about the department at fault obscured resolution of the problem. Hammond determined that the sick and wounded would not suffer because of inadequacies of the supply system. He utilized multiple sources, multiple deliveries, and purposeful waste, accepting oversupply at one point and time in order to prevent suffering from want at another. Lost supplies can be replenished, but lives lost are gone forever.

To aid in the supply of medications to hospitals and to regimental surgeons, Hammond set up a board of pharmacological experts to sim-

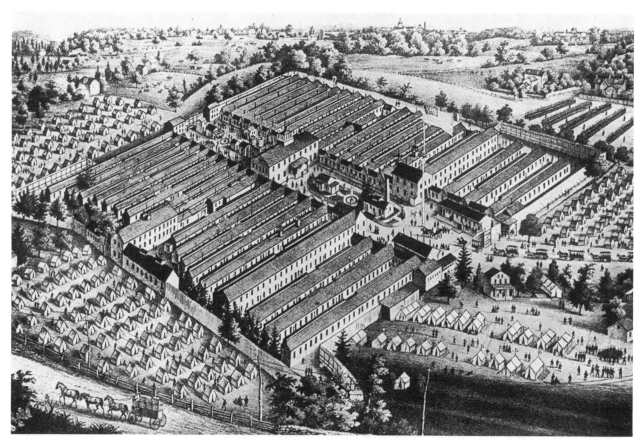

This contemporary poster shows Satterlee Hospital in west Philadelphia. Named for an elderly, career army medical officer, it was one of the largest and best-organized Union hospitals built on the pavilion system.

plify the list of drugs available to army physicians. This board issued a simplified supply table or formulary in October 1862. The new supply table remained complex; it contained, for example, four different forms of quinine. The private laboratories that produced medications expanded to fill army orders. One druggist, who had formerly been a naval surgeon, mortgaged his own home to expand his drug factory.[15] When private industry could not meet the huge demands of the Union army for medications, especially for quinine, Hammond constructed government-owned pharmaceutical laboratories.

Hammond supervised the huge enlargement of the general hospital system of the U.S. Army. In every city existing hospitals were taken over for use by the military. Other large buildings, such as warehouses or hotels, were pressed into service. But because existing structures were inadequate, the U.S. Army undertook a huge program of new hospital construction. Hammond had studied the great hospitals of Europe; his book *Military Hygiene* contained over one hundred pages describing their physical layout and specifying what was right and what was wrong with each.

Hammond believed that the goal of hospital design should be to provide ventilation so that the exhalation and secretions of the ill would be rapidly dissipated. The sick and the wounded exuded a smell of putrefaction; perhaps this smell indicated that the sick person gave off particles of illness that could be carried to others. The buildings and the beds within them should therefore be arranged so that a breeze did not carry any potential dangerous particles from one sick person to another. The ideal hospital should also have only one story, so that these infected vapors did not rise to infect patients in the upper rooms. The hospital should not rest directly upon the ground, because this type of flooring could absorb, and later release, the effluvia arising from wounds and sick bodies. Hammond placed toilet facilities at a distance from the beds.

In Philadelphia, Hammond's old friend, Silas Weir Mitchell developed a special interest in injuries to the nervous system. He was a volunteer civilian physician to a hospital on Christian Street that had been a police department. Using his extensive medical connections throughout the city, Mitchell arranged for pa-

tients with nervous system injuries to be sent to the Christian Street Hospital. Most physicians were happy to exchange patients with painful injuries or epileptic seizures for patients who were convalescing from uncomplicated wounds.

To aid his old friend Mitchell in the study of nervous injuries, Hammond arranged for a special hospital to be built. The U.S. Army Hospital for Diseases and Injuries of the Nervous System was built on Turner's Lane at the northern outskirts of Philadelphia. Mitchell convinced two other civilian physicians to join him there: a well known local surgeon named George R. Morehouse and a recent graduate of Jefferson Medical School, William W. Keen. While still a medical student, Keen had served for a month in the Union army, acting as the assistant surgeon of the 5th Massachusetts at First Bull Run. Many patients with painful nerve injuries were studied and treated with morphine injections; this was one of the few places where drugs were given by subcutaneous injection. Many patients with epilepsy and with seizures caused by head wounds also were studied; Keen said that it was not unusual for two hundred seizures to occur at Turner's Lane Hospital in a single day.[16]

Under Hammond's leadership, the medical department made strenuous efforts to retrieve the wounded promptly from the battlefield. The mortality from gunshot wounds in the Union army fell during the first three years of the War. A statistical study performed by John H. Brinton showed that only a minority of soldiers who had been wounded returned to full duty. Using reports gathered by the Union medical authorities through the end of 1862, Brinton showed that of 20,930 soldiers who had been wounded, only 5,149 returned to duty with their regiments. Soldiers who had received medical discharges numbered 2,897 while 9,960 of the wounded remained in the hospital at the time of the report. Only 856 were home on medical furlough. The remainder had died or deserted. While some of those still hospitalized might return to duty, nevertheless, at the time of the report, only one out of every four who had been wounded were back with their regiments.[17]

The contribution of the medical bureau to maintaining the fighting strength of the Union army lay predominately in the prevention of sickness. Vaccination against smallpox was

At Turner's Lane Hospital in north Philadelphia, Silas Weir Mitchell treated soldiers who had suffered injuries to the nervous system. USAMHI

carried out and that disease was not a significant problem for the Union. The two major conditions that Hammond had to worry about were malaria and diarrhea.

Malaria threatened the health and vigor of Union troops. In certain parts of the South, malaria afflicted much of the population. Lay people, as well as doctors, could identify regions where the climate did not permit troops to remain healthy. Hammond knew from a careful study of the world experience that quinine could ameliorate the symptoms of malaria. In addition, quinine taken daily by healthy persons could prevent the appearance of the symptoms of malaria. William H. Van Buren, the leading physician of the United States Sanitary Commission, reviewed scientific studies of quinine from different malarial regions of the world. Physicians had studied plantation laborers in Charleston, French colonial troops in Africa, and transport workers in Panama. In each case, one set of people had taken quinine daily and experienced much less malaria than an equivalent group who took no medication. Van Buren's pamphlet, entitled "Quinine as a Prophylactic Against Malarial Diseases," was published in 1861 and distributed by the Sanitary Commission to all Union doctors. Hammond reprinted the article in the

work he edited, *Military Medical and Surgical Essays*, which was also distributed to Union army physicians.

With this scientific underpinning, Hammond undertook to administer quinine every day to every soldier present in malarious regions of the country. The drug was quite bitter and soldiers resisted taking it. Experience showed that soldiers would take the bitter medicine if it were dissolved in whiskey. Some doctors tried to fool the soldiers, giving a drink of whiskey to the regiment as a purported stimulant before or after a march or a detail; the soldiers had no difficulty determining by its bitter taste that their whiskey reward had been laced with quinine. Other regiments gave the quinine-in-whiskey dose at a special time. The troops were called to formation by a bugle call that sounded to them like the wailing of the word "qui-eye-nine."

Diarrhea was the great symptom of the War. A chronic looseness of the bowels was called the soldier's disease. Some people even joked that every soldier had to learn to shoot from a squatting position. For many, active campaigning and diarrhea were inextricably linked. Explosive and uncontrollable watery diarrhea could break out acutely in an entire regiment; this was especially likely to occur in troops who occupied dirty encampments. The disorder could become chronic, producing a soldier who was easily fatigued. A regiment, or an army, of soldiers suffering from this disorder experienced a lack of vigor that inhibited fighting abilities.

Physicians as well as lay people knew that diarrhea had something to do with camp cleanliness. During the Crimean War, for example, the number of soldiers experiencing diarrhea had fallen when the British military medical authorities paid careful attention to sanitation. The U.S. Sanitary Commission had been formed partly to address this problem. Agents of this commission, as well as medical officers, inspected camps and on many occasions pointed to encampments fouled by dirt and human waste. The primary responsibility for camp cleanliness lay with the regimental commander, not the medical officers. Camps that were obviously disordered and unkempt suffered from high disease rates, but an apparently pristine camp could also produce diarrhea and dysentery if the latrine was located upstream from the water supply. The major treatment for a regiment afflicted by diarrhea was simply to move camp.

Throughout 1862 Hammond vigorously attacked the problems of medical care in the Union army. He improved the reputation of the medical department while he assured a permanent record of the military medical experience as a lesson for future generations. He made great efforts to counter malaria with quinine and to prevent diarrhea with camp cleanliness. With his subordinate Jonathan Letterman, he improved the evacuation and treatment of the wounded soldier. He always appeared serious and confident, perhaps too confident.

10

Medicine at Sea

MEDICAL CARE IN THE UNION AND CONFEDERATE navies presented special problems. Some actions that were routine on land could be difficult at sea. The naval doctor who tried to set a dislocated shoulder during a gale had to deal with the roll and pitch of the ship as well as the dislocation of the limb.

Naval medicine did not classify illness by the system developed by William Farr of England and used by the medical services of both Northern and Southern armies. Rather, both navies used a special system of disease nomenclature devised particularly for the U.S. Navy in 1857.[1] Medical care for the sailors of the naval forces was administratively separate from army medicine.

Most ships of the U.S. Navy had one or two medical officers aboard. The next level of medical command was the fleet surgeon of the squadron to which the ship was assigned. The fleet surgeon was analogous in position to the medical director of a field army. He gave advice to the fleet commander regarding medical matters. For example, the fleet surgeon of the East Gulf Blockading Squadron recommended in 1862 that the major outfitting port at Key West be closed because yellow fever was infecting all the ships that stopped there; the advice was not taken.[2] The fleet surgeon, on the staff of the officer commanding the squadron, reported to William Whelan, who was the senior doctor in the U.S. Navy, holding the title of chief of the bureau of medicine and surgery.[3] Dr. Whelan reported directly to Secretary of the Navy Gideon Welles.

In the smaller Confederate States Navy, the senior doctor on each ship or at each naval station sent his medical reports directly to William A. W. Spotswood, the chief of the bureau of medicine and surgery, who reported to Secretary of the Navy Stephen Mallory. Several surgeons from the old U.S. Navy, such as Spotswood, went South with their states. With few Confederate ships, they were assigned to naval headquarters in Richmond, where they chaffed, waiting for a position where they could help the Confederacy.

The two senior naval medical officers, Whelan and Spotswood, were analogous in position to Hammond and Moore. Both were in their late fifties during most of the War, being born in 1806 and 1808. They had learned their medicine by apprenticeship; neither had graduated from a medical school. Both had spent many years at sea in the old U.S. Navy. The term "old salt" often came to the minds of men meeting these rough and ready medical sailors.[4]

Naval surgeons, like their army counterparts, looked upon the treatment of wounded as their most exciting duty. Sea engagements could be bloody affairs. In land battles, the courageous commander orders his troops forward; if the casualties are too great the troops may falter and stop, or even retreat, on their own initiative. At sea, the courageous commander who brings his ship alongside the enemy vessel brings the sailors and marines with him. They cannot retreat; they must stand toe-to-toe with their enemy until one or the other ship breaks off the action and flees, surrenders, or sinks. A medical officer below decks in a wooden ship is not really a noncombatant; shells pass through the wooden barriers bring-

This drawing by Charles Elley Stedman shows the special difficulties of medicine at sea. The surgeon is setting a shoulder in a gale. From the sketchbook of Charles Ellery Stedman.

ing a blizzard of splinters with them. During the American Civil War, the surgeon was just as likely as any other person aboard to be struck by a shell, and he knew it.[5]

Most surgeons aboard naval vessels, however, were never involved in a major engagement like the *Alabama* versus the *Kearsarge*. Most medical activities involved the simplest and most boring of duties: sick call. The minor medical complaints of the healthy crew gave little difficulty to the surgeon of the vessel. Boredom afflicted the doctor as well as the rest of ship's company as they cruised the ocean. The tedium of long patrols at sea was broken by meetings with enemy vessels, involving a chase, and with friendly vessels, involving a social meeting. The exchange of visits between ships' doctors usually involved cigars and sherry.[6]

The phenomenon that made medicine at sea so difficult was not the risk of life in an engagement, but the risk of loss of the ship because of an epidemic. A strange disease could afflict a ship to such an extent that not enough healthy crewmen remained to man it. An example is the African fever that disabled the slave ship captured by the U.S.S. *Saratoga* as related in the prologue to this work. "Our crew had become so debilitated and sickly," wrote the commanding officer, Lt. John Julius Guthrie of the U.S. Navy, later of the Confederate States Navy, "that it became very difficult to carry sail and manage a ship of this size." What was this fever that almost destroyed this ship? Not enough information was recorded by Lt. Guthrie to be certain, but it may have been typhus. The horrible scourge of typhus fever could burst upon any group of people who were forced to live in close quarters for prolonged periods.

Besides typhus, scurvy and yellow fever afflicted ships on long voyages in the years before the Civil War. By 1860, however, scurvy had disappeared from the American navy. James Lind of the British navy had shown that scurvy could be prevented if the crew consumed a regular diet of fresh vegetables or fruits, especially limes. Scurvy had been a major problem for navies earlier in the century, but the change in vessel power, from wind to coal, meant a change in the characteristics of naval voyages. When ships were powered only by the wind, the duration of any cruise depended upon the perseverance of the crew. Now that coal was needed to turn the screws that supplemented wind power, the length of voyages was limited by fuel supply. Ships had to return to land to load coal, and while there they also loaded foodstuffs. So the dietetic disease, scurvy, did not afflict Civil War navies. Scurvy remained a problem for armies, but it no longer crippled a ship at sea.[7]

Although scurvy and typhus were not major problems for ships at sea, yellow fever was. Yellow fever was carried by cargo ships and by warships from the Caribbean and South America to the shores of the Confederate States of America. Epidemics occurred in Galveston, New Bern, and other ports; the most severe epidemic crippled the Union force occupying Hilton Head Island, South Carolina.

If yellow fever broke loose upon a ship, the best treatment involved rapid movement toward the North. The U.S.S. *Dacouta* was a wooden hulled warship, sailing along the coast of Cuba, searching for blockade runners. Yellow fever appeared among the crew, probably picked up in Havana when the *Dacouta* loaded coal. The surgeon of the ship, Delevan Bloodgood, discussed the epidemic with fleet surgeon Gustavus R. B. Hunter. Their recommendation to the fleet and ship commanders was taken: the *Dacouta* was to sail north as fast as possible. It was hoped that the cool breezes of a ship underway would clear the fever. If it cleared, the ship was ordered to return to duty with the fleet off Cuba. If it did not, the ship was ordered to continue to a northern port.

The next anyone heard of the *Dacouta*, she was docking in New York harbor. The ship was free of yellow fever and able to join in the search for the dreaded Confederate raider, the C.S.S. *Alabama*. There were no new full-blown cases of yellow fever with jaundice, but the disease could produce debilitation. After one month at sea, the commanding officer of the *Dacouta* reported that he was too ill to continue his sea duty; he requested six weeks of shore leave to recoup his health.[8]

Activities in Confederate naval medicine were of necessity as diffuse and adaptable as the Confederate Navy itself. The Bureau of Medicine and Surgery of the Confederate States Navy was located on the second floor of the War Building in Richmond. The office of the Secretary of the Navy was immediately adjacent. The Bureau supervised five naval

Table 8

Major Confederate Ships and Their Surgeons

Vessel	Medical Officers	Type
C.S.S. ALABAMA	Francis L. Galt, Surgeon David H. Lllewellyn, Asst. Surgeon	Cruiser
C.S.S. FLORIDA	Archer Hays, Asst. Surgeon	Cruiser
C.S.S. TENNESSEE	Daniel B. Conrad, Fleet Surgeon R.C. Bowles, Asst. Surgeon	Ironclad
C.S.S. VIRGINIA	Dinwiddie B. Phillips, Surgeon Algernon S. Garnett, Asst. Surgeon	Ironclad

Source: ORN ser. 2, vol. 1, pp. 286, 308

hospitals, in Richmond, Wilmington, Charleston, Savannah, and Mobile. Medical activities on the Confederate cruisers were largely independent of any administrative control.

Surgeons from the old U.S. Navy who went South included Daniel B. Conrad and William A. Carrington. While they were officially medical officers of the Confederate States Navy, they spent much of their time with the Confederate States Army. Carrington served aboard the Confederate ship *Baltic* and was later inspector of naval hospitals in Pensacola and Mobile. But late in the War he became the director of the general hospital system that supported the Army of Northern Virginia.

Daniel B. Conrad volunteered as surgeon of the Third Virginia and accompanied Stonewall Jackson's Corps during the 1862 campaign in the Shenandoah Valley. When Hunter Holmes McGuire convinced General Jackson that the captured Federal doctors should be treated as noncombatants, Dr. Conrad added the arguments of the medical navy to those of the medical army.[9] Conrad and McGuire had been boyhood friends in Winchester, Virginia. Later, Conrad served with the famous Confederate naval officer J. Taylor Wood, whose special expertise involved the capture of U.S. naval vessels that came too close to shore. Conrad participated in Taylor's raid on the U.S.S. *Underwriter* in February 1864 off New Bern, North Carolina. He treated the wounded after Confederates had stormed the vessel. "I examined a youth," he wrote, "and in feeling his head I felt my hand slip between his ears, and, to my horror, discovered that his head had been cleft in two by a boarding sword in the hands of some giant of the forecastle."[10]

The famous clash between the U.S.S. *Kearsarge* and the C.S.S. *Alabama* illustrates medical activities during combat at sea. When the Confederate cruiser *Alabama* sailed out of the French port of Cherbourg, the *Kearsarge* cleared for action. All material on deck was taken below or thrown overboard. The huge naval guns were loaded and prepared. The only medical person aboard, Surgeon John M. Browne, prepared to handle the wounded. He had already trained all the crew to use tourniquets to stem the flow of blood. He placed two stretchers upon the gun deck, but was unable to detail any sailors to remove the wounded. Every hand was needed at his post, to steer the ship or to service the guns. Dr. Browne

proceeded to the forehold, where he prepared for surgery.

Two surgeons were aboard the C.S.S. *Alabama*. Francis L. Galt, the senior doctor, had served with the *Alabama*'s skipper, Rafael Semmes, throughout the War. Galt had first served under Semmes aboard the C.S.S. *Sumter* and then, when the *Alabama* was ready in England, had accompanied Semmes to that vessel. A second medical officer had been added to the crew of the *Alabama*: a young English physician from Charing Cross Hospital, Dr. David Herbert Llewellyn.

Dr. Browne waited in the forehold of the *Kearsarge* as the two vessels approached each other off the French coast. He noted his watch when the firing began. Exactly eighteen minutes later, the first casualty came into the forehold. John W. Dempsey walked in, cradling his right arm with his left. He reported that a sixty-eight-pound Blakely shell had smashed through the starboard bulwarks and exploded on the quarter deck, injuring the crew of the pivot gun. Dr. Browne examined the arm; the area of the elbow had been totally destroyed and all three arm bones, radius, ulna, and humerus, were macerated. Dr. Browne informed Dempsey that amputation was required, gave him a glass of whiskey, and assisted him to a chair, because the second casualty of the explosion now hobbled in. James MacBeth had suffered a fracture of one of the bones of the lower leg, just below the knee. Dr. Browne examined the wound and determined that it was clean of shell fragments. He gave MacBeth a drink and began to dress the wound, when his attention turned to the third casualty. William Gowin crawled down the ladder into the forehold. He had been injured in the same blast that had caught MacBeth and Dempsey, but his injury was more severe.

Shell fragments had slashed through Gowin's left leg. He was unable to walk, so he dragged himself across the deck with his arms. As he crawled along, leaving a trail of blood on the deck behind him, many gunners offered to help. He waved them back to their guns, for the battle was still raging. He crawled the length of the ship, from the aft pivot gun to the forehold, then plunged down the steps into the doctor's sick bay. Browne examined the wound. The lower half of the femur had been smashed into spicules; the upper portions of the tibia and fibula were macerated and the

The officers of the *Alabama*. The commanding officer was Raphael Semmes, who is the top center sitting figure. Assistant Surgeon David H. Llewellyn is in the top row, second from the left, next to Semmes. Surgeon Francis Galt is at the far left of the bottom row. Miller

knee was completely missing. No shell fragments were present in the wound, but it was bleeding profusely. Dr. Browne gave Gowin a drink of whiskey and compressed the bleeding with a dressing; the leg would need amputation. The stretchers that Dr. Browne had so carefully placed upon the gun deck were never used.

The exchange of shells between the C.S.S. *Alabama* and the U.S.S. *Kearsarge* continued for another half hour. Shells from the Confederate cruiser came close to the U.S. naval ves-

Table 9

Confederate Naval Hospitals in 1864

Hospital	Admissions	Discharges	Deaths	Daily cost
Richmond	842	645	21	$3.64
Charleston	252	154	18	$5.82
Wilmington	135	90	3	$4.96
Savannah	394	270	15	$2.85
Mobile	372	251	12	$2.12

Admissions to the five Confederate naval hospitals during the year that ended 30 September 1864 show that the hospital in Richmond was the busiest. At that hospital, over half of the yearly total, or 464 sailors, were admitted during the sickly season of July, August, and September.

Source: <u>ORN</u>, ser. 2, vol. 2, p. 761.

A drawing by Charles Ellery Stedman shows a surgeon practicing the treatment of casualties in the wardroom. In a scene just like this, David Llewellyn was operating upon a wounded sailor when a cannonball crashed through the room from bulkhead to bulkhead. The shell struck the sailor on the operating table, killing him instantly. The doctor was not injured, but he had only about ten minutes to live.

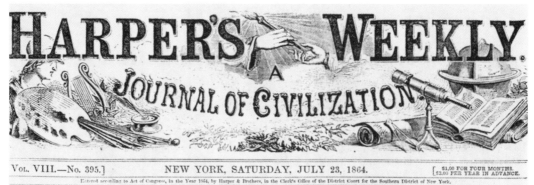

HARPER'S WEEKLY.

A JOURNAL OF CIVILIZATION.

Vol. VIII.—No. 395.]   NEW YORK, SATURDAY, JULY 23, 1864.   [$1.00 FOR FOUR MONTHS. $3.00 PER YEAR IN ADVANCE.

Entered according to Act of Congress, in the Year 1864, by Harper & Brothers, in the Clerk's Office of the District Court for the Southern District of New York.

THE SINKING OF THE "ALABAMA," OFF CHERBOURG, June 19, 1864.—[See Next Page.]

This cover from *Harper's Weekly* presents an idealized version of a longboat from the U.S.S. *Kearsarge* rescuing the crew from the foundering C.S.S. *Alabama*. In the actual situation, survivors were picked up by civilian vessels; the *Kearsarge* was too slow in launching its boats to save anyone. Dr. Llewellyn was among those who drowned.

U. S. NAVY—SINKING OF THE ALABAMA—JUNE 11th, 1864

Both the Confederate and Union wounded were transferred from the *Kearsarge* to the French naval hospital at Cherbourg. Courtesy of the Beverley R. Robinson Collection, United States Naval Academy Museum.

sel, so close that their explosions frequently knocked crewmen to the deck. The shells from the *Kearsarge* found their marks upon the *Alabama*. One huge cannonball crashed through the casualty area, killing the very sailor upon whom Dr. Llewellyn was operating.

The *Alabama* began to sink. Semmes signaled that he surrendered and that he was sending his wounded to the Federal vessel. The *Alabama* lowered her two boats, filled with wounded sailors, accompanied by Surgeon Galt. As the two boats were alongside the *Kearsarge*, the *Alabama* suddenly plunged forward, throwing her exhausted crew into the water. Semmes and most of his officers made it to a British yacht that had been observing the action. They were taken to England and eventu-

ally made it back to the Confederacy. Assistant Surgeon Llewellyn survived the gun battle, but drowned in the ocean.

Aboard the *Kearsarge*, Dr. Browne was amputating the arm of John Demsey, when Confederate Surgeon Galt came up and introduced himself. Galt and the wounded from the *Alabama* had come aboard the Union vessel. Browne could see that Galt had suffered contusions during the battle; he showed exhaustion from treating the large number of Confederate wounded. Browne ordered Galt to his own room, where he collapsed onto the Union doctor's bed. Browne turned his attention to the treatment of the Confederate casualties.

When the *Kearsarge* sailed into Cherbourg,

the French naval authorities arranged for the wounded of both sides to be admitted to the French naval hospital. There they received the best of treatment, but Gowin's wound became gangrenous; he developed pyemia and died.[11]

11

Stonewall Jackson Struck by Friendly Fire

HUNTER HOLMES MCGUIRE, THE SENIOR SURGEON in Jackson's Corps, was notified that Stonewall Jackson had been wounded. The doctor immediately moved forward with a wagon that had been reserved for use as an ambulance. The doctor found the commanding general in great pain, lying a few hundred yards from the main line, surrounded by his shaken officers.

"I am badly injured, doctor," Jackson said to McGuire very calmly but feebly. "I fear I am dying." After a pause, he added: "I am glad you have come. I think the wound in my shoulder is still bleeding."

McGuire could not perform a proper examination because of the growing darkness. Palpating the general's body, he discovered that Jackson's clothes were saturated with blood. He could feel that the shoulder wound was still bleeding, despite being heavily swathed in bandages. McGuire compressed the artery in the armpit with his finger.

After a lantern was brought, the doctor began a more thorough examination. A bandage had been wrapped around the shoulder at the scene of the wounding; it was now totally soaked with blood. McGuire removed this bandage and discarded it. Three bullets had struck the general. He had been hit in the right hand; McGuire could feel the ball under the skin of the back of the hand. Two bullets had struck the left arm. One had produced a fracture of the humerus about three inches below the left shoulder. The splintering bone, or the bullet itself, had divided the main artery and Jackson would certainly have bled to death had not the doctor compressed this artery

above the site of injury. An additional wound in the left arm was several inches in length. The ball had entered the outside of the arm, just an inch below the elbow, had then traversed the entire length of the forearm and exited between the wrist and the thumb. The arm was obviously useless and would have to be amputated.

Unfortunately, there was yet a fourth injury. While being carried from the field, Jackson had fallen to the ground. His back had struck a hard protuberance, probably a stump, and his ribs had been damaged, possibly fractured.

Jackson had been shot by his own men. His audacious attack upon the right flank of the Army of the Potomac on 2 May 1863 had caused the collapse of the Federal 11th Corps. The Union forces had been driven back two miles, but had then steadied. Jackson and his staff had gone forward to scout the terrain. Returning to their own lines at twilight, they had been mistaken for Yankee cavalry. A single volley killed a staff officer and knocked Jackson from his horse.

The staff officers shouted to the Confederate pickets, who shrank back in horror at their mistake. They dissolved into the Confederate line and have never been unequivocally identified.[1] Jackson's aides helped the general to his feet. He could walk with aid, but only slowly. He finally made it to the Confederate line and stretched out on the ground. All the Confederates were lying down as Federal shell and canister raked the area. The Yankees were attempting a counterattack. The scene was a frightful one. The air seemed alive with shrieks of shells and the whistling of bullets.

Riderless horses, mad with fright, dashed in every direction.

The commanding general of the division, William Dorsey Pender, found Jackson and suggested a retreat. Jackson stood up and responded feebly, yet clearly enough to be heard above the din of battle: "General Pender, you must hold on to the field, you must hold out to the last." He was exhausted by this effort and intended to lie down again. His aides feared that he would be captured by a Federal advance and hurried him farther to the rear.

A litter was obtained and Jackson was laid on it. Four men each grasped the two poles and started off across the rough ground. Unfortunately, one of the bearers fell, either tripping over an obstacle or hit by a Federal minié ball. As Jackson struck the earth, he screamed out in pain. He was again placed on the litter and hurried about two hundred yards to the rear, where he was met by Dr. Hunter Holmes McGuire, as already related.

Although seriously wounded, General Jackson maintained a demeanor of extreme calm. His hands were cold, his skin clammy, his face pale, and his lips bloodless. His face betrayed not a sign of suffering, however, except a slight corrugation of the brow and a compression of the lips so rigid that one could see the impression of his teeth. McGuire was struck with the general's control over his emotions; he suppressed the disposition to restlessness that McGuire had seen in many other soldiers who had lost a great deal of blood.

One of McGuire's fellow medical officers, a Dr. Straith, obtained whiskey and opium, and these were given to Jackson to diminish the pain. He was placed in a wagon alongside another wounded officer, and they started for the field hospital of the Second Corps, located in the Wilderness Tavern. The other officer was Colonel Stapleton Crutchfield, the chief of artillery of Jackson's Corps. McGuire examined Crutchfield; a minié ball had struck his femur, splaying bone fragments throughout muscle tissue. The leg must be amputated this night.

The bumping of the wagon produced excruciating pain in Colonel Crutchfield's splintered leg. Jackson ordered the ambulance to stop; additional morphine was given to Crutchfield. As the wagon slowly moved down the rutted road, McGuire sat beside the general with his finger on the artery in the armpit. The bleeding had stopped, but if a jolt renewed the hemorrhage, McGuire would again compress the artery. Jackson did not want his troops to know their commanding officer had been disabled; he told McGuire to reply to questions about who was in the ambulance with the simple phrase, "a Confederate officer."

Upon reaching the Wilderness Tavern, Jackson was placed in bed in a tent, covered with blankets, and given another drink of whiskey. After about two and a half hours of rest, at about two A.M. on 3 May, Dr. McGuire, with three of his associates present, determined that the time for surgery had come. McGuire proposed to the general an examination under anesthesia; amputation would probably be necessary. "Dr. McGuire, do for me whatever you think best," replied Jackson. Chloroform was dripped onto a cloth, which was then held over the general's nose. "What an infinite blessing," murmured Jackson as he became insensible and went limp.

Dr. McGuire first treated the wound of the right hand. He made an incision in the back of the hand and removed the ball, which turned out to be a round ball fired by a smooth-bore musket, not the Federal minié fired by a rifled barrel. The second and third metacarpal bones had been fractured. The left arm was then amputated just two inches below the shoulder. Some of the skin was brought together below the bony stump and sutured; a portion of the wound was left open to heal by granulation. McGuire noted scratches on the General's face, inflicted by tree branches; these were washed and dressed.

General Jackson was only just coming out of the anesthesia when a staff officer demanded to see him. McGuire refused to permit the exhausted patient to be further depleted by such an interview. When the officer, Major Pendleton, the assistant adjutant general, claimed that the safety of the Army of Northern Virginia required that he see Jackson, McGuire relented and allowed Pendleton within Jackson's tent. The general smiled and said, "Well, Major, I am glad to see you. I thought you were killed."

Pendleton explained the military situation; Jeb Stuart had taken command of Jackson's Corps. General Jackson asked for details of troop dispositions; he contracted his brow, set his mouth, and was obviously trying very hard to concentrate his thoughts. His nostrils di-

Thomas J. "Stonewall" Jackson is photographed after his minor wound at First Manassas but prior to his serious injury from friendly fire at Chancellorsville. NA

The place where Stonewall Jackson was wounded; the photograph was taken just a few days later. USAMHI

lated and his eyes flashed their old fire, as McGuire had seen so many times just before the General would issue a stream of orders to energize the Confederate troops under his command. But his face then relaxed and he told the major feebly and sadly: "I don't know; I can't tell; say to General Stuart that he must do what he thinks best." He closed his eyes and drifted into a deep sleep.

The next morning he was free from pain and felt he was on the road to recovery. He sent a staff officer to inform his wife of his injuries and bring her to him. An aid arrived with a note from General Robert E. Lee: "I have just received your note, informing me that you were wounded. I cannot express my regret at the occurrence. Could I have directed events, I should have chosen for the good of the country to have been disabled in your stead. I congratulate you upon the victory which is due to

your skill and energy." Jackson told McGuire that Lee should thank God, not Jackson, for the great victory at Chancellorsville.

A few hours later, Jackson was bothered by pain in his right side and asked McGuire to examine the area. The doctor could discover no evidence of injury; the skin was not broken; no bruise had yet appeared; the lungs could be inflated and deflated without apparent difficulty. A bandage was applied.

By the evening, the pain in the side had disappeared and General Jackson seemed to be doing well in all respects. He slept soundly that night and felt well the next morning. The Federals had resumed the battle and their artillery could be easily heard at the hospital at Wilderness Tavern. All the officers save one had returned to their military duties.

Dr. McGuire received orders from Lee to move Jackson further to the rear, to Guinea's

Hunter Holmes McGuire was Jackson's surgeon. After graduating from the small medical school at Winchester, Virginia, he studied in Philadelphia. Astonished by the reaction of the Northern populace to the attempt by John Brown to stimulate a bloody slave rebellion, McGuire led a secession of Southern medical students from Philadelphia. He became the medical director of Stonewall Jackson's Corps and treated the General after his wounding. **NLM**

Station. Lee feared that a Federal advance would capture Jackson. Jackson said he was not afraid of capture by Union forces. "I have always been kind to their wounded and they will be kind to me." But preparations were made to leave the next morning. Lee ordered McGuire to turn over the medical command of the Second Corps to his second and to accompany Jackson.

Travel in an ambulance wagon took all day on Tuesday. Captain Hotchkiss was sent ahead with a party of engineers to clear the road in order to make the trip smoother. Teamsters sometimes refused to move their heavy wagons to make way for an ambulance. Told that it contained Jackson, they quickly moved their loads and stood respectfully with hats off as Jackson passed. All along the route, women crowded around the ambulance with tears in their eyes. About eight o'clock in the evening, they arrived at the Chandler House and Jackson was put to bed.

The next day was very warm and the general complained of nausea. This was relieved by placing a wet towel across his stomach. The following day he felt better and ate heartily. Dr. McGuire removed the bandages and examined the wounds. The hand wound was discharging the yellowish material called laudable pus. The stump of the left arm was also healing well; union had taken place in the edges that had been brought together and the remainder of the wound showed healthy granulation tissue.

Very early the next morning, the general awoke with nausea. He asked his servant Jim to place a wet towel on his abdomen for relief. Jim asked Jackson if he could wake the doctor to be sure this was permissible, but the general refused, claiming that McGuire had barely slept these previous three nights. The towel was placed on the abdomen; others later saw this as an error that began a frightening descent.

At daylight the General was seized with a great pain in his right chest. McGuire was awakened and performed an examination. The chest moved poorly and sounded congested; McGuire diagnosed pleuropneumonia, probably resulting from a lung contusion caused by the fall just after his wounding. McGuire thought that this inflammation had been delayed by the patient's weak condition from loss of blood. McGuire applied cups to the chest wall hoping to draw any putrefaction away from the lungs.

Toward evening he seemed improved. Mrs. Jackson arrived with the general's infant son. Jackson played with the child for some time, caressing him and calling him his little comforter. "Do not be sad," he said to his wife, seeing how worried she was, "I hope I may yet recover." He declared he was prepared for death if it should come and instructed her to end each prayer with the wish for God's will to be done.

McGuire changed the dressings again on Friday, and the wounds seemed to continue healing well. But Jackson breathed with difficulty and complained of great exhaustion. One of McGuire's colleagues, Dr. Breckinridge, applied a blister. Dr. Tucker arrived from Richmond for consultation. "I see from the number of physicians," said Jackson, "that you think my condition dangerous." On Sunday morning, Mrs. Jackson told her husband that she thought he should prepare for the worst. "It will be my infinite gain to be translated to heaven," he replied. He advised his wife that, should he die, she should live with her father. He requested burial in Lexington, Virginia.

Jackson asked McGuire his condition. The doctor informed him that he would die this day. He looked at the ceiling for a moment, then said: "Very good, very good, it is all right." He tried to comfort his sobbing wife; he said he had much to tell her but was too weak.

His mind now began to fail and wander, and he frequently talked as if in command upon the field, giving orders in his old way. Then in his delirium, the scene shifted and he was at the mess table, in conversation with members of his staff; now he was with his wife and child; now at prayers. At intervals, his mind would clear. A few moments before he died, he cried out: "Order A. P. Hill to prepare for action. Tell Major Hawks. . . ." He left the sentence unfinished. A smile spread upon his pale face, and he said quietly and with an expression, as of relief: "Let us cross over the river and rest under the shade of the trees."[2]

12

"Mine Eyes Have Seen the Glory"

THE TWO GREATEST ARMIES IN NORTH AMERICA, the Union Army of the Potomac and the Confederate Army of Northern Virginia, collided at a small Pennsylvania village named Gettysburg. The huge number of casualties staggered both sides. Four months later, President Abraham Lincoln came to Gettysburg to dedicate a national cemetery for those who were killed in this bloody engagement. This is not the story of those who were buried in the new cemetery, those whom Lincoln called "these honored dead." This is the story of those who were wounded. The soldiers wounded at Gettysburg experienced such agony and terror that, by comparison, dying was easy.[1]

Justus M. Silliman awoke in a daze. He was lying on his back in a grassy field. Slowly his memory returned. He was a private of the 17th Connecticut, assigned to the Union 11th Corps. His unit had rushed forward through the town of Gettysburg to reinforce the 1st Corps after its commander had been killed. He had been firing his gun when he felt a curious sensation in his head. Now, he came to himself to discover that he was on the ground, surrounded by soldiers in gray, the enemy.

He closed his eyes and drifted off again for a few minutes. When he again awoke, the rebels were gone. He stood up shakily and walked about aimlessly. Rebel soldiers running past pointed him toward their field hospital. He walked over a mile to find a Confederate surgeon, who examined his head. He had a received a glancing blow from a ball on the side of his head, he was told, but would soon recover. The Southern doctor dressed his wound and gave him water and crackers. Silliman

marveled that "those who a short time previous had been hurling death at us, now assisted our wounded."

Two days later, Silliman and the other captured Union wounded were moved. They were taken in ambulance wagons, which Silliman compared to the wagons used by butchers in Connecticut, to the German Dutch Reformed Church in the town, being used as a hospital for the captured soldiers of the Federal 11th Corps. Captured Union doctors were present, but they seemed more interested in watching the battle through the church windows than in ministering to the wounded. The church shook as the tremendous bombardment of a hundred cannon roared.[2]

Along Seminary Ridge, the Confederates formed. A tremendous artillery duel shook the ground and transformed a sunny day into a fog of gunpowder. Everyone realized that the great climax of the battle was about to begin. Brigadier General Lewis Armistead rode along the front of his brigade, giving encouragement to his men. The brigade surgeon, Arthur Barry, asked for orders. "Set up your hospital well, doctor, you will soon have much to do."[3]

It was about four P.M. on 3 July when the divisions of Pickett and Pettigrew, including Armistead's Brigade, left the line of trees and marched straight ahead into the meadow. The huge cannonade had so filled the air with concussion waves that now the day seemed eerily silent. As the Confederates marched forward, the smoke slowly lifted. Their hearts sank as they saw a long line of blue on Cemetery Ridge directly ahead of them.

The Federal artillery launched a few cannon shots at the approaching Confederates. The soldiers could see the iron balls coming and merely stepped aside. The soldiers in the first rank, however, blocked the vision of those behind them. The huge iron balls bounced along the ground, tearing holes in the ranks, and smashing into the unaware. The assistant surgeons supervised the removal of the injured.

The Union soldiers on Cemetery Ridge fired their muskets into the onrushing mass. The Confederates reeled, as though struck with a sudden powerful wind. With the famous rebel yell, they rushed up to the Union line. Armistead's brigade fought their way up to a stone wall where Union troops fell back. General Armistead himself leaped over the wall. He waved his sword high in the air; his hat was transfixed to the sword as a signal to his troops where they should concentrate. The Union troops also saw the hat waving above the mass of gray soldiers; they concentrated their fire on the Confederate general. Just as Armistead placed his hand on the barrel of a captured Union cannon, he was struck by several minié balls and knocked to the ground. The Yankees and rebels stood only a few yards apart, pouring fire into each other, loading and firing.

Jacob Bieswanger was thirty-nine years old when he was struck by a rebel minié ball on Cemetery Ridge. A box maker before the War, Bieswanger had enlisted in the 75th Pennsylvania. His back was toward the rebel line as he plunged his rod down his rifle barrel, ramming in another charge. He noted that he was not properly pushing home the rod and realized that his left arm was hanging limply at his side. Only when he saw blood streaming down his useless arm did he conclude that he had been hit by enemy fire. With his good right arm, he grasped his left; it was numb. He let his rifle slip to the ground and began running away from the battle line. Becoming dizzy, he fell. Rising up again, he was attacked by a fit of coughing; he was alarmed to discover blood in his sputum. Medical personnel did not physically assist him, but rather just

Most of the Confederate soldiers who were wounded during Pickett's charge retreated and were cared for by the Confederate medical system. Those more seriously wounded were left on the field and were evacuated by the Union medical system. When this photograph was taken, only the dead remain. NA

pointed him to the division hospital half a mile behind the battle line.

David Schively was just a boy when he joined the 114th Pennsylvania in August 1862; he gave his age as seventeen but was probably younger. He was lying prone in the grass, aiming his rifle at the approaching line of shouting rebels, when he felt a sudden shock in his left arm. He stood up and dropped his musket. He staggered backward a few steps and fell to the ground. He lay there a few minutes, listening to the whoosh of the balls passing overhead. Thinking that his arm had been completely blown away, he palpated his left shoulder, then passed his hand down his arm. He was pleasantly surprised to find that his arm, though without feeling, was still completely whole. He halfway sat up in the grass and turned to look over his right shoulder at the battle line. His regiment was holding against the charging rebels. He reeled from a hard blow to the right side of his face. "I have been murdered," he shouted aloud when he understood that he had received a second wound. With his left arm dangling helplessly and with blood streaming down his face, he staggered toward the rear.

William Estee of the 5th Massachusetts Light Artillery was loading a Union cannon when a rifle ball struck him in the lower abdomen. Holding his hand over the wound, he walked to the rear where the regimental assistant surgeon pointed him toward the rapidly filling division hospital.[4]

General Armistead was taken to the Union field hospital. Spicules of bone exuded from his shattered arm. Amputation was obviously necessary. He waited his turn at the operating area. Operations were performed in the open air, with those about to undergo amputation watching those ahead of them in the line. Surgery was quick, bloody, and brutal. The unfortunate person being operated on was anesthetized, but those waiting for surgery were awake. They could see in others what would soon happen to them.

The surgeon wore an apron covered with blood. He held the knife between his teeth as he sutured the wound. Taking the knife in his bloody hands, he called out, "Next." Another soldier was lifted and placed, not too gently, on the operating table. He groaned as his painful limb was jostled. He might be crying or moaning, or he might be cheerful, knowing that with one limb missing, he would not again face the mass of bullets that had just been poured upon him. A cloth soaked in ether or chloroform was held over his nose, he took a few breaths, and then his entire body went limp. The surgeon took the knife in his hand, made a huge cut around the upper limb with a continuous motion, and scraped tissue away from the bone. With the bone easily seen by the surgeon as well as by the surrounding audience, he again placed the knife between his teeth, and took up the saw. Rapid sawing movements produced the loud rasping sound of saw upon bone, a familiar sound to all present because it sounded just like sawing wood. After a few seconds of this grating sound, the limb fell to the ground. An assistant carried the limb away and tossed it onto a gruesome pile. The surgeon placed aside the saw, sutured the ends of the wound around the stump of bone. "Next!" was the shout as the soldier was carried away on his stretcher. General Armistead moved up one place as another groaning soldier was tossed onto the table.[5]

A soprano voice rose above the moans of the wounded and the scratching of the saw. Helen Gilson of Chelsea, Massachusetts, stood on a table, singing the popular hymns and military songs familiar to all. The Union favorite was the "Battle Hymn of the Republic." Nurse Gilson urged everyone to sing along with her. The wounded groaned the lyrics, surgeons mumbled the words as they cut, even rebels hummed the tune. Her trained voice floated above the strange choir of the maimed. "Mine eyes have seen the glory."[6]

All night they operated. Armistead's turn did not come until the next day, 4 July. The Confederates were in retreat that day. All the Confederate wounded who could be moved headed south in a makeshift column of wagons. The Federal wounded who had fallen into rebel hands during the first two days of the battle were left behind. Many Confederate wounded remained, tended by Confederate doctors and assistants who volunteered to stay behind. Many of the captured Confederates, such as General Armistead, were already under treatment by the Union medical system. As the Confederate army followed their long line of wounded back to Virginia, the Federal wounded in Confederate hands were recovered by Union forces and rapidly transferred to Union hospitals.

Helen Gilson had been a nurse of the Second Corps for eighteen months when she was called upon to help care for the wounded at Gettysburg. She tried to counter the gruesome brutality of surgery by leading everyone in song. Holland

Surgery at Gettysburg often took place in open tents with many people observing. The man with the white beard is Reverend Winslow of the Christian Commission. NA

On the evening of 4 July, beginning about seven P.M., a tremendous thunderstorm struck. Rain fell in such torrents that it seemed to some that arteries in the heavens had ruptured. Many patients were housed outside in the open air; they became soaked. Some tents had been erected in low ground and Jonathan Letterman, the medical director of the Army of the Potomac, feared that flooding might drown those too weak to crawl to higher ground. Attendants worked all night to move patients.

The next day the food gave out. The troops had consumed all supplies of sustenance available from the army's commissary department. Fortunately, the U.S. Sanitary Commission, the Christian Commission, and a whole series of volunteers began to arrive with additional supplies. They traveled to Gettysburg by wagon because the rail lines had been cut by Confederate cavalry.

On 5 July General Armistead died. He had become pale following the amputation. He was not bleeding from the stump; perhaps he had bled internally due to another wound.

Healing takes time, but war never waits. The Army of the Potomac made ready to pursue the retreating Army of Northern Virginia. The order filtered through the hospitals; medical personnel reported to their regiments. Of 650 doctors with the Army of the Potomac, 544 accompanied the army in the pursuit of Lee. The Union military commanders expected to fight the rebels again before Lee could retreat across the Potomac; Letterman had to be prepared to handle the wounded from another major battle. Only 106 physicians were left behind to treat 20,000 wounded.[7]

The wounded at Gettysburg under Union control were spread throughout barns, taverns, churches, warehouses, and homes. Volunteers helped in the care. Father Burlando arrived from Baltimore with a group of sisters trained in nursing. The appearance of the nuns was strange to many of the rural soldiers. When one wounded man asked a nun if she

The U.S. Sanitary Commission played an important role at Camp Letterman. HW

were from the Catholic Church, she replied, "No, I am from the Methodist Church." She was referring to the building where she served as a nurse.[8]

As days passed, the wounded were consolidated in a huge tent hospital located in a flat meadow, broken by a few large trees, near the rail line. It was called Camp Letterman even though the chief medical officer of the Army of the Potomac departed with the troops pursuing the rebels. On the Confederate side of the battlefield rebel physicians treated the many rebel wounded who had been unable to retreat with Lee.

One of the Confederate doctors who remained behind was Simon Baruch, surgeon of the 3rd South Carolina. He had set up his division hospital in a building known as the Black Horse Tavern. During the battle, Union artillery shells had passed over the hospital. Baruch remained at Black Horse Tavern for six weeks. After only one or two days he ran out of all supplies; he received some much needed medicines and food from the Christian Com-

mission. When these ran out, he traveled across the old (already it was called old) battlefield to Camp Letterman. He was not only given medical supplies and foodstuffs, now arriving by train, but a Union army wagon and even a Union soldier to act as a driver under the command of the Confederate officer.[9]

Estee, the soldier who had been shot in the abdomen, developed peritonitis. He was in great pain, lying on one side with his legs drawn up in the fetal position. Attempts by the attendants to straighten the legs caused him to moan terribly. When the doctor tapped the patient's distended abdomen, he could feel fluid slosh around within. Estee was unable to eat and perspired profusely and continuously.

The wounded were evacuated by the repaired rail line. Trains left for Harrisburg and Baltimore twice a day, at 10 A.M. and at five P.M. Unfortunately, the trains were sometimes full and the soldiers had to spend the night by the rail line. As usual, the United States Sanitary Commission picked up the slack. A Sanitary Commission nurse, Georgeanna

Simon Baruch, surgeon of the 3rd South Carolina, stayed behind at Gettysburg and supervised the Confederate wounded at Black Horse Tavern. He was amazed how the Yankees provided him supplies. Officially a prisoner at Baltimore after the battle, he stayed with friends. He obtained a Confederate uniform (perhaps this one) from a Baltimore tailor. Courtesy of the Simon Baruch Collection, Archives and Special Collections, Tompkins-McCaw Library, Medical College of Virginia, Richmond.

Woolsey, set up a camp where soldiers could eat and spend the night. She estimated that in the three weeks after the battle she served sixteen thousand meals and arranged for a night's sleep for four thousand wounded soldiers. She was most amazed at how well the wounded rebels and Federals got along. They compared their locations at various times during the battle. She heard one soldier tell his former enemy, "You are a lot friendlier this close, than when you are just a little farther away."

On 13 July Estee was placed on a wagon and carried to the train. He was laid on the wooden floor of a boxcar and taken by rail to Jarvis General Hospital in Baltimore. Only a sprinkling of straw protected his painful and distended body from bouncing on the hard wooden floor of the rail car. Estee was feverish and almost delirious when examined at Jarvis. The examining physician noted the entry wound in the left abdomen and the exit wound in the right buttock. When the doctor pressed gently on the distended abdomen, gas and feces exuded from both open wounds. When Estee attempted to urinate, feces and gas escaped through the urethra. The doctor concluded that the rifle ball had cut through the bowel and the bladder. Feces in the lower bowel leaked into the free abdomen and exited from both wounds; feces also flowed into the bladder and exited during urination. The doctor informed Estee that his wound was mortal and he would soon die. Dressings were placed on both the entry and exit wounds and changed frequently because they were continuously dirtied by fecal material. The doctor cut away dead material from the edges of the wounds and prescribed frequent irrigation of the wounds and of the bladder with tea. The tea was boiled, but then cooled to a lukewarm temperature before it was injected.[10]

As Estee lay in pain in Baltimore, other soldiers were in pain back at Camp Letterman. Schively, the soldier who had been wounded twice, was never in danger of dying. His facial wound healed rapidly, though his right eye socket was empty. His arm remained lying across his abdomen. He would let no one touch the arm because the slightest pressure caused excruciating pain. This seemed to the physicians to be some sort of nerve pain, and Schively was evacuated to Turner's Lane Hospital, the special hospital for nerve injuries,

in Philadelphia. Jacob Bieswanger also developed nerve pain and was evacuated to Turner's Lane.

At Camp Letterman the number of wounded was decreasing. The official statistics compiled by Letterman before his departure showed 14,193 wounded Union soldiers and 6,802 wounded rebels cared for by the Union medical system. An inspection by the Sanitary Commission on 22 July reported that 13,050 Northern and 1,810 Southern wounded were receiving Union medical care, mainly at Camp Letterman. Across the battlefield were the Confederate medical facilities caring for 5,452 wounded rebels.[11]

As these Confederate wounded improved and were able to travel, they were evacuated by rail to the Union hospital for prisoners of war: DeCamp General Hospital on David's Island in New York harbor. The first groups of wounded had to bypass Manhattan by boat because of draft riots convulsing the city. Between 17 and 25 July DeCamp Hospital received over three thousand Confederate wounded. Many of those who had undergone amputation on the battlefield suffered from gangrene in the stump. The doctor at David's Island treated these wounds with frequent washing. Each prisoner was given his own sponge and was told not to exchange or share it with other wounded soldiers. Some secondary amputations were required, but the wounds healed by granulation. The terrifying complication of gangrene slowly disappeared among the prisoners.[12] The Confederate doctors who had stayed with their wounded were held as prisoners of war for several weeks; Simon Baruch was taken to Baltimore, but he stayed in town with friends rather than in a stockade. The Confederate doctors were eventually released and returned to the Army of Northern Virginia.

All the Union wounded who could be evacuated from Camp Letterman were taken to Baltimore, Philadelphia, or New York. Many of those who were too sick to move wasted away. They were buried in the newly commissioned military cemetery. In November 1863 only about one hundred wounded remained in the Gettysburg hospitals when President Lincoln came to dedicate the new cemetery. Most of the military doctors were away in Virginia with the Army of the Potomac. The volunteer nurses who remained in Gettysburg came to hear the president. In his speech, Lincoln praised "these honored dead" interred within the new cemetery. He encouraged his listeners to continue to pursue the cause for which the dead had given "the last full measure of devotion."

Estee survived, contrary to his doctor's pronouncement, but feces continued to escape through his painful urethra. Schively and Bieswanger held their painful arms as they lay quietly groaning in Turner's Lane Hospital in Philadelphia. The dead had given their last measure of devotion, but the miseries of the wounded were just beginning.

13

Northern versus Southern Medicine at Vicksburg

THE UNION HAD OCCUPIED MEMPHIS BY ADVANC-ing down the Mississippi River from Illinois. The United States Navy had forced its way up the Mississippi from the Gulf of Mexico and had taken New Orleans. Vicksburg remained the great rebel fortress that prevented the free flow of the products of the Midwest down the Mississippi River to world markets. Medical support for the campaign to wrest the Gibraltar of the West from Confederate hands challenged Northern medical resources. The Southern defensive effort was poorly served by inadequate Confederate medical support.[1]

The Union force assigned the mission of taking Vicksburg was named the Army of the Tennessee because of their previous successes along the Tennessee River. They should not be confused with the Confederate Army of Tennessee, named after the state. The Union forces numbered about 155,000 men and were under the command of Ulysses S. Grant.

Grant's initial plan called for an overland movement from Memphis to Vicksburg along the line of the railroad. Rebel forces cut this rail communication, however, and Grant feared that his army might be isolated deep within Confederate territory. He therefore retreated to Memphis and decided to advance by water down the great Mississippi River. In December 1862 the Confederate defenders repulsed a hurried assault upon the northern ramparts of the Vicksburg defenses. The following spring, Grant moved his fighting forces down the Mississippi, landing on the western shore opposite Vicksburg. Hiring thousands of former slaves as laborers, the Union army attempted to dig a canal that would bypass the Vicksburg fortress. When this attempt failed, Grant determined upon a daring plan.

In May Grant transported a major portion of his force downriver, past the huge guns of Vicksburg. They landed upon the eastern shore of the Mississippi and rapidly moved overland toward Jackson, the capital of the state of Mississippi, fighting major skirmishes. Grant and his army were loose in rebel territory without support and without a clear line of retreat.

Grant was opposed by the Confederate force called the Department of Mississippi and East Louisiana. John C. Pemberton commanded this force until May, when he was superseded by Joseph E. Johnston. When Johnston arrived at the state capital, he was met by the Union Army of the Tennessee and a battle ensued. Johnston was forced to retreat and was unable to link up with Pemberton's forces in Vicksburg. The Vicksburg defenders came out of the city to engage Grant at the major battle of the campaign, fought near a plantation called Champion's Hill. Pemberton retreated back into Vicksburg with about twenty-seven thousand men, where he became surrounded. With thirty-five thousand Confederate soldiers under his command, Johnston retook the state capital as Grant moved toward Vicksburg. Grant's troops surrounding Vicksburg numbered about seventy-five thousand; the remainder of the Army of the Tennessee were guarding the river, the city of Memphis, and western Tennessee. The Confederate troops under Johnston were unable to lift Grant's siege and Vicksburg surrendered on 4 July 1863.

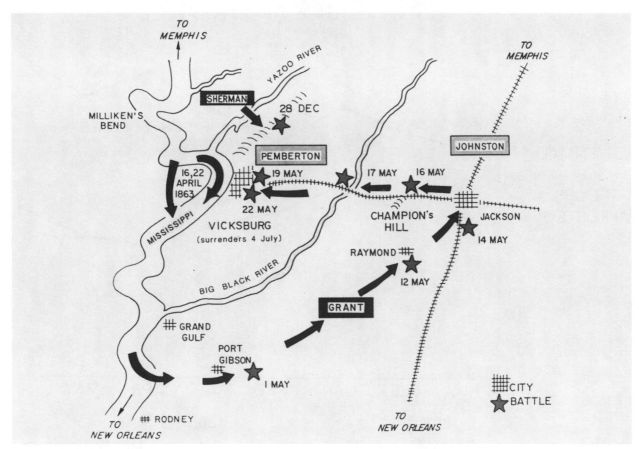

A map of the Vicksburg campaign shows how Grant advanced into the interior of the countryside. He had no system to evacuate his wounded.

Grant's troops experienced a high rate of sickness. Until May the sick and wounded were evacuated to the huge hospital complex in Memphis, but no farther. Grant was worried that the various Sanitary Commission vessels might carry slightly wounded or sick soldiers to St. Louis, or Cairo, or Cincinnati; improper medical evacuation could bleed the strength of the Army of the Tennessee. Therefore, Grant refused to let his medical authorities evacuate any of the sick and wounded further north than Memphis.

A secondary base was set up on the west side of the Mississippi River just north of Vicksburg, at a site called Milliken's Bend. This area was so devoid of solid ground that no structures could be built. The hospital vessel *D. A. January* moored at Milliken's Bend and acted as a floating hospital. From March through June, almost five thousand sick or wounded soldiers were admitted to the floating hospital; many were transferred to other vessels and carried to Memphis. The hulk of the old steamer *Nashville* was towed to Milliken's Bend after being fitted out as a hospital capable of holding one thousand sick soldiers.

When Grant determined to cut off all connection with his base of supply, he was naturally faced with the problem of how to evacuate his wounded. Against the advice of his medical director, Madison Mills, Grant decided to leave the wounded behind to be cared for within Confederate lines. This was without precedent in military annals as purposeful policy, but no other method of handling the wounded allowed Grant to penetrate to the central region of the state, occupy the state capital, and attack Vicksburg from the east. The Union wounded were placed in buildings in towns and cared for by Union medical officers. At the same time, in the same cities, other buildings were occupied by Confederate wounded and cared for by Confederate doctors. The large number of Union wounded from the Battle of Champion's Hill were carried to farm buildings near the battlefield.

TOTAL SICK AND WOUNDED

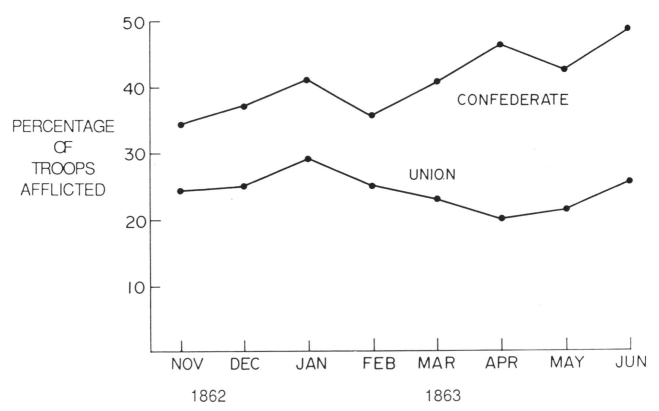

This graph of the total sick and wounded shows that the Confederates started with a greater proportion of their forces disabled; about one of three Confederates and about one in four Yankees were sick in November 1862. During the course of the campaign the proportion of the Confederate force that was sick grew. The Northern forces grew healthier from January to April. By June, the proportion of Confederate troops disabled by sickness or injury was twice that of the Union.

Union surgeons treated Confederate as well as Union wounded.

While Grant's army invested Vicksburg, Union wounded were left over a wide area of central Mississippi that was controlled by Confederate military forces. Since the Union expedition had again made contact with the Mississippi River, medical supplies could be obtained in quantity; they were sent under flag of truce to the hospitals under Confederate control. The official Union medical report sent to Surgeon General Hammond stated that 2,161 wounded soldiers had been left "within the lines of the enemy," where they were being treated by nineteen Union medical officers; four other Union doctors had been detailed to assist the rebel surgeons to care for their wounded.[2]

After the fall of Vicksburg, Medical Director Mills repatriated the Union wounded from rebel control. "A large proportion of our wounded," he reported, "left from necessity at Raymond, Champion Hills, and Black River, have been brought forward, and today fifty ambulances and a supply train have been sent by flag of truce to these places, and I expect that nearly all of those remaining will reach this camp tomorrow evening."[3]

Both the Union and the Confederate armies kept medical statistics. Each regimental surgeon was responsible for filling out the medical returns of his regiment. These were collated and sent to Washington or to Richmond.[4] These reports reveal that the opposing armies in the Vicksburg campaign were both quite ill. Between 20 and 30 percent of the Union Army of the Tennessee was sick or wounded at any given time. But during every month of the campaign, the Confederate Department of Mississippi and East Louisiana had a greater proportion of troops disabled. In November 1862 about one in three Confederate soldiers in the Department were on the sick list; by June 1863, just before the surrender of Vicksburg, almost half the troops were ill. The proportion of the Confederate force unable to perform military duties was greater than the proportion of the Union force; this relationship existed for every month of the campaign, from November 1862 through June 1863. In addition, during the course of the campaign the Confederate force grew sicker; a higher percentage of the troops were afflicted each month. The opposing Union force grew healthier until April.

What diseases were responsible for this health difference between the two opposing military organizations? The number of soldiers wounded was quite small. Except for the month of May, when the Union recorded over six thousand wounded, only a few hundred of the disabled were wounded. The injuries recorded by the medical departments and sent to Washington or Richmond make up a very slight fraction of huge armies numbering many thousands.

The available source material allows analysis of the most significant disease processes. Both Union and Confederate medical authorities used the same nosological system, the British Farr system. The two major medical conditions that afflicted both armies were diarrhea and malaria.[5]

The proportion of Union forces afflicted by diarrhea steadily decreased during winter and spring. In June diarrhea hit the Union forces in epidemic form. This epidemic probably resulted from poor control of human waste in the makeshift Union camps surrounding Vicksburg. One medical inspector of the besieging lines reported that "the men have been in the habit of going out into the bushes, and not infrequently only 30 or 40 feet from some of their tents, and relieving themselves; in fact, human excrement has been promiscuously deposited in every direction until the atmosphere, as the dampness of evening and night approaches, is so heavily loaded with the effluvia that it is sickening."[6]

The Confederates had a fluctuating percentage of their troops sick from diarrhea; however, a greater proportion of the Confederate than the Union army was afflicted by diarrhea during each month of the campaign. The Confederate force had a greater percentage of their troops afflicted by malaria each month also. Malaria decreased among the Union forces throughout winter and spring, but rose suddenly in June. The percentage of Union forces in the Army of the Tennessee afflicted with malaria continued to rise after the surrender of the Vicksburg fortress and the conclusion of the campaign.

While diarrhea and malaria made up about half the sick and wounded, the other half consisted of a large number of injuries and illnesses. Of these separate diagnoses, varying from catarrh to epilepsy to gunshot wound, each involved only a few soldiers. Measles and smallpox are examples of these numerically insignificant but interesting disorders.

During the Vicksburg campaign, measles af-

Table 10

The Number of Soldiers Wounded Each Month
during the Vicksburg Campaign

Month	Union	Confederate
November 1862	159	170
December	823	747
January 1863	847	295
February	218	134
March	128	129
April	136	64
May	6489	552
June	676	317

Sources: <u>MSH</u>, Medical Volume, pt. 1, p. 240, table 38; and "Returns, Department of Mississippi and East Louisiana," Joseph Jones Papers, folder 109, Howard-Tilton Memorial Library, New Orleans, La.

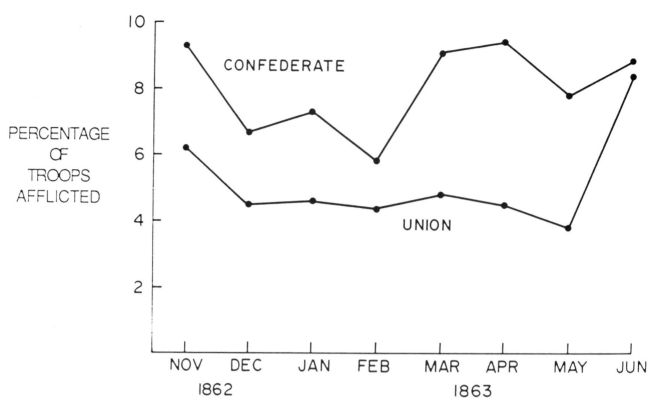

This graph shows that malaria disabled a greater proportion of Confederate than Union troops throughout the campaign. In June, malaria began to become a problem for the Yankees.

flicted about one in one hundred soldiers of the Union Army of the Tennessee but never even one in two hundred Confederate soldiers of the Department of Mississippi and East Louisiana. The disease appeared suddenly among Union forces in November, then rapidly disappeared. The Confederate experience with measles was quite different. New cases of measles occurred among the Confederates during every month of the campaign.

J. J. Woodward's study of measles among Union recruits in 1861 explains these results. Most people, North and South, had acquired measles as children and were immune to further infection. The few Northerners who had not had measles as children developed the disease early in the Vicksburg campaign. No additional recruits were added to the Union besieging force; therefore, no additional cases of measles were recorded. The Confederates, on the other hand, attempted to reinforce the Department of Mississippi and East Louisiana; young soldiers were continually added to the defenders and some of these new recruits

had not previously been exposed to measles. Therefore, measles never disappeared from among the Confederates as it did among the Union soldiers.[7]

A similar phenomenon explains the differing response of the two armies to smallpox. Smallpox first appeared in Confederate forces in December 1862. The infection then occurred in the Union forces, rising slowly until reaching a peak of 0.2 percent (one in five hundred soldiers) in March. This peak was broad but single, as the disease spread throughout all soldiers who had not been successfully vaccinated against smallpox. The infection in the Confederate forces had exacerbations after the initial peak in January, due to the steady arrival of new recruits, some of whom had not been vaccinated.

Measles first reached a peak in Union forces, then spread to the Confederates. Smallpox peaked first among the Confederate soldiers and only later in the Union Army of the Tennessee. One could hypothesize that the two diseases passed each other during the cam-

SMALLPOX

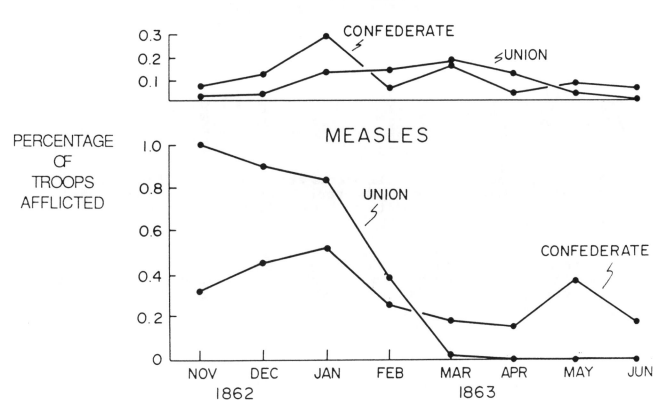

MEASLES

PERCENTAGE OF TROOPS AFFLICTED

This graph shows the incidence of smallpox and measles in Union and Confederate armies during the Vicksburg campaign. These disorders only afflicted a few soldiers, but their epidemiology is interesting. Measles appeared first among the Union troops and smallpox first among the Confederates; it seemed as though the two sides traded diseases. Both disorders disappeared in the Union army before the end of the campaign; their continuation among the Southerners suggests that the Confederates received a steady trickle of new recruits, fresh from their immunologically isolated farms.

paign; smallpox moved from Confederate to Union forces, while measles crossed battle lines in the opposite direction.

Although the Confederate military forces in the Department of Mississippi and East Louisiana had more soldiers ill at all times than did their Union opposition, the percentage of the afflicted who died was very similar. The lethality of various specific diseases, defined as the number of deaths from a particular disease divided by the total number of cases of that same disease during the entire eight months of the campaign, varied widely from disease to disease but remained remarkably similar between Union and Confederate forces. The total deaths as a percentage of total reported illnesses over the entire campaign were 2.48 percent for the Confederacy and 2.15 percent for the Union.[8]

The available Confederate medical statistics allow one to calculate how sick soldiers were lost by medical transfer. Soldiers sent home on medical furlough or sent to hospitals in other departments (and lost to Pemberton's command) are presented in the accompanying graph. In February 1863 almost 97 percent of the disabled were returned to duty.[9] Thereafter, however, the ability of the medical authorities to return troops to duty rapidly deteriorated. In May 10 percent of the forces dwindled away because of medical furlough or medical transfer. If the Confederates had been 10 percent stronger at the Battle of Champion's Hill, the entire campaign might have had a different course and even a different outcome. In June, 14 percent were lost to duty for medical reasons.

In summary, both armies engaged in the Vicksburg campaign had a significant proportion of their forces on the sick list at all times.

Table 11

Mortality from Various Causes
during the Vicksburg Campaign

	UNION	CONFEDERATE
Died from Wounds	6.2 %	7.0%
Diarrhea & dysentery	1.6	1.5
Malaria	0.8	0.7
Pneumonia	13.4	17.2
Smallpox	10.5	12.6
Typhoid fever	25.9	29.0
Overall	2.15	2.48

Mortality from cause x is all deaths attributed to x divided by the number of cases of x over the period from November 1862 through June 1863. Overall mortality is all deaths divided by all recorded episodes of illness.

Sources: Calculated from data in <u>MSH</u>, Medical Volume, pt. 1, p. 240, table 38; and "Returns, Department of Mississippi and East Louisiana," Joseph Jones Papers, folder 109, Howard-Tilton Memorial Library, New Orleans, LA.

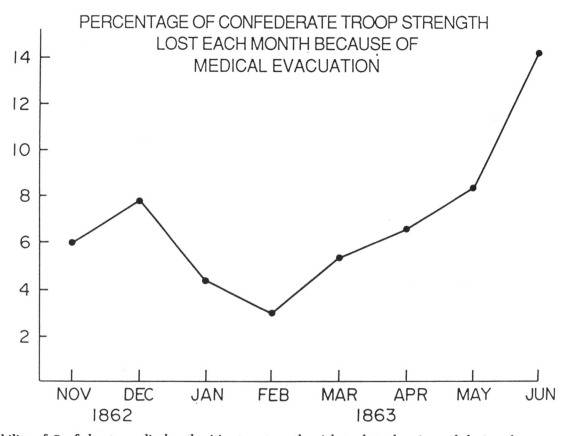

PERCENTAGE OF CONFEDERATE TROOP STRENGTH LOST EACH MONTH BECAUSE OF MEDICAL EVACUATION

The ability of Confederate medical authorities to return the sick to duty deteriorated during the course of the Vicksburg campaign. This graph shows the percentage of total troops evacuated outside the control of the Confederate Vicksburg defenders each month. Only a few of these evacuated soldiers ever returned to the Vicksburg defense. The Union figures are not known, but Grant ordered that no sick soldier could be evacuated farther north than Memphis, a base under his command.

About one in every four Union soldiers were sick; the Confederate proportion of ill soldiers rose from about one in three to about one in two. Medical furlough and medical evacuation to other departments caused a serious loss of military manpower just when it was most needed.

14

Confederate Medicine Deteriorating

LATE ON 3 JULY 1863 ROBERT E. LEE CONCLUDED that the Army of Northern Virginia would have to retreat from Gettysburg. The cavalry brigade commanded by John D. Imboden had not been engaged with the enemy during the vicious fighting of the past three days. Lee ordered Imboden to load all the Confederate wounded onto wagons and begin an immediate retreat. The Army of Northern Virginia would follow the next day.

Imboden's troops seized every wagon and cart from the surrounding countryside. They lined these vehicles up along the road to Cashtown until they stretched for over seventeen miles. Some of the more seriously wounded Confederates stayed behind with a few Confederate doctors; one was Simon Baruch. Most of the injured were loaded into the wagons in great haste. Some of the soldiers who had been wounded during Pickett's charge had not even had their wounds dressed. As the retreat began, the column was rocked by crashing thunder and lightning. A downpour drenched the wounded; it seemed to Imboden as though the very windows of heaven had opened. The noise of thunder and moaning drowned out all attempts by officers to issue commands. The teamsters could not control the frightened horses and mules.

The unsprung wagons bounced along the muddy and rutted road, torturing the wounded passengers. The train of wagons limped along in a madhouse of confusion and misery. Over the sound of the rain, the thunder, the creaking of wagons, and the bleating of the terrified animals, the screams of the wounded cut into the heart. Some prayed aloud; others swore incessantly. These phrases were riveted upon the minds of the accompanying cavalry:

"Stop one minute and take me out, and leave me to die on the roadside."

"Oh God! Why can't I die?"

"My God! Have mercy and kill me."

"My poor wife, my dear children! What will become of you?"[1]

As the terrible retreat passed through the hamlet of Fairfield, Pennsylvania, local residents came out of their houses to watch the groaning caravan. Young boys pushed sticks through the wagon wheels, ripping out the spokes. Imboden ordered that the next boy who destroyed a wagon would be hung. Some wagons were discarded; their loads of wounded soldiers were left behind in the Fairfield church. Imboden ordered the retreat to continue without rest. He feared enemy pursuit and he had to clear the road for the rest of the army. "Many of the wounded in the wagons had been without food for 36 hours," he said. "Their torn and bloody clothing, matted and hardened, was rasping the tender, inflamed, and still oozing wounds." Imboden summarized this terrible retreat of the maimed: "During this one night I realized more of the horrors of war than I had in all the two preceding years."[2]

The wagon loads of wounded soldiers were hauled overland to Williamsport, Maryland, where Imboden organized a desperate defense against an attack of Federal cavalry. The wounded were ferried across the Potomac on rafts and carried to Winchester, Virginia, where a support hospital had been set up, us-

124

John D. Imboden was in charge of the column of ambulances that carried the Confederate wounded from Gettysburg to Virginia. During the first horrible night of the retreat, he learned more of the horrors of war than in all his prior military experience. NA

ing doctors and supplies from the Hanover Junction Hospital. The huge number of wounded were treated as best as possible, then transported by wagon to the railhead, where they were carried in boxcars to the R and D in Gordonsville. There they were distributed throughout the Virginia hospital system. Some went southeasterly to Richmond and Petersburg, others southwesterly to Charlottesville and Lynchburg.

After the horrendous Gettysburg campaign, the creaks in the Confederate Medical Department became more noticeable. From his headquarters on the second floor of the War Building, Surgeon General Moore attempted to deal with these problems:

First, *supplies* grew short as the Northern naval blockade tightened. The response was an effort to use the products of the Confederacy as replacements for imported items.

Second, *medical furlough* was too easily obtained, draining the fighting forces of potential strength. A series of War Department orders, amplified by laws passed by the Confederate Congress, regulated medical furloughs.

Third, *supervision* of widely scattered doctors and medical facilities was difficult. Moore responded with a new organization and efforts at continuing medical education in the midst of destructive war.

Fourth, *coordination* with other Confederate military departments became more and more difficult as each department faced its own problems in the deteriorating Confederacy.

In its Trading with the Enemy Act of 13 July 1861, the North had declared that medical supplies had potential military uses and could be intercepted by blockading naval vessels. At the first meeting of the Northern American Medical Association to occur during the War, Augustus K. Gardner of New York offered a resolution to make medical supplies freely available to the Confederacy; the resolution was immediately tabled.[3] Southerners believed the rumors that Dr. Gardner's motion was met with hisses by the civilian medical authorities of the North.[4]

From the very beginning of the War, the Confederate government arranged for its medical department to have a separate fund available in Europe solely to purchase medical supplies. Agents in London and Paris, with funds in British pounds, obtained supplies and openly shipped them to such places as Halifax, Bermuda, or Cuba. They were then transferred to Confederate blockade runners, which slipped past the U.S. naval blockade into Southern ports. Medical supplies for the portion of the Confederacy west of the Mississippi were shipped from Europe to Matamoras, Mexico, then taken across the Rio Grande to Brownsville, Texas.[5]

The Confederate States Army obtained some medical supplies via the capture of Federal stores, a procedure that was especially successful in Virginia. Medical Director Lafayette Guild complained to Surgeon General Moore that his doctors were seizing medical stores from the enemy for their own use, rather than turning them in to the medical purveyor for distribution where they were most needed. One regimental surgeon obtained such a supply of a certain ointment that he sent some of it to a civilian medical colleague back home: "I have more of it than I could use in two years," he said.[6]

Smuggling was a major source of medical supplies for the Confederate forces in Tennessee. The South may have received more supplies from Memphis after it had fallen into Union hands than while it remained a Confederate city. A whole series of ruses were used to smuggle quinine from Memphis into Confederate territory. Women hung bottles of the medicine from racks within their hooped skirts. Dead horses and mules were filled with containers of quinine; Confederate sympathizers then dragged these carcasses past Union sentries, supposedly to be buried. In addition, open exchange sometimes took place; corrupt civilian and military authorities in the city traded medical supplies for valuable Southern cotton. In spring 1862 a rumor circulated that the quinine smuggled through Memphis had been poisoned by the nefarious Yankees. The rumor proved untrue but some perfectly good quinine was discarded.[7]

Although captured and smuggled supplies were happily received, they could not be counted on. Running supplies through the blockade, though generally successful, added cost to scarce items and became less reliable as the Union naval force grew. Coffee was very soon in short supply. This substance was thought to have therapeutic properties as a stimulant and much of the coffee that came through the blockade was turned over to the medical department. The surgeon general heard that doctors sometimes drank the coffee themselves and issued a strict order on 2 December 1863. Coffee was not a beverage for use by the healthy, but should "be used solely for its medicinal effects" for the sick and wounded.[8]

The Confederacy hoped to become self-sufficient for its major needs. In the case of alcohol, the South was successful in supplying its needs, and these needs were huge. Alcohol was considered a stimulant and often was given to a patient who appeared exhausted or who was about to undergo surgery.

The medical department constructed its own distilleries. The alcohol distillery in Salisbury, North Carolina, consumed so much grain that the North Carolina governor complained to the Richmond government that not enough grain remained to feed the civilian population.[9] Salisbury was the site of a bread riot when the hungry populace reacted to the price and scarcity of corn and other staples.

The medical authorities also purchased a vast amount of alcohol from private distillers. In 1863 the Confederate Congress authorized the purchase of two hundred thousand gallons of alcohol for medical use at three dollars per gallon. The medical department had to pay the market price, however, and inflation soon pushed the price above the Congressionally approved three dollars. Surgeon General Moore personally authorized paying a greater amount, but he advised his medical purveyors to assume the role of private citizens, not government agents, when purchasing liquor in order to get a better price.

The medical department sought substitutes for imported products. Surgeon General Moore appointed Francis Peyre Porcher to survey the flora of the Confederacy for therapeutic properties. Porcher was professor of materia medica (pharmacology) at the medical school in Charleston; before the War, he had contributed an article to *Debow's Review* on the possible therapeutic uses of plants and trees growing throughout the Southern states. In 1863 Porcher published a six-hundred-page compendium on the flora and fauna of the Confederate States that suggested many therapeutic uses.[10] Several Confederate laboratories manufactured drugs from Southern flora, especially morphine from poppies. The most successful laboratory was run in Columbia, South Carolina, by John and Joseph LeConte.[11]

The major deficiency in the Southern pharmacopeia was quinine. Most physicians in 1860 knew that patients with malaria who were treated with quinine recovered more quickly than those who were not so treated. Furthermore, the symptoms of malaria were less likely to develop in healthy individuals who took quinine every day. Joseph Jones proved this observation in April 1863 with an experiment involving the 25th South Carolina, a regiment stationed in a very malarious region near Charleston. Dr. J. N. Warren, the regimental assistant surgeon, selected two hundred men and forced all of them to swallow four grains of quinine each day. Of the soldiers so treated, four developed malaria and only one developed typhoid fever. The remainder of the regiment, some three hundred to four hundred men, experienced over three hundred episodes of malaria and twenty-three cases of typhoid fever, with two deaths.[12]

Despite the scientific evidence that quinine could prevent malaria if taken daily, not enough of the medication was available for widespread use. Moore ordered that quinine should be used to treat individuals suffering from malaria, but not to be given prophylactically to healthy troops. By 1864 quinine was selling on the open market for four hundred dollars per ounce.

Good surgical instruments were difficult to obtain. One surgeon had to use the bent prong of a fork to elevate a depressed skull fracture. But the problems with supply led to the development of new medical devices. Necessity is the mother of invention. J. J. Chisolm constructed a small device to save anesthetics during surgery; the cotton was placed within the device and soaked with chloroform or ether; two small prongs directed the anesthetic into the nostrils. Confederate surgeon John J. Bolton devised special rods to stabilize fractures of the leg. A civilian dentist devised a series of straps, individualized for each patient, to aid in the stabilization and subsequent healing of fractures of the jaw.[13]

The material needed to vaccinate against smallpox had always been produced locally. In late fall 1863 another smallpox epidemic threatened. Because he was unsure if his previous vaccination attempts had been successful in all cases, Surgeon General Moore decided to vaccinate each soldier in the Confederate Army, despite the fact that for many soldiers this would be a second vaccination. He told a surgeon named C. W. P. Brock to reproduce vaccine material in volunteers.

Table 12

Regulations Regarding Medical Furloughs,
Confederate States Army

Year	Date	Order number	Content
1861:	9 June	9	MF must be signed by senior surgeon and regimental commander.
	7 Nov	17	MF must also be signed by the commanding general of the field army.

[Period of easing regulations]

1862:	31 May	48	In Richmond, MF can be granted by a hospital surgeon and the area commander.
	29 Sept	72	The commandant of each post can grant MF.

[Regulations tighten from this point forward]

	17 Dec	107	Surgeons should grant MF only if required for the health of the soldier.
1863:	3 Feb	14	MF over thirty days requires approval of the regimental commander.
	29 April	51	In larger hospitals, a surgical board, not a single surgeon, must approve MF.
	23 May	69	Smaller hospitals should band together to form a board to approve MF.
	2 Oct	130	Medical officers are admonished to comply strictly with rules of MF.
	29 Oct	141	The soldier on MF upon arriving home must report to an army representative.
1864:	29 Feb	25	A soldier can be given MF only if he will be ill over sixty days.
	1 Nov	83	No extension of MF for enlisted men.
1865:	6 Jan	1	A soldier on MF who fails to report will be arrested.
	30 March	18	No extension of MF for officers.

Abbreviation: MF=medical furlough

Source: OR, ser. 4, vol. 2, pp. 4, 98, 243, 380, 570, 693, 913 and vol. 3, pp. 175, 749, 999.

This doctor and a colleague went through Richmond, knocking on doors, asking mothers to have their children vaccinated in order to vaccinate the army. No mother refused. Vaccine material was injected in six places on each arm of each child. Two weeks later, these twelve crusts were removed, wrapped in tin foil, and sent throughout the army. All soldiers were vaccinated within six weeks. "In no case," reported Brock, "was any other disease communicated by vaccine."[14]

Medical furlough became a more and more serious problem as the War continued. Soldiers recovering from a wound or from a serious illness were sent home to recuperate. Unfortunately, they often stayed home when they were needed to reinforce the dwindling manpower resources of the Confederate armies. The Confederate military authorities recognized this problem and promulgated a series of regulations to restrict the use of medical furlough. Many doctors found it very difficult to turn down the request of a wounded soldier to return home to see his family and recuperate under their loving care. One Confederate physician wrote to his wife that the most difficult problem he faced with the army was bearing the hatred men felt for him when he denied their requests for medical furlough.[15] Some doctors awarded leave when it was not really medically required in order to avoid this antipathy. One of the first reforms, therefore, required a board of doctors, not just a single physician, to award a furlough to a soldier for medical recuperation.[16]

The need of the field armies for manpower affected the medical department directly. At the beginning of the War, soldiers who were recovering from a bout of illness served in the hospital as nurses, guards, and other hospital workers. As the Confederate hunger for troops grew, more and more of the convalescents were shipped back to their regiments. White women, often of the upper class, served in their places as nurses and matrons. Free blacks and slaves acted as nurses, orderlies, cooks, and laundry workers. The Confederate hospital system could not have functioned without black labor. Both free blacks and slaves were paid a monthly wage; for example, laundry workers received twenty-five dollars per month.[17]

Despite the efforts to empty the hospitals of all patients who could perform some sort of military duty, the doctors were unable to discharge some patients who developed shifting symptoms and new complaints to justify a continued hospital stay. The more recalcitrant among them were called "hospital rats." Some of these were outright malingerers. Dr. A. A. Lyon at Chimborazo attempted to treat a soldier named Parsons for "aphonia"; he could not speak above a whisper. After many months of unsuccessful therapy, Lyon awarded the soldier a medical discharge. The next day, the doctor encountered him in the street loudly auctioning off his uniforms. When Lyon suspected that another soldier was faking epileptic seizures, he threw a bucket of ice water upon his shaking body and the "seizure" immediately terminated. Ordered back to his regiment, the soldier deserted. Lyon concluded that the young man had gone to a place "where bullets ceased to fly and fits need never come."[18]

Toward the end of 1863 Surgeon General Moore reorganized the Confederate medical administration. Dr. David Yandell became medical director of the Trans-Mississippi Department, that portion of the Confederacy cut off by Yankee control of the Mississippi River. Yandell was largely free of supervision from Richmond. Moore arranged hospital systems to serve as support for the Confederacy's two great armies: the Army of Northern Virginia and the Army of Tennessee. Lafayette Guild remained medical director of Robert E. Lee's Army of Northern Virginia. The hospital system in Virginia to which this army evacuated its sick and wounded was placed under the direction of William A. Carrington, a doctor with the old U.S. Navy. Andrew Foard remained the medical director of the Army of Tennessee; Samuel H. Stout controlled the hospital system in Georgia and Alabama to which Foard sent his sick and wounded. Edwin S. Gaillard, who had lost his arm to a Federal minié ball, was made inspector of hospitals over the entire Confederacy.

Confederate physicians, especially those not in Richmond, needed continuing medical education. Moore and fellow Richmond physicians started an organization called the Association of Confederate Army and Navy Physicians. Under Moore's stimulus, a new journal was begun, *The Confederate Medical and Surgical Journal*. The editorial functions were the responsibility of a committee consist-

Table 13

Workers at Chimborazo Hospital, January 1863

	Personnel	Number
Hospital stewards:	White Confederate soldiers	166
Matrons:	White women volunteers	25
Nurses:	Free blacks and slaves	264
Cooks:	Free blacks and slaves	58
Laundry workers:	Black women	123

Source: J. H. Brewer, The Confederate Negro: Virginia's Craftsmen and Military Laborers, 1861-1865. (Durham, N.C.: Duke University Press, 1969), 98.

ing of Moore, William Middleton Michel of Charleston, and James B. McCaw of the Chimborazo Hospital, who had edited the *Virginia Medical and Surgical Journal* before the War.[19]

The *Confederate Medical and Surgical Journal* contained several different types of articles. Some concerned medical science and would interest civilian as well as military physicians. Others, written by military doctors, concerned interesting cases from the field or observations from military hospitals. One article from the Surgeon General's Office included all the medical statistics from the first two and one half years of the War.[20]

At the very beginning of the War, J. J. Chisolm had written a military medical manual that became popular with Confederate military officers. Other manuals were available to Confederate surgeons, including works by Union and by British doctors. Nevertheless, Surgeon General Moore thought that all these works were too difficult to use for some Confederate surgeons, who were forced by circumstances to perform surgery that they had never before seen. The surgeon general set up a committee to produce a simpler manual. This work was published in Richmond in 1863 and distributed throughout the Confederate army. The most remarkable aspect of the Confederate *Manual of Military Surgery* was the pictorial section. The drawings of operations were as simple as cartoons. A doctor with very little surgical experience could be guided by this work.

Moore's administration of the Medical Bureau was clear and vigorous. His relationships to other departments of the Confederate bureaucracy were more problematic. Moore's

hospital directors generally bypassed the Confederate Commissary Department to obtain food directly from farmers. The Treasury Department sometimes did not pay Moore's bills even when money was present in the medical account. After the first year of the War the Confederate Congress appropriated medical funds regularly at six month intervals, but in May 1863 Moore ran out of money and supplemental appropriations were needed. By 1864 currency inflation was so severe that many people would not accept Confederate government script. When medical requisitions went unfilled, Moore complained to Secretary of War James A. Seddon, who merely forwarded the complaint to the Treasury Department, which did nothing.[21]

The medical department of the Confederate States Army had great difficulty working with the army authorities responsible for producing and delivering material to hospitals and to the medical directors of field armies. To obtain various forms of transport, Moore had to contact one or more of these quartermasters in Richmond: Captain E. Carrington, whose office was on Bank Street, the third door from 10th Street, was in charge of transporting medical supplies; Captain W. Weisiger, whose office was on 9th Street near Main, was in charge of supplying fuel to hospitals and camps; Major R. P. Archer was in charge of ambulances; his office was in Bacon's Quarter Branch; and Captain W. E. Warren, whose office was at the corner of Bank and 10th Streets, was in charge of hospital construction and repair.

While these officers tried to cooperate with Moore and accede to his desires, they all had other responsibilities. Anyone familiar with

A MANUAL

OF

MILITARY SURGERY.

PREPARED FOR THE USE OF THE

CONFEDERATE STATES ARMY.

ILLUSTRATED.

BY ORDER OF THE SURGEON-GENERAL.

RICHMOND:
AYRES & WADE,
ILLUSTRATED NEWS STEAM PRESSES.
1863

The title page from the Confederate *Manual of Military Surgery*, written by a committee.

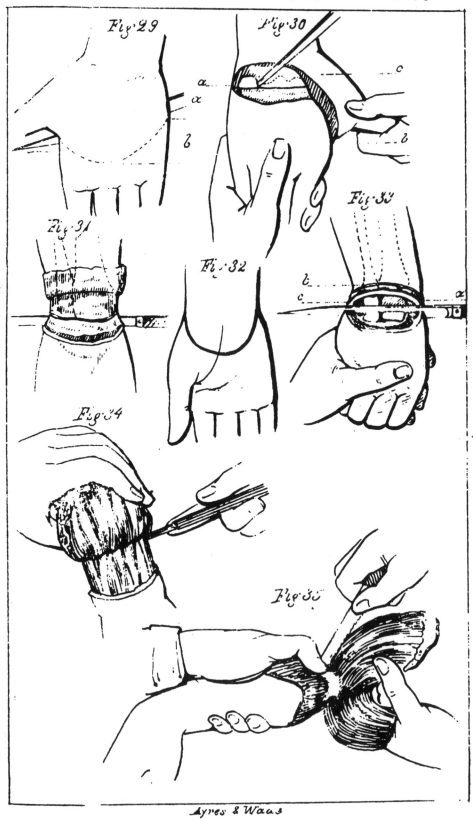

The *Manual* presented surgical procedures in pictures that have an almost cartoon-like quality.

Table 14

Confederate Medical Appropriations

Appropriation passed		Amount	Stated purpose
1861:	21 May	$350,000	Budget to 18 February
	21 August	$50,000	Contract physicians
	4 September	$1,000,000	Unrestricted
	24 December	$250,000	Additional supplies
1862:	15 February	$120,000	Supplies
	3 April	$2,400,000	Budget to 30 November
	9 October	$400,000	Additional supplies
	13 October	$1,500,000	Retire deficit
			Budget to 30 June 1863 for:
1863:	10 February	$2,500,000	Supplies
		$150,000	Hospital costs
		$890,000	Salaries
			Budget to 31 December 1863 for:
	1 May	$3,500,000	Supplies
		$150,000	Hospital costs
		$985,000	Salaries
			Supplemental appropriations for:
	1 May	$625,000	Hospital clothing
		$605,000	Additional alcohol
		$1,000,000	Special supplies
			Budget to 30 June 1864 for:
1864:	17 February	$15,420,000	Supplies
		250,000	Hospital costs
		$1,150,000	Salaries
			Budget to 31 Dec 1864 for:
	13 June	$14,820,000	Supplies
		$100,000	Hospital costs
		$1,400,000	Salaries

The Confederate States Congress appropriated considerable monies for the use of the medical department of the army. The sums are in Confederate currency, which underwent inflation.

Source: OR, ser. 4, vol. 1, pp. 339, 580, 599, 812, ser. 4, vol. 2, pp. 112, 120, 392, 532, and Ser. 4, vol. 3, pp. 139, 480.

bureaucracy can imagine how one of these officers, Captain Weisiger, for example, reacted when faced with supplying fuel to the camp of a major general or to a hospital. He undoubtedly gave greater attention to the requests of the major general than to those of Moore, who only held the army rank of colonel. If Moore wanted to go over Weisiger's head in the army chain of command, he had to route his complaint through his superior, the secretary of war, who probably felt little desire to referee a fight between a captain and a colonel.

With all these problems, the Confederate medical department continued the struggle to provide medical care to the wounded and to the sick of their deteriorating army.

15

Union Enclaves along the Confederate Coast

COMBINED OPERATIONS BY THE U.S. ARMY AND THE U.S. Navy seized several important points along the coast of the new Confederate States of America. Many people North and South thought that these locations would be springboards for the deep penetration of the Southern interior. Along the Carolina coast, a tenacious Confederate defense never allowed the Union forces to move more than a few miles from the ocean. A series of fevers and illnesses assisted the Confederate defense. The Northern force in New Orleans feared that yellow fever, the stranger's disease, might threaten their occupation.

The initial Union landings were made on Roanoke Island, North Carolina. Surgeon Frederick S. Wells of the 9th New Jersey was drowned on 15 January 1862 while attempting to rescue food from a foundering boat for his starving regiment.[1] From Roanoke Island, Union forces moved to take Newbern, North Carolina.[2] The Yankee troops, made up of New England regiments, settled down for a long occupation.

A hospital was built as a local support facility. Stanley General Hospital, named in honor of Edward Stanley, the Union military governor of North Carolina, was located in several buildings in the center of Newbern. In addition, several wooden pavilions were constructed. The total hospital system contained 520 beds. The surgeon-in-chief, J. Baxter Upham, was proud to report that all the buildings that made up the hospital allowed the circulation of air required by Surgeon General Hammond's order. In a directive dated 24 November 1862, Hammond had ordered that hos-

pitals in existing buildings should have twelve hundred cubic feet of space per patient; in a pavilion hospital building with better ventilation, six hundred cubic feet of space was required. Stanley General Hospital was manned by six surgeons and by nurses from the Sisters of Mercy Convent of New York.[3] As always, the U.S. Sanitary Commission was present to assist the medical support of the Union troops.

Almost as soon as the hospital was completed, a strange and deadly illness afflicted the Newbern garrison. Young men were seized with pain in the head, back, and legs. Within a day, they were bedridden, usually lying on one side and groaning continuously. Vomiting, delirium, and small red spots over the skin presaged death. The majority of the afflicted were under twenty-one years old. Most went from complete health to death in less than four days.[4]

To better understand this strange and deadly affliction, the Union physicians performed autopsies. If the disease had killed in just a day or two, the brain was covered with a thin film of creamy material. Soldiers who had survived for several days before succumbing to this terrible illness showed an increased amount of this sticky substance; it had spread over the entire brain and even surrounded the spinal cord. The symptoms and the autopsy findings identified the disease: epidemic spinal meningitis.

The deadly disease continued to afflict both troops and local civilians, especially children, for several days, but then it disappeared as mysteriously as it had come. Dr. Isaac F. Galloupe, the surgeon of the 17th Massachusetts,

The U.S. Sanitary Commission had its representatives at Newbern, North Carolina. **USAMHI**

tried to make sense of this terrifying epidemic. From discussion with local people, including the town's civilian physician, he determined that no disease such as this had ever before appeared in Newbern. It was not related to the most common febrile illness, malaria, because the fever of this new epidemic was continuous from beginning until death rather than coming in paroxysms. In addition, no improvement followed the administration of massive amounts of quinine. He thought that the disease was caused by "living in barracks made of green lumber and insufficient ventilation."[5]

No sooner had spinal meningitis stopped, then Newbern was afflicted with a sudden epidemic of yellow fever. The mortality was frightful. Dr. Nathan Mayer, in charge of the effects of the dead, claimed to have "two trunks full of watches."[6] The Newbern yellow fever epidemic seemed to show a special virulence for physicians. Of the eighteen assistant

surgeons of the occupying force, nine died during this epidemic. Yellow fever continued to terrorize Newbern until the first frost. No one ever determined exactly how it had so suddenly appeared, nor why it had ended so abruptly.

Another epidemic afflicted Union troops stationed along the Carolina coast. The major Union base on Hilton Head Island, South Carolina, had been free of deadly epidemics until the arrival, on 26 August 1862, of the U.S.S. *Delaware*. The ship had taken aboard coal and supplies at Key West, leaving on 14 August. One passenger, Assistant Surgeon Cornick, had been ill with yellow fever earlier in the summer while on duty in the Dry Tortugas, but he thought that he had recovered. Because Key West and the Tortugas were subject to yellow fever, and because it was the sickly season of late summer, the *Delaware* was held at quarantine at the end of the long dock. Sev-

The long dock on Hilton Head Island was the site where the yellow fever epidemic began. That might be the U.S.S. *Delaware* at the end of the wharf. USAMHI

eral soldiers aboard were ill, supposedly with a nonspecific bilious fever. After the expiration of the quarantine, the sick soldiers debarked from the ship, which loaded supplies and sailed north. After lying at the end of the wharf for about twelve hours, the sick were taken by rail to Hilton Head Hospital on another part of the island.

Under the supervision of Medical Director Charles H. Crane, Drs. Thomas T. Smiley and A. A. Moulton treated the sick soldiers from the *Delaware*. Four were admitted to the hospital the evening of 8 September. The doctors harbored no apprehension that these fever patients represented a serious illness until the following day, when Private D. K. Ripley of the 7th New Hampshire suddenly underwent circulatory collapse and died. Dr. Smiley performed a postmortem examination; he noted that the skin was yellow and mottled. When he opened the stomach of the cadaver, black vomit spewed out. These findings indicated to Dr. Smiley that he was facing a yellow fever epidemic. Over the next few days, seven more soldiers were admitted to the U.S. Army hospital. Of the total of eleven patients admitted, nine died.

No new cases of yellow fever occurred after 17 September, and the medical authorities felt that they had escaped a serious yellow fever epidemic. On 9 October, twenty-two days after the admission of the last case of yellow fever, John Lowney, a civilian working in the Quartermaster's Department, developed a high fever and applied for treatment at the Hilton Head Hospital. Dr. Smiley arrived about 7 P.M. and examined him by candlelight. Lowney's eyes were bloodshot, his face red and bloated, his abdomen tender. Since the patient was accompanied by three other civilian workmen who were slightly drunk, Dr. Smiley thought that the patient merely suffered from an alcoholic debauch.

The next morning, however, Mr. Lowney vomited about two quarts of black material and suddenly died. At autopsy, the skin had a yellow appearance, not noted during life, and the stomach was full of black vomitus. It was obvious to Dr. Smiley that yellow fever had killed this man and he feared greatly that an epidemic would follow.

Later that same day, seven more patients were admitted to Hilton Head hospital with symptoms of yellow fever. One of these was a soldier of the 47th New York; the others were all civilian employees of the Quartermaster's Department. The Quartermaster Building was near the end of the dock where the *Delaware*

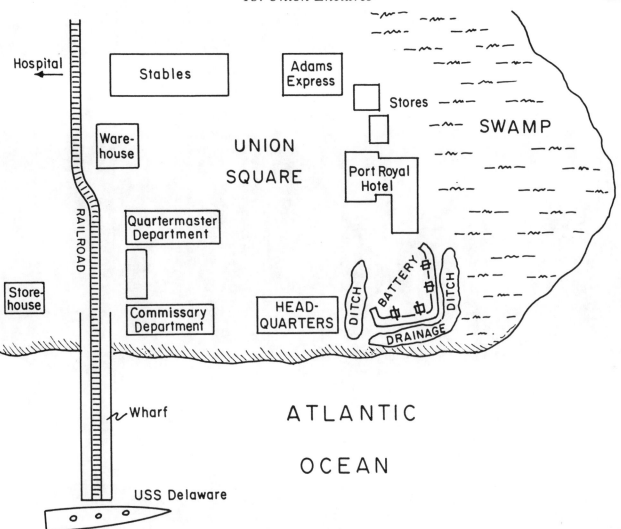

This map of Union Square on Hilton Head Island shows the main focus of the epidemic. It spread from the dock to the officers at headquarters, to the workers at the quartermaster building, and to the residents of the Port Royal House Hotel. Swamps and ditches surround the area where the epidemic flourished.

had been moored. Before the yellow fever epidemic was over, a total of thirty-seven people were admitted to the army hospital on Hilton Head. In addition, several officers assigned to general headquarters were afflicted and taken to nearby Beaufort for treatment. These officers, who had resided in the Port Royal House Hotel, included the commanding officer of the Third Rhode Island, who died from fulminant yellow fever.

The commander of all military forces on Hilton Head Island was Major General Ormsby Mitchel. In his army career Mitchel had utilized the scientific training he had obtained at the U.S. Military Academy to become the leading American astronomer. At the outbreak of the Civil War he had put aside his

telescope to return to the command of army troops. Epidemics know no rank, and the senior U.S. Army officer on Hilton Head Island was struck with virulent yellow fever. Just before he became delirious, he said: "God has called me, and I cheerfully obey the summons." He died on 29 October.

The first frost of 1862 at Hilton Head occurred on 7 November. No new cases of yellow fever occurred after that. The terrible epidemic subsided, and Dr. Smiley turned to its analysis. He carefully mapped out where each of the victims worked or lived. The predominant locations were all at the end of the long wharf within an area called Union Square: the Quartermaster Building, general headquarters, the Port Royal House Hotel, and the sta-

Dr. A. A. Moulton assisted Dr. Thomas Smiley in their struggle against yellow fever. If he had known that Hilton Head would suffer such an epidemic, he probably would not have arranged for his wife and child to share his tent with him on the island. USAMHI

bles. Much of this square had been built on sand heaped up over a swamp. A defensive battery had been built off Union Square. Dr. Smiley noted that the ditches in front of the battery were always filled with stagnant water. He concluded that new forts and posts in conquered areas of the Confederacy should not be built upon swamps because morbific substances arising from the remains of the swamp spread yellow fever. Smiley was unable to fathom why an illness-free period of 22 days occurred between the last of the yellow fever cases from the ship and the first from the island.[7]

Meningitis and yellow fever were the great killers. They could sweep through a regiment, sucking out courage as well as life. The chap-lain stood at the door of the hospital ward, threw religious tracts on the floor inside, and hurried on. These epidemics were terrifying but transient. The disease that debilitated the entire army along the Atlantic seaboard, how-ever, was malaria. It did not kill individual soldiers, but made them so sick that it de-stroyed any possibility of a military offensive.

The 17th Massachusetts, occupying New-bern, reported in one month eleven hundred attacks of malaria in a regiment of less than nine hundred. According to the regimental surgeon, "the regiment became so much re-duced as to be hardly able to perform camp duty." Only three soldiers from the 17th Mas-sachusetts died from malaria, but in many "the constitution was completely broken

Major General Ormsby Mitchel was an internationally famous astronomer before the War. He was the commanding officer of all U.S. troops on Hilton Head Island when he died from yellow fever. From F. A. Mitchel, *Ormsby Macknight Mitchel, Astronomer and General*, Boston: Houghton, Mifflin, 1887.

Table 15

Malaria among Federal Troops
along the Atlantic Coast

Year	Troop strength	Cases	Incidence	Deaths	Mortality
First	27,453	5,375	19.6%	109	2.0%
Second	36,458	23,882	65.5	141	0.6
Third	33,800	37,841	112.0	67	0.2
Fourth	29,166	29.622	101.6	99	0.3

Definitions: Incidence is the number of cases of malaria (all forms) that occurred during the year divided by the average number of troops present that year.   Since each person can experience malaria more than once, the incidence calculated in this manner can give a result greater than 100 percent. Mortality is the number of soldiers who died from malaria divided by the number who were diagnosed as suffering from malaria. These numbers do not include returns from black regiments.

Source: Medical and Surgical History, Medical Volume, pt. 1, pp. 48, 54, 186, 192, 336, 342, 502, and 508, tables 9, 10, 30, 31, 53, 54, 79, and 80.

down, and the men were discharged from the service." The doctor thought that quinine was good treatment for malaria, but he was dissatisfied with the use of the agent for prophylaxis. "Companies which took these medicines daily appeared to be as much affected by the disease as those who did not take it," he concluded, but he did not make any special effort to ensure that the soldiers took the bitter medicine.[8]

The medical returns from the Union Department of the South, making up the areas occupied by Union forces along the Confederate Atlantic coast (plus islands off Florida), showed how malaria debilitated the troops. The affliction rate every year was greater than 100 percent because some soldiers had more than one attack. With virtually every soldier afflicted by malaria, it is not surprising that this sickly army could make no significant advance inland. The Confederate military commander of the area, Pierre G. T. Beauregard, told President Jefferson Davis that the fevers of the Atlantic coast would destroy any potential Yankee offensive.[9]

While malaria debilitated the Northern troops along the Carolina coast, the Union authorities in New Orleans on the Gulf coast expected to be struck by a deadly epidemic of yellow fever. The United States Navy had

pushed past the forts at the mouth of the Mississippi in April 1862 and captured the largest city of the Confederacy. Unfortunately, New Orleans was also the sickliest city of the Confederacy; yellow fever had ravaged the city almost every year in the 1850s. The epidemic of 1853 had killed over eight thousand people and an epidemic in 1859 had killed almost five thousand.[10] A yellow fever epidemic in New Orleans like the ones that stuck Newbern and Hilton Head Island on the Atlantic coast would cause great loss of life among civilians and among Union troops.

A notable and important characteristic of yellow fever concerned a difference in virulence for different populations. People who had lived in the region for a long time were relatively immune to the ravages of the epidemic; these lucky ones were said to be acclimatized to the disease. Yellow fever so frequently and severely afflicted newcomers to the region that it was called the "stranger's disease." Medical authorities were divided concerning whether a person could eventually become acclimatized or whether only those born in the region were relatively safe from the disease, but all agreed that yellow fever attacked newcomers, especially Northerners, with great violence. In the past, the citizens of New Orleans had prayed that the horrible scourge of yellow fever would spare their city. But now, under the galling Federal occupation, some churches of the city openly prayed for a cleansing scourge that might afflict the acclimatized Southerners only slightly but could devour the occupying Union Army.[11]

The commanding general of Union forces in New Orleans, General Benjamin Butler, knew the danger of a yellow fever epidemic. He vowed to use medical knowledge to prevent an epidemic that might threaten the Federal occupation. Medical authorities had two interacting theories for the appearance and propagation of the epidemic. One theory held that it came from the outside; it was brought from South America or the Caribbean to New Orleans by infected sailors or passengers on ships. From them it spread, in an unknown manner, to helpless citizens ashore. The disease could be prevented, according to this theory, by holding ships at a quarantine station until medical authorities could be sure that no one aboard was sick. The second theory held that the disease arose from decaying garbage and could be prevented by rigorous sanitation.

Since Butler did not know which of these two theories was correct, he adopted them both. He used his military authority to force all ships to stop at the mouth of the Mississippi until they could be inspected by a physician. The doctor then wired Butler that the ship was free of disease; only when Butler personally wired the quarantine station was the vessel allowed to proceed up the river to New Orleans. Secondly, Butler used the occupying military force to clean up the city. Decaying garbage was removed; standing water was drained. Despite these efforts, a few cases of yellow fever appeared in the city. In 1863 sailors who had passed the quarantine station became ill and were admitted to the Charity Hospital; medical evaluation, including autopsy examination, showed that these few sailors had acquired yellow fever. If this disease were to spread to the general population of New Orleans, the Federal force would be decimated and the occupation endangered.[12]

16

The Trial of William Hammond

In the military chain of command, surgeon General Hammond reported directly to Secretary of War Edwin M. Stanton, yet Stanton had been opposed to Hammond's appointment. The secretary of war felt that the Sanitary Commission and other civilian do-gooders had forced Hammond upon him. Stanton told several people that Hammond was "the Sanitary Commission's Surgeon General, not mine."[1] The ambulance corps was eventually taken from the quartermasters and placed under medical control, but only after Hammond had accused his superior of a disregard of the comfort of the wounded. Hammond's letter after Second Bull Run virtually accused Stanton of willful neglect of Union wounded. Disagreement and distrust festered between these two strong-minded individuals.

Hammond's support from the civilian medical community dissipated overnight. On 4 May 1863 Hammond ordered the removal of calomel and tartar emetic from the official formulary of the U.S. Army, called the army supply table. Hammond became convinced that these drugs killed more patients than they helped. The excessive use of calomel caused salivation, gum sores, and tooth loss. The vomiting produced by tartar emetic could further dehydrate a person already limp from chronic diarrhea. The vomiting and purging of debilitated soldiers worsened their conditions. But when Hammond removed these medications from the army formulary, much of the civilian medical community arose in revolt. For a generation, medical doctors had competed with a series of other healers, with botanists and homeopaths, whose only unifying creed was that regular medicine used too much calomel. Now, the leading army doctor seemed to corroborate the criticism of all these sect practitioners. Hammond, whom they had praised as a fine example of the best that modern medicine had to offer, now seemed to be trying to destroy mainstream medical practice.

Stanton sent the surgeon general on a series of inspection tours: to Hilton Head, South Carolina, then by ship around the entire Confederacy to New Orleans. While Hammond was away from Washington, Stanton appointed Joseph K. Barnes as the acting surgeon general. During the past year, Barnes had become Stanton's personal physician and then his friend; the two men and their wives vacationed together.

Hammond traveled up the Mississippi on the U.S. Hospital Steamer *D.A. January*, recently renamed the *Charles McDougall* after an elderly career army doctor. He left New Orleans on 28 October and arrived at Cairo on 2 November. Only one hundred sick soldiers were aboard, so the medical commander of the vessel, Alexander Hoff, had plenty of time to talk with the touring surgeon general. Late in 1862 Hoff had written from this very vessel that soldiers coming aboard were showing evidence of the effects of too much calomel. "This treatment, as far as my experience goes," he concluded, "cannot be necessary."[2] Hammond had followed Hoff's lead and had restricted the use of this most potent of remedies. In discussing the situation on this trip, Hoff could only suggest that the army should obtain better doctors.[3] But Hammond had to use the doc-

Table 16

Schedule of the <u>D. A. January</u> for 1863

Embarkation		Debarkation		Number of Sick and Wounded
Date	Place	Date	Place	
14 Jan	Arkansas Post	28 Jan	St. Louis	432

March to June: moored at Milliken's Bend, near Vicksburg.
July: refurbished, with new boilers, at St. Louis,
  renamed U.S. Hospital Steamer <u>Charles McDougall</u>.

11 Aug	Milliken's Bend	18 Aug	St. Louis	378
27 Aug	Vicksburg	31 Aug	Memphis	387
5 Sept	Vicksburg	8 Sept	Memphis	377
15 Sept	Vicksburg	18 Sept	Memphis	244
29 Sept	Vicksburg	7 Oct	Memphis	78
28 Oct	New Orleans	2 Nov	Cairo	100
23 Nov	Memphis	28 Nov	St. Louis	345
9 Dec	Nashville	12 Dec	Evansville	344

During 1863, the <u>D. A. January</u>, officially renamed the <u>Charles McDougall</u>, supported the Vicksburg campaign, then evacuated sick and wounded from Vicksburg to Memphis. Toward the end of the year, the vessel traveled the full extent of the Mississippi from New Orleans to St. Louis. During one portion of this trip, Surgeon General Hammond was aboard.

Source: <u>MSH</u> Surgical Volume, pt. 3, pp. 979-80.

tors available; he hoped to improve the health of debilitated soldiers by restricting excessive therapy, but he had not expected how his order would arouse the medical community.

While Barnes was acting surgeon general in Washington, Hammond traveled from Cairo to Nashville to inspect the medical facilities at that major Union center in Tennessee. When leaving a hospital in Nashville after an inspection, Hammond tripped and fell down the stairs. Abrasions were present on his legs, but the fall was only a few steps, and he did not think he was seriously injured. Hammond was frightened to note, however, that he could barely move his legs. He traveled to Philadelphia to see the leading expert in nerve injuries, his old friend Silas Weir Mitchell. Mitchell noted weakness and loss of sensation in both legs. When Mitchell asked Hammond to identify where on the leg he felt the examiner's touch, the surgeon general indicated a point about six inches higher up the limb. Mitchell and his Turner's Lane colleagues could not uncover the exact reason for the weakness, but with time leg strength returned to normal.

This temporary leg paralysis may have been due to Hammond's mental strain at his approaching battle with Stanton.[4]

To understand Stanton's point of view, one must note that Hammond was a difficult subordinate. To many people, the surgeon general appeared excessively serious and self-important. One of Hammond's physician colleagues claimed that "those who knew him rarely found him anything but captious, irritable, and pompous." When Hammond inspected a hospital in Philadelphia, one assistant surgeon claimed that "a more arrogant and pompous individual had never visited the hospital."[5] Hammond himself later admitted that he had been "a bit puffed up" during this period of his life.[6]

Recovering from his leg paralysis, Hammond returned to Washington for a showdown with Stanton. He demanded that either he should be returned to full control of the Surgeon General's Office or that a formal review should evaluate his tenure as head of army medicine.[7] Stanton suggested that Hammond resign his office and retire without undergoing the trauma of a formal hearing. Hammond was certain that his handling of the medical affairs of the Union army would meet with approbation from a panel of fair officers, so he demanded a trial.

Several weeks were spent in formulating specific charges against Hammond. Judge Advocate General Joseph Holt, the chief army prosecutor, under the direction of Stanton, did not charge the surgeon general with running his organization poorly. Holt did not even accuse him of insubordination to his superior in the chain of command. Rather, Hammond found himself formally charged with a series of bureaucratic irregularities.

The court-martial board examined three charges, with eleven specifications. Two of the charges involved the purchase of goods that were purportedly inferior and unnecessarily expensive. None of the specifications accused the surgeon general of direct financial gain, but some intimated that his personal friends had benefitted from transactions with the Surgeon General's Office. Several medical purveyors, particularly one named George E. Cooper, claimed that Hammond had directed them to make purchases from one supplier, implying that better or cheaper materials were available from other suppliers.[8] A typical specification concerned the food supplement provided by the company Wyeth and Brother:

Charge 1, specification 7: In this that he, the said Brigadier General William A. Hammond, Surgeon General, United States Army, about the eighth day of October in the year of our Lord one thousand eight hundred and sixty two at Washington City in the contempt of and contrary to the provisions of the act entitled, An act to reorganize and increase the efficiency of the Medical Department of the Army, approved April 16, 1862, did corruptly and unlawfully direct Wyeth and Brother of Philadelphia to send 40 thousand cans of Extract of Beef to various places, to wit: Cincinnati, St. Louis, Cairo, New York, and Baltimore and send the account to the Surgeon General's Office for payment and which Extract of Beef so ordered was of inferior quality, unfit for hospital use, unsuitable and unwholesome for the sick and wounded in hospitals, and not demanded by the exigencies of the service.

The prosecution placed upon the stand several civilian physicians assigned to general military hospitals. They testified that Wyeth and Brother's food supplement, a meat ex-

tract, was spoiled and inedible. The defense countered with a series of witnesses, military doctors from field armies, who testified that this excellent beef extract nourished exhausted troops. Among these witnesses was Jonathan Letterman, medical director of the Army of the Potomac.

Hammond was found guilty of the charge and of the particular specification, but was found innocent of elements of the specification. The final guilty specification removed the statement of corruption and all suggestion that the extract was unwholesome. The court found that Hammond "did unlawfully direct Wyeth and Brother of Philadelphia to send 40 thousand cans of their Extract of Beef to various places, to wit: Cincinnati, St. Louis, Cairo, New York and Baltimore and send the account to the Surgeon General's Office for payment, and not demanded by the exigencies of the service."[9] Hammond was found guilty of all ten specifications of this type. He had cut through red tape to rush needed supplies to the field. Now the danger of this action in a bureaucratic world became clear.

The final charge was officially termed "conduct unbecoming an officer and gentleman." Hammond was accused of lying to medical officer George Cooper, who had been the medical purveyor in Philadelphia. Hammond told him that he was being removed from that position because the general-in-chief, Henry W. Halleck, had requested that Hammond appoint a friend of his to this position.

The following facts came out at the trial. Halleck testified that he did not recall telling Hammond to appoint his friend to the post. The person appointed to the post, replacing Cooper, was an old acquaintance of Halleck's who had never met Hammond. The following additional facts were not admitted at the trial. While Hammond was on his inspection trip, a burglary had occurred at the Surgeon General's Office. Hammond claimed that the written order from Halleck to appoint his acquaintance had been stolen. In addition, Cooper later admitted that he had lied at the trial; his military career was in jeopardy as much as Hammond's. "It was Hammond's head or mine," he told John Brinton.[10]

From these findings it appears that Hammond appointed Halleck's friend or acquaintance to Cooper's post in response to Halleck's request. The court found, however, that Hammond had lied to Cooper about the reason for his dismissal and that this lie was "conduct unbecoming to an officer." From Cooper's subsequent statement, and from the idea that a burglary had stolen important papers, it seems that the trial was rigged.[11]

The chairman of the court-martial board was Richard J. Oglesby, a political general from Illinois. In 1861 Oglesby had raised a volunteer regiment, the 8th Illinois, and had become its colonel. He had been promoted to brigadier general, but in 1863 he had attempted to resign his military commission in order to run for governor of his home state. Chairing the court-martial board was his final military duty. It seems that this duty was a quid pro quo for allowing his resignation and, perhaps, for supporting his candidacy for the Republican nomination for governor.

During the course of the trial, Chairman Oglesby was faced with a military bureaucratic hurdle somewhat similar to Hammond's. He received a communiqué from the Bureau of Ordnance, questioning his handling of ordnance received by the 8th Illinois while he had been its commanding officer. Captain George T. Balche, assistant to the chief of ordnance, notified Oglesby that he had not submitted the quarterly return of ordnance stores for the third and fourth quarters of 1861. Oglesby was informed "that you have this day been reported to the adjutant general of the army as a delinquent." The adjutant general of the army was Colonel Joseph Holt, Hammond's prosecutor, who saw Oglesby every day at the trial.

In many ways Oglesby's dereliction was similar to Hammond's. During the stresses of this fratricidal war, efficient officers dispensed with traditional bureaucratic procedures. Where were the ordnance stores of the 8th Illinois? Obviously they had been fired at the enemy. Oglesby did not respond to the threat from the Bureau of Ordnance. Almost at the same moment that Oglesby's court-martial board was returning its guilty verdict on

A military trial is pictured in *Harper's Weekly.* This represents the court-martial of Fitz-John Porter, but Hammond's trial must have involved a very similar scene. Judge Advocate General Joseph Holt, the second person from the right, sitting at the end of the table, was the prosecutor in both trials. HW

Hammond, Captain Balche of the Bureau of Ordnance notified Oglesby that he had still not explained what he had done with the ammunition issued to his regiment. Not only had Oglesby not responded to Balche's demand concerning the final two quarters of 1861, he was also delinquent for the first quarter of 1862.[12]

The court-martial board found Hammond guilty on 7 May 1864. Judge Advocate General Joseph Holt was promoted from colonel to brigadier general on 22 June 1864.[13] Oglesby resigned his military commission on 26 May 1864, received the Republican nomination, and was elected governor of Illinois in November.

The verdict could not become official until it was reviewed by President Lincoln, however. Over summer 1864, while giant armies were struggling in Georgia and Virginia, Hammond pressed to have the verdict overturned. The United States Sanitary Commission mounted an effort to support Hammond, obtaining the signatures of many prominent American physicians and scientists on a petition to President Lincoln. But the political power of the Sanitary Commission was waning. Hammond's wife tried to present her husband's case directly to the president; he returned her card with this note written in his own hand: "Under the circumstances, I should prefer not seeing Mrs. Hammond." Lincoln approved the court-martial guilty verdict on 18 August 1864. Hammond was dismissed from the military service and forever forbidden to hold any office of the government of the United States.

The New York Times reported that Hammond's trial had been one of the most thorough and patient in history. His discharge from the army was far too mild a punishment for someone who had sunk to such a state of "utter villainy, bartering away the comforts and periling the lives of the sick and wounded soldiers" in exchange for "a little paltry pelf." But just two days later, the Times published a personal letter from Hammond, stating that he intended to publish the full facts of the case, in order to "submit to the judgment of the world as to how far he has been guilty of the offenses charged, and how far he has been the victim of conspiracy, false swearing, and a malignant abuse of political power." The editor of the Times admitted that his conclusion about "utter villainy" might have been premature.[14] Hammond did print and distribute at his own expense a seventy-three-page defense of his actions.[15] The court-martial board accepted a copy as an addendum to the official trial transcript.[16]

Despite their disagreement with the calomel order, the civilian medical profession generally supported Hammond after his court martial conviction. The American Medical Times of Philadelphia and the Buffalo Medical and Surgical Journal editorialized their conviction that Hammond was innocent.[17] Even the editor of the Boston Medical and Surgical Journal, who had condemned former Surgeon General Hammond immediately after his conviction, changed his opinion after he read Hammond's privately printed pamphlet.

Hammond was terribly shaken by this conviction. He had exhausted his personal finances paying for his lawyers and for the publication of his defense. With help from his old mentor, William Van Buren, Hammond moved to New York City and entered the private practice of medicine. The War continued without him.

17

Confederate Medical Support during the Atlanta Campaign

IN MAY 1864 A HUGE NORTHERN ARMY UNDER THE command of William T. Sherman moved south into Georgia from its base at Chattanooga. Opposing the Union force was the much smaller Confederate Army of Tennessee under the command of Joseph E. Johnston. The Northern troops slowly advanced down along the rail line from Chattanooga to Atlanta. Johnston retreated when outflanked, but he held his army together. When the Union army reached the northern outskirts of Atlanta, John Bell Hood replaced Johnston as Southern commander. Hood attacked the Union forces as they attempted to flank Atlanta to the east. The flanking movement was stopped but the Confederates suffered many casualties. The Union army shifted to the west and began another flanking movement. Unable to stop this advance, Hood abandoned Atlanta on 1 September 1864. The Army of Tennessee retreated into Alabama.[1]

Dr. Andrew J. Foard, the medical director of the Army of Tennessee, was in charge of all regimental medical officers. He was an 1848 graduate of Jefferson Medical College in Philadelphia. The physicians under his command provided treatment for sick and wounded soldiers of the field army. If a soldier were too sick or too severely wounded to return to duty, the regimental physician transferred him to the general hospital system. The general military hospitals supporting the Army of Tennessee were under the command of Dr. Samuel H. Stout. Following the evacuation of Chatta-

nooga, Atlanta became the major medical support center.[2]

The sick and wounded of the Army of Tennessee traveled by rail to the main station in downtown Atlanta; they were then taken by wagon or walked to the nearby Receiving and Distributing Hospital. Dr. George H. Pursley, the surgeon in charge of the R and D, and his associates examined and classified each patient. They were then distributed to the general hospitals throughout central and southern Georgia and eastern Alabama that were under the authority of Dr. Stout. These hospitals kept Dr. Pursley informed concerning the number of empty beds available in their facilities.

Sometimes the press of patients was so great that Dr. Pursley was forced to send more sick and wounded to outlying hospitals than they were prepared to accept. On 28 May 1864 George B. Douglas, the doctor in charge of the hospitals in Columbus, Georgia, wrote to Dr. Stout about the problems caused by a massive influx of sick and wounded soldiers. "I have this day telegraphed you," he wrote, "requesting that no more sick and wounded be sent here until those already here can be properly cared for. During the past 24 hours, over 700 have been sent to this post for whom no adequate preparations have been made and it will require several days to provide quarters for them."[3]

Stout referred this problem to Surgeon Joseph P. Logan, in charge of the hospitals of

147

Andrew J. Foard was the medical director of the Army of Tennessee. NLM

Samuel H. Stout was in charge of the hospital system that supported the Army of Tennessee. NA

Table 17

Support Hospitals for the Army of Tennessee,
Summer 1863

Location	Hospital name	Bed capacity	Surgeon-in-charge of post	Surgeon-in-charge of hospital
Chattanooga			Samuel H. Stout	
	Foard	300		F. Thornton
	Academy	-		F. Hawthorne
	Newsome	300		Alex. Hunter
	Gilmer	250		C. E. Michel
Ringgold			Cary B. Gamble	
	Buckner	200		W. T. McAllister
	Bragg	300		G. E. Redwood
	Foard	200		G. W. Cursey
Catoosa Springs		500	Robert C. Foster	
Tunnel Hill		335	Benjamin M. Wible	
Dalton			Faulkner H. Evans	
	Cannon	200		D. H. Morrison
	Oliver	250		J. M. Henson
	St. Mary's	250		W. J. Holt
Atlanta			J. P. Logan	
	Grant	100		J. C. Mullins
	Gate City	400		Paul F. Eve
	Medical College	200		W. Westmoreland
	Empire	250		W. P. Harden
	Fair Grounds 1	400		H. W. Harden
	Fair Grounds 2	500		Robt. Battey
Kingston		50	Thomas Mattingly	
Rome			Louis T. Pim	
	Lumpkin	229		E. M. McDonald
	Quintard	206		unknown
	Bell	225		W. C. Nichol

Sources: "Official List of the Chief Medical Officers, Hospitals, and Laboratories, Armies of the Southern Confederacy, During the War of 1861-1865," Joseph Jones Papers, folder 41, Howard-Tilton Memorial Library, New Orleans, La., and "List of All C.S.A. Medical Officers," manuscript F56, National Library of Medicine, Bethesda, Md.

Atlanta. "It has frequently occurred recently," Stout told Logan, "that patients have been sent to hospital posts which do not report empty beds. You are requested to call the attention of Surgeon Pursley to this fact and to take such action as will provide against the recurrence of similar improper treatment of our sick and wounded soldiers."[4]

After informed of this complaint by Dr. Logan, Dr. Pursley replied to Dr. Stout:

Respectfully, I have never sent 700 sick to Columbus during any 24 hours. I am informed by Surgeon Sumter that sick have been sent to Columbus from Macon, which accounts for the large number sent there in so short a time. I have often during the present emergency sent sick and wounded to posts reporting no empty beds and at times when *all* the empty beds would not have accommodated those in this hospital ready to be distributed. I respectfully ask what I am to do in such cases? I am compelled to receive all sick and wounded sent here, varying from 200 to 400, 500, and 600 daily with a hospital of only 250 capacity. And if I am not permitted to send to posts where no empty beds are reported, then this hospital will remain for days crowded to the great injury of the sick and wounded, as is the case at this time.[5]

Table 18

Admissions to the Atlanta
Receiving and Distributing Hospital

Date	Number of admissions	Percentage of admissions due to gunshot wounds
December 1863	3,271	20%
January 1864	1,990	9%
February	3,151	12%
March	570	13%
April	1,242	8%
May	14,725	16%
June	13,735	26%
July*	8,157	38%

*moved from Atlanta to Macon

Source: Joseph Jones Papers, folder 109, Howard-Tilton Memorial Library, New Orleans, La.

Dr. Stout responded to this communication from Dr. Pursley with a letter to Pursley's superior, Dr. Logan: "It is not improbable that these sick may have been transferred from Macon or Montgomery, in which case, of course, no blame should attach to Surgeon Pursley. But he cannot exercise too much care to avoid sending sick and wounded to posts already full."[6]

One may note how carefully the chain of command is maintained: from medical director, general hospitals of the Army of Tennessee (Stout), to surgeon-in-charge, Atlanta (Logan), to surgeon-in-charge, R and D Hospital (Pursley). Although Dr. Stout concluded that no blame should attach to Surgeon Pursley, he never responded to Pursley's heartfelt cries for support or direction.

An analysis of the admissions to the R and D corroborates Surgeon Pursley's complaints. The number of admissions in the first month of operation, December 1863, was over three thousand. Twenty percent of these were wounded. They had been wounded in the battle of Chattanooga on 25 November, but some had not made the long trip to Atlanta until early December. At the beginning of 1864, with the army in winter quarters, both the number of admissions and the percentage of those admissions due to gunshot wounds fell. With Sherman's advance in May, however, the number of hospital admissions leaped up to over fourteen thousand. It was during this month that Dr. Pursley asked for help because he was "compelled to receive all sick and wounded sent here, varying from 200 to 400, 500, and 600 daily." The actual statistics show that for each of the 31 days of May, the R and D averaged 475 admissions to its 250 beds. One can imagine Dr. Pursley's consternation when he tried to supervise the examination and classification of each one of this massive influx of patients. Yet when he tried to distribute them to other hospitals, he was told the other hospitals were too full. His Receiving and Distributing Hospital was not only jammed full, but he was expecting another deluge of patients the next day.

In the middle of July, when Federal artillery began lobbing solid shot cannonballs into downtown Atlanta, the R and D was relocated to Macon. From the middle of July to the fall of Atlanta, the distribution function was carried out directly in the railroad station.

Although the number of wounded soldiers admitted to the R and D rose from May through July, the majority of admissions were always due to disease. For the period from December 1863 through June 1864, only 19 percent of hospital admissions were due to gunshot injuries. About four in five soldiers evacuated from the Army of the Tennessee through the Atlanta R and D were sick, not wounded. The most common illness was nonspecific diarrhea, which produced almost the same loss to the army as gunshot wounds. The next most common diagnosis was debilitation or, as it was officially called in the Farr system,

Table 19

Reasons for Admission to the Atlanta R and D Hospital,
December 1863 through June 1864

| | Admissions: | |
Diagnosis	Number	Percent
Gunshot wounds	7,415	19%
Diarrhea (all types)	7,273	19%
Debilitation	6,514	17%
Malaria (all types)	3,720	10%
Pneumonia	1,424	4%
Typhoid fever	1,334	3%
Chronic rheumatism	714	2%
Hepatitis	557	1%
Measles	425	1%
Total admissions	38,684	100%

Source: Calculated from returns in Joseph Jones Papers, folder 109, Howard-Tilton Library, New Orleans, La.

debilitas. This was a descriptive term to describe the soldier who was losing weight and was so exhausted that he was unable to fulfill his military duties. Most cases were probably due to physical exhaustion with chronic diarrhea compounded by poor diet. Malaria accounted for only about 10 percent of the admissions. This illness was much less common in the Army of Tennessee than among the troops in the Mississippi Valley or along the Carolina coast. A large number of other diseases made up the remainder of the sicknesses that caused hospitalization, but no one remaining diagnosis made up more than four percent of the total.

Passing through the hands of Dr. Pursley and the R and D, this huge mass of sick and wounded were dispersed throughout the general hospital system of the Army of Tennessee. Dr. Stout supervised almost sixty hospitals throughout Georgia and eastern Alabama. These hospitals were located in all the major cities and in some minor villages along the rail lines. Some of these hospitals were named for Confederate generals, some for doctors such as Foard and Stout, some for women who had helped Confederate wounded, and one for the chaplain, Quintard. Many were named for the major building they occupied; they kept the same names even if forced to relocate.

Some of the medical problems of the campaign can be appreciated more fully by an evaluation of the admissions to some of these military hospitals. City Hall Hospital opened in the government buildings of Macon in January 1864 with Albert H. Sneed as the chief surgeon and Theodore Parker as his assistant. Admissions each month throughout the winter and spring were less than 200. But almost 500 sick and wounded soldiers were admitted in May 1864 when Sherman began his advance, leading to the construction of a second hospital. This second administrative unit was called Stout Hospital; Parker was promoted to become its chief surgeon. In June these two hospitals admitted 662 patients, of which only 74 went to the newly opened facility. July was the peak month with 1,359 admissions; 787 patients were admitted to City Hall Hospital and 572 to Stout Hospital. In August and September the number of admissions to Macon hospitals fell to about 700.

Dr. Willis F. Westmoreland organized Medical College Hospital in the buildings of the Atlanta Medical College in February 1862. The old medical college had closed the previous year when all its students entered the Confederate army. Most of the college faculty, including Westmoreland and Joseph P. Logan, became Confederate physicians. In 1862 and much of 1863 this hospital was far in the rear of military activities. The number of admissions rose when the Army of Tennessee was involved in a major battle; for example, a large number of wounded soldiers were admitted in January 1863 after the Battle of Stone's River near Murfreesboro, Tennessee. The greatest number of admissions in any one month occurred in September 1863 after the horrendous Battle of Chickamauga. Excess patients were housed in tents. Admissions increased again after the Battle of Chattanooga. Few patients were admitted to the Medical College Hospital during winter 1864, but when Sherman's advance began, the hospital again overflowed. The number of admissions was over four hundred in May and June and only slightly less in July when the hospital moved to Barnesville, Georgia. When this town was threatened by Federal forces, the hospital moved again, this time to Milner, Georgia.

The Confederate medical system made immense efforts to handle the huge overflow of the sick and wounded. The initial response to the problem of overwhelming numbers was simply to enlarge. A hospital divided into two, with the assistant director of one hospital becoming the director of a new one adjoining. City Hall Hospital in Macon created the adjacent Stout Hospital. Fair Ground Hospital, located on the Atlanta fair grounds, split into two hospitals, unimaginatively named Fair Ground Number 1 and Fair Ground Number 2. Civilian doctors were hired to help staff these new hospitals. The pay, established years earlier by the Confederate Congress at eighty dollars per month, was so worthless in the inflated economy of 1864 that these doctors essentially donated their services.

The continuing influx of sick and wounded translated into a continuous need for more of everything: more doctors, more hospitals, more beds, more bedding, more food. "We cannot accommodate any more sick men at present," wrote the surgeon in charge of the hospital at Thomaston, Georgia on 16 June 1864. "I am hurrying on my arrangements as rapidly as possible but cannot keep up with the unexpected numbers sent here. Could you supply us with 50 tents? You could not do better for the sick than send them here to this place," he promised, "but if you send any more we must have tents. P.S. Please send me assistant surgeons—two or three."[7]

Stout attempted to respond to requests like this one from Thomaston, but his resources were rapidly dwindling. Not only was Confederate currency almost worthless, but the Commissary Department was unable to respond to Stout's requisitions. Some surgeons purchased supplies for their patients using their own personal funds and credit. When credit and currency were exhausted, the medical authorities reverted to the barter system. Dr. Stout had taken a newspaper printing press with him when Chattanooga was evacuated in order to print hospital forms. He printed a large supply of forms, then traded the press for food. Dr. Stout sent doctors to Charleston to barter donated cotton for drugs that had passed the U.S. naval blockade. Stout even hired a fisherman, Cousin John Thrasher, to travel to Florida to catch fish to feed the hospitalized soldiers.[8]

In addition to the press of patients and the failure of the Confederate supply system, another problem faced by the hospital support system of the Army of Tennessee was the need to move hospitals. The advance of Sherman's army forced Stout to relocate hospitals from Chattanooga and northern Georgia. Some of these institutions moved several times. The Academy Hospital under Frank Hawthorne moved from Chattanooga to Atlanta and then to Auburn, Alabama. The Newsome Hospital under Surgeon Charles E. Michel moved from Chattanooga to Marietta and then to Thomaston, Georgia. These hospitals were moved from one set of buildings to another, but retained the same doctors, nurses, patients, supplies, and records.

The medical difficulties compounding these evacuations were immense. The volunteer nurse Fannie Beers described the movement of the Buckner Hospital from Ringgold to Newnan, Georgia:

> Dr. McAllister was everywhere, superintending the removal with the energy natural to him," she wrote. "Sick and awfully wounded men were hurriedly placed upon stretchers and their bearers formed an endless procession to the rough cars, some of them lately used to transport cattle and dreadfully filthy. Here they were placed upon straw mattresses, or plain straw, as it happened. No provisions were to be had except sides of rusty bacon and cold corn bread. These were shoveled into carts and transferred to the floor of the cars in the same manner.

During the trip of several days along the deteriorating Confederate railroad line, the volunteer nurses had to beg supplies from nearby farmers. At one stop, "the only water to be procured lay in ruts and ditches by the roadside, and was filthy and fetid."[9]

_— now and always
your devoted friend
and comrade
Fannie A. Beers_

Mrs. Fannie A. Beers was a volunteer Confederate nurse who described the valiant efforts to move hospitals from the path of the Yankee advance. From Beers, *Memories: A Record of Personal Experience and Adventure during Four Years of War,* **Philadelphia: J. B. Lippincott, 1888.**

The Atlanta Receiving and Distributing Hospital was located near the railroad station. When Atlanta began to receive solid-shot artillery shells, the function of classifying patients and distributing them to the hospital support system took place directly in the railroad yard. Miller

The rail yard in Atlanta after the Confederate evacuation. The damage done by Sherman's artillery is evident. NA

The worsening medical conditions forced the Confederate medical authorities to improvise. Stout had originally intended that Grant Hospital in Atlanta should be a place to concentrate patients with smallpox. But in July 1864, 153 patients were admitted to Grant Hospital; 142 had suffered gunshot wounds; none had smallpox. Stout had established a hospital in Augusta especially for officers. In July 1864 Officers Hospital in Augusta admitted 46 wounded soldiers; all were enlisted men.[10]

The medical authorities of the Army of Tennessee made use of a wide variety of volunteer labor. Of special value was the donated service of a number of women who acted as nurses. In her diary, volunteer nurse Kate Cumming described how she traveled throughout the countryside to coerce donations of food and clothing for the sick and wounded soldiers. "We stopped at a small farm house to try and procure some milk," she described a typical foraging expedition; "We were unsuccessful, but the lady of the house gave us a watermelon, for which she would take no money."[11] Railroad trains carrying the sick and wounded would often stop in small towns so that volunteers could board the train and distribute donated food to the sufferers.

The three great characteristics of the hospital support system of the Army of Tennessee were improvisation, the barter system, and reliance upon donated labor and material. Despite immense efforts by many people, the hospital support system of the Army of Tennessee failed in its most important mission: to maintain the health and strength of the army.

From a military viewpoint, the major function of the hospital system was to return to duty as large a proportion of the sick and wounded as possible. In the last two months before the fall of Atlanta, the general hospital system of the Army of Tennessee was unable to fulfill this mission successfully. Stout's general hospital system received over 23,000 admissions in July 1864. During this month the system discharged 22,891 patients to make room for the expected deluge in August. Of these, only 9,832 were returned directly to the army for the defense of Atlanta. The next month the system admitted over 21,000 soldiers. Under the pressure of crowding, overwork, movement of hospitals, and combat action, Stout's system discharged 25,665 patients in that month but only 6,568 returned to duty.[12]

What happened to those who did not return to duty with the fighting forces? Some, of course, remained hospitalized, but those discharged fell into five categories: medical discharge, medical furlough, death, desertion, and transfer to hospitals outside the control of the Army of Tennessee. Only a very tiny frac-

Table 20

Admissions to Confederate Hospitals in Macon, Georgia in 1864

Date	Admissions		Soldiers who left hospital to return to duty		Soldiers who deserted	died
January 1864	186		64	(65%)	0	0
February	165		36	(33%)	0	0
March	82		47	(30%)	7	1
April	46		18	(53%)	1	1
May	496		43	(11%)	3	11
June	662	(74)*	111	(31%)	5	8
July	1,359	(572)	164	(13%)	2	20
August	748	(364)	161	(16%)	45	44
September	679	(298)	115	(16%)	17	43

*admissions to the Stout Hospital, which opened in June, are in parentheses.

Source: Joseph Jones Papers, folder 109, Howard-Tilton Memorial Library, New Orleans, La.

tion of patients received medical discharges from the army. Many convalescents were sent home on medical furlough to recuperate. The number of soldiers who died in the hospital was fairly small, less than 5 percent of all discharges. Some, of course, died during medical furlough or after transfer to other hospitals outside the jurisdiction of the Army of Tennessee. The number of soldiers who deserted from the army while patients in the hospital remained quite low until the last two months of the campaign. Most of the patients were transferred to other hospitals, outside the jurisdiction of the Army of Tennessee.

The problem of returning hospital patients to military duty is illustrated by the experience of the hospitals in Macon. The percentage of discharged soldiers who returned directly to duty with the front line troops decreased whenever admissions rose. The fraction of the soldiers discharged from Macon hospitals who returned to duty remained above one-third until the beginning of Sherman's advance. In May 1864 only 11 percent of soldiers leaving City Hall Hospital returned to military duty; this rose to 31 percent when a second hospital was opened the next month. However, the huge influx of new patients in July created such disorganization that the percentage of discharged soldiers who returned to duty never again rose above 16.

The longer existence of the Medical College Hospital shows even more clearly how an increase in the number of admissions produced a decrease in the percentage of discharged soldiers who returned to duty. The proportion of the patients discharged from Medical College Hospital who returned to the army fell after Stone's River and Chickamauga, but rose to 50 percent in April 1864. The steady influx of new admissions after the beginning of Sherman's advance in May decreased the percentage of soldiers returning to duty to a very low level, fluctuating between 9 and 16 percent.

In all these hospitals, the number of desertions and deaths rose under the stress of the huge influx of new admissions during the Georgia campaign. Only in the Medical College Hospital, however, did the number of desertions approximate the number of admissions. In June and July the number of deaths at the Medical College Hospital rose to almost 100 each month; the highest previous value had been 57. In the final month of its existence,

the hospital changed its location and 78 hospitalized soldiers deserted. The highest previous monthly total of desertions was only 15.

Statistics are illuminated by following the course of an individual patient. Carroll Henderson Clark was nineteen years old when he enlisted in the 16th regiment of infantry in the army of the state of Tennessee. This unit, with the rest of the state army, was mustered into Confederate service and participated in the 1862 invasion of Kentucky. Private Clark was with the 16th Tennessee during the battles of Stone's River and Chickamauga. He served during the entire Atlanta campaign until 22 July when, as part of Hood's massive attack upon the advancing Federals, he was wounded.[13]

Clark was preparing to fire his rifle when he suddenly noted blood flowing from his arm. Examining the cause of the bleeding, he found he had been struck by a Federal minié ball. He headed toward the rear, looking for a field hospital. He stopped by a stream to wash his wound. At the field hospital, he was examined by a physician whom he knew, a Dr. Leek. The doctor dressed the wound and gave him a drink of whiskey. Clark remained in the field hospital overnight, but the cries and moans of the wounded kept him awake. The next day, he walked to the railroad station in Atlanta and, with other wounded, was shipped to Macon. There, he was admitted to City Hall Hospital and finally given morphine to ease the pain. In a few days his arm, including his fingers and hand, became immensely swollen. Pus oozed from his wound. The surgeon in charge told him that his arm would have to be amputated. Clark decided to desert rather than to lose his arm. He was quite weak, but with the help of another patient, he made it to the train station. He traveled to Dawson, Georgia, where he stayed with a friend. The local civilian doctor changed his dressing frequently and his wound slowly healed.[14]

After the fall of Atlanta the headquarters of the Army of Tennessee general hospital system was moved to Macon. When this city was threatened by Sherman's March to the Sea, Stout moved his headquarters to Columbus, Georgia. A system of hospitals was organized along rail lines throughout western Georgia, Alabama, and eastern Mississippi. When the Army of Tennessee marched back to its home state in the disastrous campaign that ended in

Table 21

Admissions to Medical College Hospital, Atlanta

Date	Admissions	Discharges	Percentage who returned to duty	Soldiers who: deserted	died
-1862-					
February	94	1	0%	0	1
March	170	181	92%	0	15
April	107	26	46%	0	3
May	57	108	84%	0	12
June	no report	–	–	–	–
July	no report	–	–	–	–
August	no report	–	–	–	–
September	no report	–	–	–	–
October	204	214	26%	0	1
November	no report	–	–	–	–
December	124	139	7%	4	9
-1863-					
January	481	225	14%	3	18
February	59	111	61%	15	8
March	136	103	71%	2	10
April	192	200	28%	2	18
May	137	181	60%	4	15
June	no report	–	–	–	–
July	201	202	54%	1	13
August	233	162	73%	2	10
September	1357	1227	20%	2	12
October	108	209	16%	0	48
November	433	333	27%	2	2
December	313	351	20%	1	57
-1864-					
January	102	128	35%	3	36
February	126	246	34%	3	9
March	88	86	47%	2	18
April	183	159	50%	1	31
May	407	308	16%	1	46
June	463	428	9%	1	99
July*	353	411	11%	0	97
August**	101	214	11%	78	36

*moved from Atlanta to Barnesville, Ga.
**moved from Barnesville to Milner, Ga.

Source: Joseph Jones Papers, folder 109, Howard-Tilton Library, New Orleans, La.

the battles of Franklin and Nashville, however, there was no effort to evacuate sick and wounded to this hospital system. The wounded from the Battle of Franklin underwent surgery at a large house outside of town, the Carnton House, and were then left with friendly citizens of the town. Many were treated by local private physicians.[15]

After the Battle of Nashville, most of the soldiers of the Army of Tennessee went home. A few stalwarts gathered under Joseph Johnston and made a last stand in North Carolina. Dr.

Table 22

Soldiers Lost to the Army of Tennessee
for Medical Reasons, July and August 1864

	July	August
Total hospital admissions	23,736	21,248
Number returned to duty	9,832	6,568
Number lost	13,059	19,097
Reasons for loss from the Army of Tennessee:		
Transfer to other hospitals	8,346	12,357
Awarded medical furloughs	3,717	5,244
Awarded medical discharges	6	70
Deserted from the hospital	177	646
Died in the hospital	813	780

Source: James O. Breeden, "A Medical History of the Later Stages of the Atlanta Campaign," <u>Journal of Southern History</u> 35 (1969): 31-59.

Table 23

Support Hospitals for the Army of Tennessee,
March 1865

	Number of sick and wounded present on:	
Location	2 March 1865	11 March 1865
Georgia:		
Milledgeville	182	125
Macon	787	820
Columbus	782	766
Albany	42	closed
Americus	107	112
Cuthbert	267	258
West Point	90	97
Atlanta	26	36
Fort Valley	42	51
Griffin	not open	80
Forsythe	not open	254
Alabama:		
Auburn	264	moved to Forsythe
Montgomery	1171	987
Opelika	264	273
Eufaula	192	183
Notasulga	112	77

Source: "Final Returns, 1865," Samuel H. Stout Papers, Southern History Collection, University of North Carolina, Chapel Hill, N.C.

Samuel H. Stout was still on duty, trying to hold the hospital support system together. His last report summarized the hospital system as it existed on 11 March 1865. The general hospitals of the Army of Tennessee were spread from Georgia to Alabama, even though the army was fighting its last battle in North Carolina.

18

Preparing for the Final Union Campaigns

WHEN HAMMOND WAS DISMISSED FROM THE ARMY in August 1864, Joseph K. Barnes became the new surgeon general. He did not comment upon the problems of his predecessor, but immediately reorganized the Surgeon General's Office. He had already appointed a career army physician as his personal assistant. This was Charles Henry Crane, born in 1825, the son of a career army officer. After graduation from the Harvard Medical School in 1847, he joined the army. He had been the medical director of the Department of the South from June 1861 to July 1863.

When Crane was senior physician on Hilton Head Island, he was impressed with the careful medical and surgical treatment provided to the 27th Massachusetts by its surgeon, George A. Otis, who had decided to dedicate his life to military surgery after his young wife died in July 1863. Impressed with this determination, Crane arranged for Otis to join the staff of the Surgeon General's Office. Born in Boston in 1830, Otis studied medicine by apprenticeship under Dr. F. H. Deane of Richmond and graduated from the medical faculty of the University of Pennsylvania in 1851. After postgraduate study in surgery in Paris, Otis became the founding editor of the *Virginia Journal of Medicine and Surgery*. When he moved to Massachusetts, the editorship was taken over by James B. McCaw, who was now in charge of the Chimborazo and a leading Confederate physician.

Barnes brought in several other new people. John Shaw Billings was put in charge of the library of the Surgeon General's Office, containing some six hundred medical volumes.

Born in 1838, Billings had graduated from the Medical College of Ohio in 1860. He did so well at the examination before the Army Medical Board that he received a commission in the regular army. Billings served with the Army of the Potomac; at Gettysburg, he was in charge of the hospital of the 2nd Division, Fifth Corps. Throughout most of 1864 he was an assistant to the Medical Director of the Army of the Potomac, in charge of collating statistics. In December 1864 he joined the Surgeon General's Office.

Edward Curtis, born in 1838, graduated from Harvard College and was attending the College of Physicians and Surgeons in New York when the War started. He served as a medical cadet, working at the Army Medical Museum. After graduating from the medical faculty of the University of Pennsylvania in 1863, he served with the Army of the Potomac before reporting to the Surgeon General's Office to be in charge of the portion of the Army Medical Museum dealing with microscopic specimens.

Alfred Alexander Woodhull, born in 1837, graduated from the medical faculty of the University of Pennsylvania in 1859 and practiced medicine in Kansas. In September of 1861 he became a doctor with the regular army. He served as a medical inspector with the Army of the James before joining the Surgeon General's Office in late 1864. He was also assigned to catalog surgical specimens for the Medical Museum.

Several doctors remained at the Surgeon General's Office after Hammond's departure. Robert C. Wood was made the assistant sur-

The personnel of the Surgeon General's Office early in 1865. Sitting left to right are George Otis, Charles H. Crane, John Shaw Billings, and J. J. Woodward. Standing are William Canfield Spencer, A. A. Woodhull, Joseph K. Barnes, and Edward Curtis. USAMHI

geon general and given full authority over medical activities west of the Appalachian mountains. Headquartered in Louisville, he was able to fill supply orders and distribute medical resources throughout the west without checking with Washington. J. J. Woodward was placed in charge of collating the huge collection of medical statistics coming in from all the departments and field armies.

In addition to these officers, some enlisted men and civilians were important members of the staff of the Surgeon General's Office. Artists A. Pohlers and E. Stauch visited hospitals and painted from life; they drew from photographs as well. William Bell was the chief photographer. Frederick Schafhirt and his son Adolph prepared bone specimens. The elder Schafhirt had performed this same task for many years at the anatomical cabinet (medical museum) of the University of Pennsylvania. As he worked, Schafhirt hummed and sang patriotic and romantic German songs.

John H. Brinton resigned as head of the Medical Museum. He was sent to Nashville as inspector of hospitals. Jonathan Letterman resigned his position as the medical director of the Army of the Potomac and, after brief service elsewhere, became a railroad executive in California.

The War continued to grind on, with no end in sight. Some soldiers in the Army of the Potomac thought that perhaps the War might go on for generations; they would spend their lives fighting the rebels, and then their sons would fight the sons of the South. But wars cannot go on forever. Eventually one side or the other decides that the groaning misery is not worth the potential benefit of the war's successful conclusion.

A peace movement arose among many Northerners. Violence simmered. The 1863 New York City draft riots so convulsed the city that rebel prisoners wounded at Gettysburg had to be diverted around Manhattan on their way to DeCamp Prison Hospital on David's Island. The peace movement was particularly

TABLE 24

Senior Medical Officers,
U.S. Surgeon General's Office

Office	Date Assumed
Surgeons general	
Colonel Thomas Lawson	30 November 1836
died 15 May 1861	
Colonel Clement A. Finley	15 May 1861
retired 14 April 1862	
Brigadier General William A. Hammond	14 April 1862
on tour of inspection from 3 September 1863	
discharged by court-martial 18 August 1864	
Brigadier General Joseph K. Barnes	18 August 1864
acting, 3 September 1863 to 18 August 1864	
Assistant surgeons general	
Colonel Robert C. Wood	14 June 1862
retired 31 October 1865	
Colonel Charles H. Crane	28 July 1866
Medical inspectors general	
Colonel Thomas F. Purley	1 July 1862
Colonel Joseph K. Barnes	10 August 1863
Colonel Madison Mills	1 December 1864

Sources: Official Records, ser. 3, vol. 1, p. 964; vol. 2, p. 957; vol. 3, p. 1199; vol. 4, p. 1035; and vol. 5, p. 581; and Harvey E. Brown, The Medical Department of the United States Army from 1774 to 1873 (Washington, D.C.: Surgeon General's Office, 1873), 286-99.

strong in the Midwest. Union troops on leave harassed persons suspected of peace inclinations. A Union army doctor, Surgeon Shubal York, was killed in the violent altercation that occurred in Charleston, Illinois, on 28 March 1864 between troops on leave and peace Democrats.[1]

A great event loomed on the horizon that promised to limit the duration of the War. The U.S. Constitution demanded that the American populace select a president on the first Tuesday after the first Monday in November 1864. No nation had ever held an election during a major war, and some commentators recommended that the requirements of the Constitution should be put aside during this great hour of national peril. This action would certainly have enraged the peace movement and led to even greater civilian violence. Preparations for the election proceeded.

The people would decide if Lincoln was on track in bringing the Southern states back into the Union by force of arms. The peace faction of the Democratic Party managed to nominate their man to oppose Lincoln: General George B. McClellan. Here was a man who had fought the War, yet he did not want to crush the South. He said he wanted to discuss with the Southern states a peaceful means for their reincorporation into the Union; it was obvious, however, that most people in the South did not want to return to the Union. Their actions had demonstrated their desire for independence about as decisively as could be shown. Any attempt to negotiate with the rebels gave away the premise that the Confederate States of America existed as a nation. Negotiations would soon change from how to reincorporate the errant states to how much territory the United States would cede to its new neighbor. And once the principle of the right of secession was accepted, other regions of the United States, as well as portions of the Confederate States, would soon break into separate enclaves. The great American Union could break into a collection of culturally similar but politically separate nations.[2]

But before the election in November, great battles would occur, great battles that might change the temper of the Northern public and lead to Lincoln's reelection. These battles would be decided by generals and soldiers, by strategy and tactics, by marksmanship and courage. The medical department must fulfill its mission by maintaining the strength and health of the Union military force.

The Northern army expanded with an influx of new soldiers. The huge number of slaves pouring into Federal lines provided one source of new manpower. Even this was not enough, however, and the nation resorted to conscription for the first time in its history. The medical authorities played a role in the expansion of the Union army.

The use of blacks, most of them former slaves, produced special medical problems. The medical officers of the U.S Colored Troops were white. For example, Charles Edward Briggs, a graduate of the Harvard Medical School, had spent two years as assistant surgeon with the 24th Massachusetts. When the Massachusetts black regiment, the 54th Massachusetts, was formed in 1863, Briggs became its surgeon.[3] This position paid the same as the surgeon of a white regiment, $163 per month, but held some special danger. The government of the Confederate States considered the white officers of black regiments to have somehow poisoned the minds of loyal slaves; the officers should be shot on the field if captured. In addition, some black regiments were sent to very unhealthy regions of the occupied Confederacy because it was believed that blacks were better able to resist diseases that were common in the South. For example, the 2nd regiment of U.S.C.T. became the Key West garrison. Eleven of its twenty-eight white officers died of yellow fever.

Martin R. Delaney was the first black officer in the United States Army. He was a doctor, trained by apprenticeship after being expelled from the Harvard Medical School because of his race. But he did not serve as a medical officer. Like many white doctors, he became a line officer in a combat regiment. He was the major of the 104th regiment, U.S.C.T.

In summer 1863 military authorities, including the medical authorities, were unsure if former slaves were military material. Even Surgeon General Hammond had reservations. In his work on *Military Hygiene*, Hammond gave voice to the racist ideas that were shared by many people both North and South. "No doubt can exist relative to the great superiority of the Caucasian or European race for all the purposes of war," he wrote. "In endurance, in strength, in courage, in intelligence, in susceptibility to discipline, in a knowledge of the art of war, and of the arts and sciences applicable to war, this race is pre-eminent, and has always, when occasion required, made its superiority apparent." While the book was being prepared for publication, however, Hammond added a footnote intimating that his restriction of warlike qualities to the white race may have been premature. The growing military power of the former slaves probably changed many minds.[4]

In Vicksburg the medical director of the Army of the Tennessee ordered one of his surgeons, James Bryan, to survey the new colored troops. Bryan observed that their camps were clean and the new black soldiers had a military bearing. He concluded that "the experiment of making the negro a military power will be a success." He made several specific recommendations. Too much food was being issued to black troops, he thought; the usual government rations "are too large in quantity and too varied in quality for the simple habits of the negro, who does not ordinarily consume as much as the white man." From his observations, Bryan concluded the black soldier was not exempt from local diseases, such as malaria. "He suffers from the same maladies, and ought to be treated with the same remedies."[5]

Yankee physicians were quite ignorant about blacks as soldiers, as patients, or even as people. Unlike Bryan, many doctors thought blacks were immune to malaria, yellow fever,

Martin Delaney was the first black army officer. He had been a doctor in civilian life, but did not serve a medical role in the army. He was a major in the 104th regiment, U.S.C.T. USAMHI

and other diseases endemic to the South. Dr. John Gardner Perry of Boston graduated from the Harvard Medical School in 1863; he could not diagnose measles among the colored troops because their skin "was so confound-edly black" that he could not make out the measles spots.[6]

Some Northern doctors even doubted that blacks were Americans. Army physician Isaac Smith Jr., stationed in New Iberia, Louisiana, delivered twins from a black woman. He thought that the appearance of the babies showed that they had two different fathers, one black and one white. He wrote this up for the medical literature to show that fraternal twins could have different fathers. The darker of the two babies had "the true African build," he thought, while the lighter "would have done honor to an American mother."[7]

The number of free Blacks and former slaves in the army grew until about one of seven soldiers was black. Even this influx of manpower was not adequate to fill the demand for troops. The God of War stood with arms extended, crying: "More!" The North resorted to conscription. Starting in July 1863 the government sent draft notices to 776,829 men. This acted as a stimulus to volunteering more than an actual source of troops since only 46,347 of these men entered the army. The remainder escaped service in one of several ways: they hired a substitute to take their place, they paid a commutation fee, or they failed the physical examination. Many upper-class Northerners used personal or family funds to remain civilians. Silas Weir Mitchell served at Turner's Lane Hospital, but in a civilian capacity; when he received his draft notice, he hired a substitute for $300 rather than serve as a private.[8]

All males aged twenty to forty-five were subject to the draft. Each Congressional district had to supply a certain number of men; if volunteers failed to reach this number, draft notices were sent out. These men were then examined by special civilian physicians appointed by the Provost-Marshal-General Bureau. Many of these doctors noted that substitutes wanted to pass the physical, so that they could receive their payment for joining the army, while draftees wanted to fail. Every doctor commented on how often the draftees feigned illness.[9]

Written guides for examining physicians addressed the problem of malingering among draftees. The text written by Roberts Bartholow devoted one-fourth of its pages to a chapter entitled "Pretended Disqualifications for Military Service."[10] John Ordronaux purposely wrote his handbook in abstruse medical language so the lay reader would not learn how to malinger more successfully. "Many passages in the manual bear an impress of obscurity," Ordronaux explained, "which, it is almost needless to say, has been purposely given them, in order not to furnish any instruments of deception to those who might seek here for assistance in accomplishing themselves in the art of malingering."[11]

The humorist Petroleum V. Nasby presented the view of the person undergoing examination for military service. Nasby was not only bald, he told the examining doctor, and obliged to wear a wig for twenty-two years, but he was afflicted with dandruff in what "scanty hair still hangs around my venerable temples." He had poor teeth, he said, as well as bronchitis, catarrh, and varicose veins. He was hollow chested, short winded, and ruptured in nine places, being "entirely enveloped with trusses."[12]

The problem of malingering did not end after the draftee became a soldier. The doctor in the Union army frequently encountered a soldier with medical complaints whose major goal was to escape from dangerous and onerous military duties. The basic method used by the military physician to uncover feigned illness involved careful observation of the patient under a variety of conditions. The mute soldier replies to a passerby's greeting, revealing that he was faking his inability to speak. The soldier with a paralyzed arm is observed as he walks about the hospital grounds; the wind blows off his hat and the "paralyzed" arm reaches up to catch it. The deaf soldier flinches as the doctor discharges a handgun behind him.[13]

Much malingering masqueraded as dysfunction of the nervous system: blindness, deafness, paralysis, epilepsy. The U.S. Army Hospital for Injuries of the Nervous System at Turner's Lane developed special methods for detecting feigned illness. One method involved examination while the patient was coming out of ether anesthesia. A malingerer often revealed his true abilities before fully awake.[14]

Many physicians specifically admitted that they concluded the patient was malingering if he was not definitely suffering from a known illness or condition. In his textbook, Ordronaux recommended that "in cases of doubt, it is always safest to assume the disease as feigned, rather than real." Northern physicians accepted the righteousness of their cause and believed that the need of their armies for manpower overrode the need of their patients for medical protection. "The Army of the Potomac received a reinforcement of one," said William W. Keen after concluding that a soldier's symptoms were not due to disease.[15]

Northern Whites, stimulated by conscription, filled up old regiments. The new regiments of U.S. Colored Troops reinforced armies around the nation. Railroad lines were protected, forts were garrisoned, and great armies prepared for the decisive campaigns of 1864.

19

Union Medical Support for the Decisive Campaigns of 1864

THE GRITTY, GROANING, GRINDING STRUGGLE OF 1864 involved separate campaigns across the entire sweep of the Confederacy. The South was reeling, but the Northern public was weary of the War. Could the Union put the final choke hold on the dying South, or would the South summon the last ounce of resistance that was needed to convince its enemies that their war aims were just not worth the misery? November 1864 was the great constitutional terminus of these campaigns. If the armies failed, the Northern populace would elect McClellan and the Confederacy would survive.

Four military and naval actions would decide the outcome of this fratricidal War. U.S. naval forces proposed to push into Mobile Bay, cutting off the city of Mobile. Grant's army was poised to march into northern Virginia and take Richmond. Sherman planned to enter Georgia and take Atlanta. Finally, much hope was placed upon the occupation of Arkansas and Louisiana. The medical services of the Union army and navy were ready to support these invasions.

The Battle of Mobile Bay challenged the medical system of the U.S. Navy. Admiral David G. Farragut was in his flagship, the U.S.S. Hartford, as his fleet pushed past Fort Morgan, guarding the entrance to the bay. One of the ironclads, the U.S.S. Tecumseh, hit an underwater mine and capsized. Once inside Mobile Bay, the Union fleet was challenged by the C.S.S. Tennessee, supported by three small vessels. The Tennessee put up a vigorous resist-

ance. It was raked by the fire of many ships and repeatedly rammed. The Federal flagship U.S.S. Hartford purposely collided with the Confederate ironclad, slid alongside it, and poured a broadside into the Confederate vessel at a distance, estimated by Admiral Farragut, at not more than twelve feet. The steering mechanism of the Tennessee was blown away, the ship lay helpless in the water. Faced with such a hopeless situation, the Confederate fleet commander, Admiral Franklin Buchanan, ordered the colors struck. Buchanan had suffered a compound fracture of the lower leg.[1]

Among the prisoners from the Tennessee were two doctors. Assistant Surgeon R. C. Bowles had been the vessel's physician. Since the Tennessee was the flagship of Admiral Buchanan, also on board was the fleet surgeon, Dr. Daniel B. Conrad. These surgeons examined Admiral Buchanan and determined that amputation of the leg was necessary.

In addition to those lost on the Tecumseh, the U.S. Navy had suffered a total of 22 killed and 170 wounded in the exchange of fire with the fort and with the Tennessee. Among the Union casualties were two medical personnel killed and two injured. Nurse George Stillwell was killed by a shell while serving aboard the flagship Hartford. The medical officer of the Tecumseh, Acting Assistant Surgeon H. A. Danker, was drowned when his vessel capsized.[2] Surgeon's steward Oliver Crommelin was severely scalded when a boiler exploded aboard the U.S.S. Oneida. Surgeon's steward Holbert Lane suffered splinters in his scalp

DESTRUCTION OF THE MONITOR "TECUMSEH" BY A REBEL TORPEDO, IN MOBILE BAY, August 5, 1864.—[Sketched by Robert Weir.]

During the battle of Mobile Bay, the U.S.S. *Tecumseh* struck a mine and capsized. Loss of life was heavy. HW

when a shell struck the U.S.S. *Monongahela.* The Confederate naval casualties, as reported by fleet surgeon Conrad, were 10 killed and 16 wounded.

After the battle, the Union fleet surgeon, Dr. James C. Palmer, went around the fleet by boat, offering his surgical services. Confederate and Union wounded were all taken aboard the U.S.S. *Metacomet.* The Federal vessels were inside the bay, having run under the guns of Fort Morgan. They were unable to depart because of those same guns. At the request of Admiral Farragut, the Confederate commander ashore allowed the *Metacomet* to proceed past Fort Morgan under flag of truce, carrying all Confederate and Union wounded to the U.S. Naval Hospital at Pensacola.

The first reports of the battle stated that the leg of Admiral Buchanan had been amputated. But the Union fleet surgeon, James C. Palmer, undertook the direct care of Buchanan, who was a distant relative, and the leg was saved. The Union fleet surgeon thought that his Confederate relative owed his leg to him.[3]

Sherman drove down from Chattanooga toward Atlanta. He commanded three great armies named after the three great rivers of the central United States: the Armies of the Cumberland, the Tennessee, and the Ohio. His entire force was dependent upon a single rail line. The Commissary Department was unable to keep the army supplied with fresh vegetables, and scurvy broke out. While never more than a few hundred soldiers received the diagnosis of full-blown scurvy, this was only the tip of the iceberg. Many thousands of soldiers, perhaps most of the Union army, had the easy fatiguability of minor scurvy, or as it was called by doctors and soldiers, the scorbutic taint. The problem was alleviated when the U.S. Sanitary Commission brought onions and potatoes to Sherman's army. Many of Sherman's officers wondered how the Sanitary Commission, using the same rail line, could provide these antiscorbutic dietary items, while the official army Commissary Department could not.

Sherman's forces experienced a steady

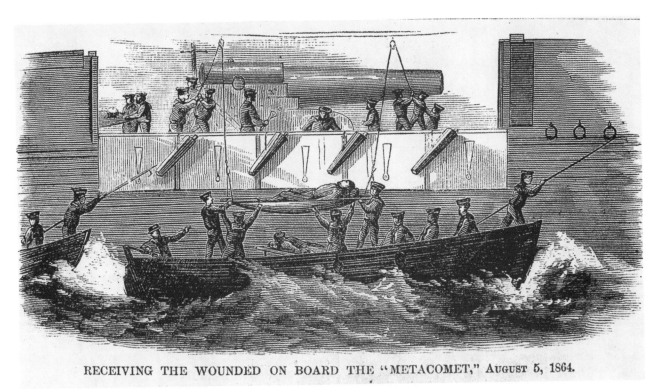

RECEIVING THE WOUNDED ON BOARD THE "METACOMET," August 5, 1864.

After the battle, both Northern and Southern wounded were ferried to the U.S.S. *Metacomet* and were taken to the U.S. Naval Hospital at Pensacola. HW

Table 25

Scurvy in Sherman's Army

Month	Cases of Scurvy
1864:	
May	363
June	636
July	914
August	869
September	620
October	229
November	52
December	35
1865:	
January	65
February	11
March	14
April	56

If a few hundred soldiers received the diagnosis of full-blown scurvy, many thousands were suffering from the lassitude and fatigue of dietary deficiency. Nutrition improved in August, but remained a problem for Sherman's army even after the fall of Atlanta. By the time of the March to the Sea in November and December, scurvy had almost disappeared.

Source: <u>MSH</u>, Medical Volume, pt. 1, pp. 459 and 542, tables 72 and 85.

RAILROAD DEPOT AT RESACA, GEORGIA.

ADAIRSVILLE, GEORGIA.

KINGSTON, GEORGIA.

Sherman's army received all its supplies down a tenuous rail connection to Chattanooga. The sick and wounded were evacuated up the same line. USAMHI

The locomotive of the hospital train was painted red. By 1864 the hospital train ran on a regular schedule, three times per week from Chattanooga to Nashville. HW

A sketch of the interior of a hospital railroad car shows that the beds are litters hung by straps. The patients were carried into and out of the car on these same litters. HW

stream of combat casualties. These were taken by rail to Chattanooga, then on to Nashville and to cities in the North. The special hospital trains ran from Chattanooga to Nashville on a regular schedule, three times a week. The locomotives of the hospital trains were painted red to identify them to roaming bands of Confederate guerrillas, who usually, but not always, let them pass.[4] The first trains had bunks three deep but surgeons had difficulty ministering to the patients in case of an emergency such as a secondary hemorrhage. Subsequent hospital train cars were built with the bunks two deep. Stretchers were carried aboard and hung from straps; upon arrival in

Nashville, the same stretchers were carried off. This arrangement made unnecessary the painful shifting of the wounded from stretcher to bed, and then again to stretcher.[5]

After the fall of Atlanta, Sherman prepared for his famous March to the Sea. He assigned two corps to guard against a Confederate offensive into Tennessee. From his remaining troops, he culled out all those who were sick or were likely to become sick. These were sent North into the hospital system. With his remaining seventy thousand men, he abandoned Atlanta and headed off into the rich agricultural hinterland of Georgia. As Sherman's army moved across the Confederacy, living off

Table 26

The Sick and Wounded of Sherman's Army

Month	Total troop strength	Number wounded	Died of wounds	Number sick	Died of illness	Percent sick and wounded
1864:						
May	142,206	8,254	188	21,682	51	21.1%
June	141,749	5,765	238	27,170	71	23.2
July	137,176	5,331	355	27,354	274	23.8
Aug	132,296	2,690	447	27,375	294	22.7
Sept	129,405	1,415	256	22,274	300	18.3
Oct	118,800*	520	84	14,967	305	13.0
Nov	78,927	234	20	8,315	49	10.8
Dec	77,585	356	37	7,682	144	10.4
1865:						
Jan	75,851	53	12	10,912	161	14.5
Feb	70,707	227	29	5,986	169	8.8
March	69,818	1,648	155	7,021	162	12.4
April	75,184	47	28	10,116	111	13.5

The number of Union soldiers wounded in combat continued at a high level until Atlanta was taken, but soldiers disabled by illness always greatly outnumbered those disabled by combat. Sherman's army during the March to the Sea had only about 10 percent of its troops on the sick list, making it the healthiest army of the American Civil War.

*The number of troops in Sherman's army dropped greatly in November when two corps were detached to protect Tennessee.

Source: <u>MSH</u>, Medical Volume, pt. 1, pp. 459 and 542, tables 72 and 85.

the land, it was the healthiest army of the Civil War. The health was due to the culling of those soldiers who were sickly, to the good diet provided by the farmlands of Georgia, and to the fact that they never remained in one camp long enough for the food or water to become contaminated with human waste.

As Sherman drove down from Chattanooga to take Atlanta, Grant drove southward from Washington to the outskirts of Richmond. Grant's Army of the Potomac experienced a great number of casualties.[6] In just the first month, May, the Medical Bureau registered 22,596 wounded Union soldiers. An additional 13,173 soldiers were wounded in June. The terrible cost of the campaign included many sick. A total of 19,902 soldiers registered sick in April, before the campaign began, as Grant purposely weeded out those who were unable to undertake the rigors expected. But in July,

after the horrendous battles of May and June, an additional 19,607 soldiers registered as too sick to carry out their duties.

The first great battle of the campaign was fought in the Wilderness. Unlike Gettysburg, where an observer could see the entire field of battle, the forests of the aptly named Wilderness broke up the battle into hundreds of deadly little contests. The dense underbrush caught on fire and the wounded who could not be evacuated were burned to death. Grant's army moved on to fight the Battle of Spottsylvania, and another great bloodletting occurred.

The new medical director of the Army of the Potomac was Thomas A. McParlin, who had been the chief surgeon of the Naval School Hospital at Annapolis. He first arranged for the wounded from the Wilderness to be loaded into the 488 ambulances that he had accumu-

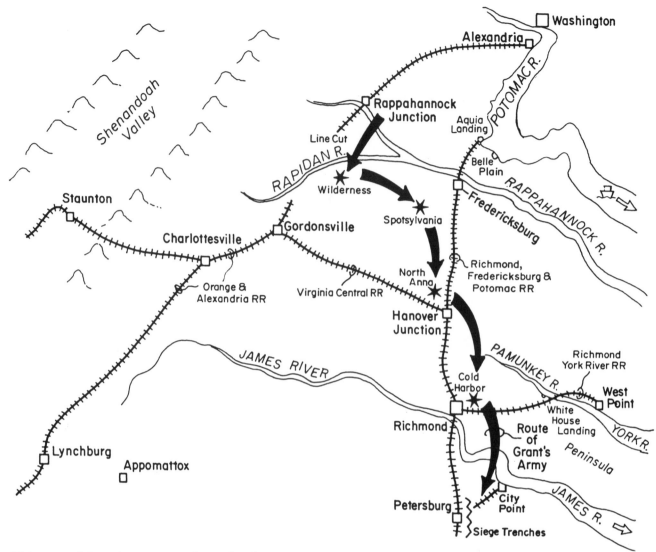

This map of Grant's campaign shows the changing medical evacuation routes. The initial base at Rappahannock Junction had to be abandoned. The wounded from the Wilderness, Spottsylvania, and North Anna were evacuated to Fredericksburg and on to Aquia Landing or Belle Plain. From these locations, they traveled by steamer up the Potomac to Washington. The wounded from Cold Harbor were taken by rail to White House Landing on the Pamunkey or on to West Point on the York River. After laying siege to Petersburg, Grant evacuated his wounded by a specially constructed rail line to City Point. From West Point or City Point, the sick and wounded went by sea to the Northern port cities. The Confederates evacuated their wounded along the rail system to Richmond or westward to Charlottesville and Lynchburg.

lated. Unfortunately, the huge number of wounded filled these and he had to obtain 320 wagons to handle the overload. This column of vehicles at first headed for the medical support area at Rappahannock Station. But when Grant moved South, abandoning the defensive line along the upper Rapidan River, this area became militarily untenable. McParlin shifted his base to Fredericksburg.

The column of vehicles containing many thousands of wounded arrived in Fredericks-

burg at 11 A.M. on 9 May, but found that no medical supplies, not even food, were present. Supplies had been sent to the expected support center at Rappahannock Station. The medical authorities of the U.S. Army tried valiantly to succor the wounded, but again the U.S. Sanitary Commission provided most of the needed supplies. The Sanitary Commission was assisted by volunteers from the Christian Commission and several unattached volunteers including Clara Barton. The U.S.

Charles K. Irwin was the brigade surgeon of the Excelsior Brigade, made up of New York regiments. After the battle of the Wilderness, he crossed into rebel territory under flag of truce. He operated for several days near the Wilderness church. Several amputations were canceled because the wounded soldiers were so ill that, in Irwin's words, they had "no other prospect than speedy relief by death." This photograph taken in camp before the campaign shows Dr. Irwin sitting outside his tent with his hospital steward. NA

Navy established a port facility at Belle Plain, as the closest point to Fredericksburg. Supplies began to pour in.

Additional wounded from the battles of Spottsylvania and North Anna were transported, or made their own way, to Fredericksburg, where temporary hospitals were frantically being set up. The road to Fredericksburg became crowded with a mass of suffering humanity. One of the civilian doctors who came to help was a pioneer in the use of ether for anesthesia: William T. G. Morton. As he made his way down the muddy road toward the front, Morton encountered the wounded walking toward medical help at Fredericksburg.

Morton had spent a lifetime in medicine, but nothing had prepared him for this.

It is the most sickening sight of the war, this tide of wounded flowing back. One has a shattered arm, and the sling in which he carries it is the same bloody rag the surgeon gave him the day of battle; another has his head seamed and bandaged so you can scarcely see it, and he weaves like a drunken man as he drags along through the hot sun; another has his shoe cut off, and a great roll of rags around his foot, and he leans heavily on a rough cane broken from a pine tree; another breathes painfully and holds his hand to his side, where you see a ragged rent in his blouse; another sits by a puddle, dipping water on a wounded leg, which, for want of dressing since the battle, has become inflamed; another lies on a plot of grass by the roadside, with his browned face turned full to the sun, and he sleeps.[7]

Most of the wounded from the Wilderness, Spottsylvania, and North Anna were taken to Fredericksburg. Photographers recorded the treatment in the open. A male nurse is dressing a wound to the left in the photograph. The soldier resting against the tree has his right foot swathed in bandages. Miller

And these were the walking wounded; the seriously wounded were carried in ambulances and wagons.

The wounded were treated in tents or in the open air near Fredericksburg, then loaded on trains to be taken to Washington, Philadelphia, or places further north. Some were taken by wagon to Belle Plain, then loaded on ships to be taken to New York, Boston, or other port cities. When Grant advanced after the horrible

May battles, the evacuation route was adjusted. The old site of White House on the Pamunkey, a key point during the Peninsula Campaign of 1862, became the main supply base of the Army of the Potomac. The building that gave the place its name, the white house that had belonged to the Custis family and had been so important a historical site that it could not be used as a hospital in 1862, was now just a pile of blackened bricks. Ships em-

Another photograph of treatment in the open air at Fredericksburg during May of 1864 shows several wounded soldiers. The lad in the foreground on the stretcher has just undergone an amputation of his right lower leg. **USAMHI**

The white house that was protected when first encountered in 1862 was nothing but burned ruins when Grant's army used White House Landing as a medical support area in 1864. See page 72 for the white house in better times. **NA**

barked wounded at White House and carried them down the Pamunkey and York Rivers and out into the Atlantic, where they were taken to Washington, Baltimore, Philadelphia, New York, or Boston.

During the Peninsula Campaign of 1862 most of the ships were leased by the Sanitary Commission. Medical Director Tripler argued with Frederick Law Olmsted about what soldiers were on what ship and where they were going. Tripler was now semiretired in Cincinnati, Olmsted was starting a new career in California, and the new medical director of the Army of the Potomac controlled the hospital transports. The *Joseph K. Barnes* was the first ship built from the keel up as a hospital ship. It transported wounded northward, but no surgery was attempted aboard. The doctor in charge was Alexander H. Hoff, who had transferred from the old *D. A. January* on the Mississippi.

Cold Harbor was perhaps the greatest un-

necessary bloodletting of the War. The soldiers of the Army of the Potomac were exhausted, their physical and numerical strength depleted by the terrible battles of May. After a ferocious back and forth struggle, the Union troops retreated to their original positions. Between the Confederate and Union lines lay a vast number of seriously wounded soldiers, most of them Federals.

Grant asked Lee for a truce to collect the wounded. The subsequent series of missed communications would be comical if wounded men had not been lying in no-man's land, begging for succor. Grant's first letter was sent in the early morning hours of 5 June; Lee's reply was received too late to put a truce into effect. Grant wrote again the next day, but it was not until the following day that Grant and Lee could agree to a truce. Long before the official truce, soldiers of both sides, on their own, without official approval, advanced into the area between the lines waving white flags.

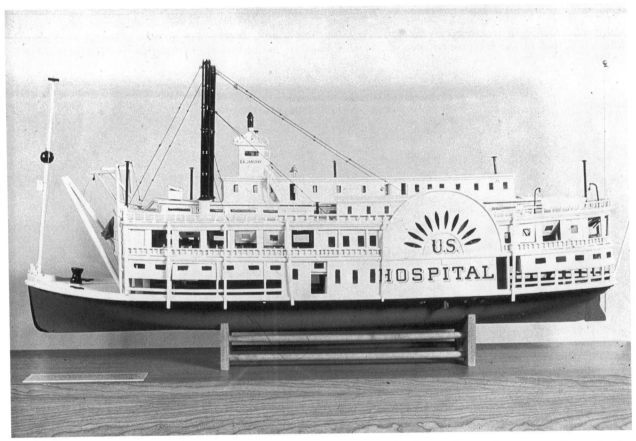

A model of the *Joseph K. Barnes*, a U.S. Army vessel, the first ship built as a hospital transport from the keel up. There was no operating room aboard. Courtesy of the Historical Collections, National Museum of Health and Medicine.

After the terrible failure at Cold Harbor, Grant moved the Army of the Potomac across the James River to lay siege to Petersburg. The exhausted Army of the Potomac attempted to break the Confederate lines in many fierce struggles, most notably the Battle of the Crater. Medical Director McParlin set up a new evacuation route via City Point. Special rails were laid on the ground, without cross rails, for temporary train travel. These trains traveled very slowly, rising and falling with slight undulations of the ground. City Point became a center of supplies, warehouses, camps, and hospitals. But the wounded poured in and some of the warehouses had to be hurriedly converted to hospitals. Many of the same volunteers were still there still nursing their boys in blue; among them was Helen Gilson, who had cheered the wounded at Gettysburg with her singing.

Former slave Charles Brown, now a private with the 23rd United States Colored Troops, was wounded on 13 July 1864 in an attack on the Petersburg fortifications. He heard minié balls zipping over his head, when suddenly he noted blood streaming down his face. He dropped to the ground and palpated his head to discover that a minié ball had creased his scalp. Weak from loss of blood, Private Brown was carried from the field and taken to the hospital of the 4th Division, Second Corps. He was evacuated by the specially built rail line to the colored hospital at City Point. On 17 August 1864 he was placed on the steamer *Baltic* for transportation to Philadelphia, where he was to be admitted to Satterlee Hospital. While the vessel was underway, however, Brown began to have repeated epileptic convulsions. These seizures became continuous and Private Brown died aboard the vessel on 18 August 1864.[8]

The great Army of the Potomac had been worn down by combat and by disease. Its strength, despite reinforcements, dwindled

Table 27

The Sick and Wounded of Grant's Army

Month	Strength	Number wounded	Died of wounds	Number sick	Died of illness
1864:					
March	104,916	87	8	13,670	136
April	136,115	123	9	19,902	131
May	115,385	22,596	322	12,754	35
June	98,384	13,173	549	14,188	119
July	74,589	2,043	124	19,607	270
August	55,105	2,322	198	16,560	220
Sept	60,897	958	43	14,855	152
Oct	72,581	1,477	101	14,110	167
Nov	74,561	299	56	14,207	152
Dec	97,235	349	51	15,107	171
1865:					
Jan	104,436	132	26	14,940	261
Feb	105,635	1,158	78	12,853	157
March	109,707	3,082	153	13,659	160
April	110,233	4,357	293	12,127	104

Grant's army almost bled to death from sickness and from combat during the horrible summer of 1864. The effective strength dropped from 136,115 in April to 55,105 in August. Additional troops reinforced the Army of the Potomac throughout the fall and winter.

Source: <u>MSH</u>, Medical Volume, pt. 1, pp. 324 and 490, tables 51 and 77.

from a high of 136,115 in April 1864 to a low of 55,105 in August. Many of the soldiers who still reported for duty were too ill to carry on a vigorous campaign. The Sanitary Commission physician who inspected the Army of the Potomac during late summer 1864 reported that "the men look perfectly exhausted, the results of this long campaign are beginning to show themselves in worn out nervous systems, in utter lack of energy, and in emaciated faces."[9] The Army of the Potomac could only wait in its trenches until the spring brought reinforcements, renewed health, and new vigor.

President Lincoln held out great hope for a campaign in the Mississippi Valley in 1864. He hoped that Union military successes in the states just west of the Mississippi would swell sentiment among the local people to rejoin the Union. Despite the occupation of Little Rock, the southern half of Arkansas remained in rebel hands, and much of the northern half was disrupted by guerrilla activity. Union forces abandoned the goal of occupying Louisiana after their failure to advance up the Red River in spring 1864. The inability of the Union to accomplish its goals in the Mississippi Valley was caused, in part, by the deteriorating health of Union armies in the region.

The Union forces in Arkansas and Louisiana were virtually paralyzed by illness in summer and early fall. During this sickly season over 40 percent of the troops were too ill to perform military duties; many sick soldiers were sent North, but their replacements soon also fell ill. During a typical month, August 1864, in Arkansas, 15,206 Union soldiers were too sick for duty out of a total strength of 35,764; 42.5 percent of the troops were disabled by illness. Malaria accounted for 48.7 percent of these sick soldiers. Compared to the effect of illness, combat wounds had no effect on the battle readiness of the Union forces. Of over 15,000 Union soldiers in the hospital or in convalescent camps in August, only 65 were disabled because of gunshot wounds.[10]

The review of an individual with the debilitating symptom of diarrhea shows how a sick soldier had difficulty performing his military duties despite his best intentions and, furthermore, shows how convalescence at home can deplete the army of troops. Charles B. Johnson was the hospital steward of the 130th Illinois. In July 1863 he suffered a fit of vomiting and diarrhea, which he attributed to drinking water directly from the Mississippi River. His diarrhea became chronic; he thought he was as weak as "the classical dishrag." He lost so much weight and became so listless that the regimental physician sent him to a nearby convalescent camp to recover. After just a few hours among strangers who all looked as thin and as sallow as he did, Johnson became lonely and returned to his regiment. His diarrhea worsened, however, and he obtained a medical furlough. He traveled by steamer from New Orleans to Cairo, by train to Vandalia, Illinois, and then by wagon to his home in Greenville. He spent almost six months enjoying the healthful conditions at home, including his mother's cooking. On his own initiative Johnson returned downriver and found his regiment in Baton Rouge.[11]

Malaria as well as chronic diarrhea took the vigor out of fighting troops. The terrible shaking chill that came in paroxysms exhausted the most military of soldiers. Troops of the 33rd Iowa, stationed in Arkansas, could tell when their bugler had developed malaria by the quivering of the notes; the sound of taps quivered with a shaking chill. Almost every day a new bugler replaced the one sent to the hospital, but by the next night, taps again quivered. The soldiers joked that the bugle itself was the source of the malaria.[12]

During 1864 Union physicians in Arkansas ran out of quinine. Joseph Smith, the medical director, complained to Assistant Surgeon General Robert C. Wood, in charge of medical supplies in the west. The stockpile of quinine at Memphis had been destroyed in a fire. In July 1864 Smith ordered his medical officers to husband their dwindling quinine; they were to desist from prophylactic administration and reserve the available quinine to treat soldiers already stricken with malaria.[13]

In 1863 General Grant had ordered that the sick of his army in the Mississippi Valley should go no further North than the medical base at Memphis. He feared that his soldiers would disappear on medical furlough. In 1864 in the Trans-Mississippi region, that is exactly what happened. The case of Charles B. Johnson, going home to his mother's cooking, was multiplied a thousand times. The Massachusetts physician in charge of the Union army hospital in Baton Rouge sent his sick soldiers by ship to New England. He longed to return there himself, where he could practice "the

Charles B. Johnson, hospital steward of the 130th Illinois, experienced a severe and chronic problem with diarrhea. From Charles B. Johnson, *Muskets and Medicine,* **Philadelphia, F. A. Davis, 1917.**

One of the best Union military hospitals built on the pavilion pattern was located in Little Rock, Arkansas. During the campaign of 1864, it became full of soldiers sick with malaria and diarrhea; very few patients were hospitalized due to gunshot wounds. **USAMHI**

healing art where malaria is not inhaled at every breath, where nature is not always antagonistic to the physician, and where a vigorous, rapid, and complete convalescence is not an impossibility."[14] While the transfer of sick soldiers to the North may have helped individuals, the continuous hemorrhage of the sick and the convalescent sapped the military strength of the Union army in Louisiana and Arkansas during 1864.

Despite the military failures in Louisiana and Arkansas, Lincoln defeated McClellan in the presidential election of November 1864. Grant was stymied in Virginia, but held the Confederate army in siege. The naval victory at Mobile Bay and the fall of Atlanta had shown the Northern populace that the Confederacy was doomed.

20
The Last Full Measure of Devotion

BY SPRING 1865 EVERYONE, NORTH AND SOUTH, knew that the end was near. Sherman was loose in the Carolinas. The city of Mobile was about to fall. The Confederates waited for the great spring offensive in Virginia that would end their experiment at nationhood. Each soldier waited, hoping that he would not be the last casualty of the War.

During winter 1864/65 the Army of the Potomac grew stronger. Reinforcements arrived from the North: more black troops, more drafted men. Each division constructed its own field hospital, housing the patients in large tents. New rail lines connected the field hospitals to the small port of City Point. At that location, a complex of warehouses, supply depots, and hospitals, all temporary wooden structures, sprouted up like spring buds. The medical authorities of the Army of the Potomac supervised the construction of six thousand new hospital beds at City Point. Medical Director McParlin and his colleagues were

BEFORE PETERSBURG—FIELD HOSPITAL OF THE FIRST DIVISION, NINTH ARMY CORPS.—[FROM SKETCHES BY A. M'CULLUM.]

A series of tent hospitals were erected behind the fortification lines around Petersburg. This drawing from *Harper's Weekly* shows ambulances bringing wounded to the field hospital of the 1st division, Ninth Corps. HW

181

INTERIOR OF A HOSPITAL WARD.

The wards of the field hospitals were in large tents. The doctor is taking the pulse of a patient. HW

ready for any combat or sickness that the Army of the Potomac might encounter.

Corporal Edson D. Bemis received his third gunshot wound during the winter of waiting. He had enlisted in the 12th Massachusetts at the beginning of the War. At the Battle of Antietam in September 1862 he received his first wound. A round musket ball struck his left upper arm, fracturing the humerus. The fracture healed normally except that the left arm was about an inch shorter than the right. He returned to duty, but received a second wound at the Battle of the Wilderness on 6 May 1864. A musket ball struck him in the right lower abdomen. He was evacuated to Chester Hospital near Philadelphia; much inflammation occurred in the wound, but it eventually healed. He returned to duty for the great spring offensive.

Bemis received his third wound on 5 Febru-

ary 1865 at the Battle of Hatcher's Run. He was shot in the left temple and knocked unconscious. He was carried to the field hospital of the 1st Division, Second Corps. Surgeon A. Vanderveer of the 66th New York examined the corporal and noted that brain matter was oozing from the wound. The patient was stuporous, with slow respirations and a pulse rate of 40. The right side of the body was limp and motionless, while the semidelirious patient jerked his left arm and leg frequently. Surgeon Vanderveer thought that the ball within the brain was producing swelling and bleeding, so he decided to remove the offending agent. On 8 February Dr. Vanderveer anesthetized the patient and undertook the surgery. First with his fingers, then with a long metal instrument, he searched within the brain substance. He found and removed the bullet, which proved to be a minié ball. Imme-

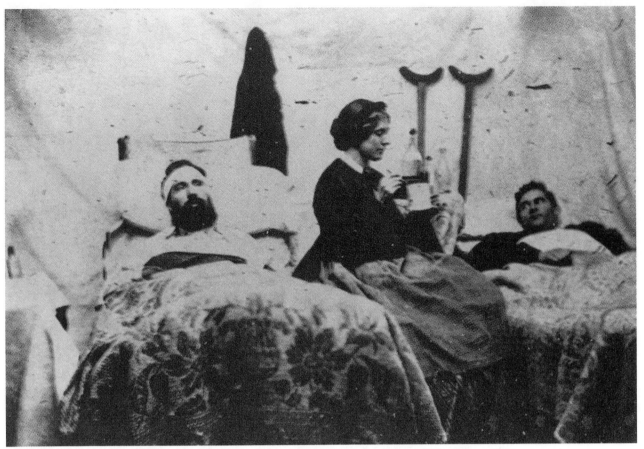

A photograph shows a female nurse inside a tent ministering to two wounded soldiers. NA

diately, the patient improved. He told the surgeon his name and looked about him, but said nothing else.

Within ten days, the patient had improved to such a degree that he could answer direct questions, but not carry on a conversation. By 18 February the weakness of the right arm and leg had disappeared and by the twenty-eighth was able to walk around the ward. On 18 March the patient went on medical furlough by hospital steamer to New York. In May he returned to his home at Huntington, Massachusetts. On 13 July 1865 he visited the Army Medical Museum and a photograph was taken.

The physicians at the Museum examined the patient. They thought that his mental faculties were normal; the brain pulsations could be felt if one placed one's fingers over the healed wound. In 1870 former Corporal Bemis wrote to the Army medical authorities: "I am still in the land of the living. My health is very good considering what I have passed through at Hatcher's Run. My head aches some of the

time. I am married and have one child, a little girl born last Christmas. My memory is affected and I cannot hear as well as I could before I was wounded."[1]

Private Pembroke Scott, 198th Pennsylvania, age twenty-five, was wounded on 29 March 1865. A minié ball struck his skull, knocking him unconscious. He was carried to the field hospital of the 1st Division, Fifth Corps. He was evacuated by rail to the Ninth Corps depot hospital at City Point. On 2 April he traveled by ship to Harewood Hospital in Washington, where a picture was taken. On 15 May he was transferred to Satterlee Hospital in Philadelphia and was discharged from the service on 5 July 1865. The following year, the former soldier was examined by Dr. Wilson Jewell. He noted that Scott suffered from a poor memory and from an inability to speak normally, called by Jewel a partial aphasia. Scott received a disability pension.

Corporal C. H. Grant of the 43rd New York was 19 when he was wounded at the siege of

City Point, Virginia was the main support base for the siege of Petersburg. A mass of ships transferred war material to a melee of wagons. Some of the ships took on the sick and wounded for transfer to the North. NA

Petersburg on 27 March 1865. He was taken to a field hospital of the 2nd Division, Sixth Corps. Examination showed that a minié ball had destroyed the right elbow. Amputation was required. Surgeon George T. Stevens of the 77th New York sawed off the arm midway between elbow and shoulder. The patient was taken by rail the next day to the Sixth Corps depot hospital at City Point. He remained there until 14 May 1865, when he boarded the steamer *State of Maine* and was taken to Carver Hospital in Washington.

Corporal Grant seemed to be doing well, although the stump had not completely healed, so he was transferred closer to his home. He arrived at the Ira Harris Hospital in Albany, New York, on 27 June 1865. The stump continued to fester and drain inflammatory material, so Assistant Surgeon J. H. Armsby decided to explore the wound. He passed a probe through the wound up into the central canal of the humerus. Dr. Armsby thought that the bone must be necrotic, since the probe passed so easily. On 6 July 1865, Dr. Armsby anesthetized Grant with chloroform, cut open

the stump, and removed several pieces of dead bone with a forceps. The new stump healed by granulation and Grant was discharged from the hospital, and from the army, on 5 October 1865. He settled in Springfield, Massachusetts, and received a pension.

Sergeant C. A. Winser, 6th Wisconsin, was twenty-two years old when, on 31 March 1865, he was hit in the right shoulder by a Confederate minié ball during the siege of Petersburg. He was examined by Surgeon John C. Hall, the senior medical officer of his regiment, who determined that the ball had ripped through the upper part of the arm, fracturing the humerus near its junction with the shoulder. On the day of the injury, at the field hospital, Dr Hall performed an excision of the upper portion of the humerus. With Sergeant Winser under anesthesia, the surgeon made a long incision along the shoulder and upper arm. He moved the head of the humerus out of the shoulder joint, noted that it had been seriously damaged by the ball, and sawed off the most proximal two or three inches. He dressed the wound, leaving most of the bone intact.

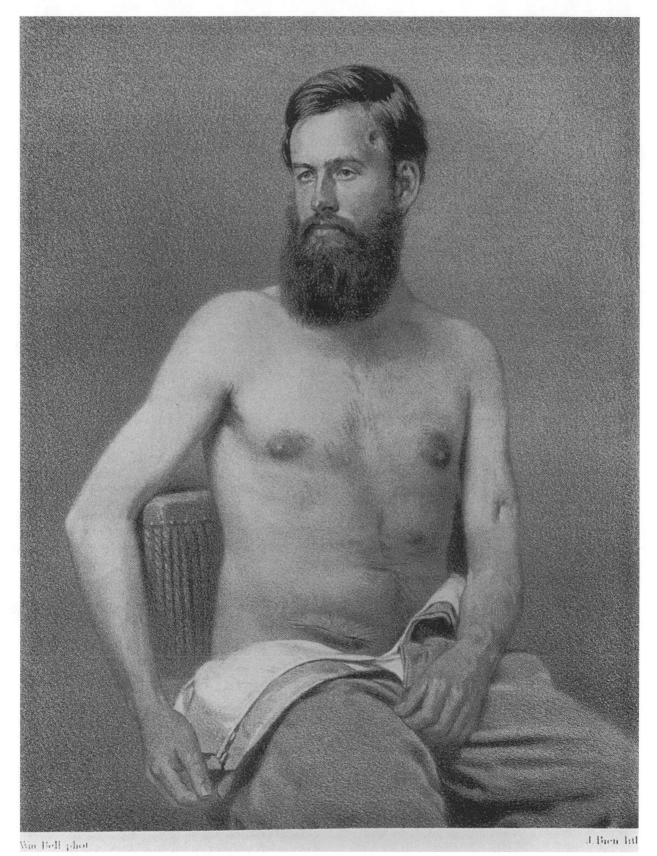

Edson D. Bemis received his third wound of the War on 5 February 1865. This drawing shows his wounds of the right lower abdomen, the left upper arm, and the left temple. MSH

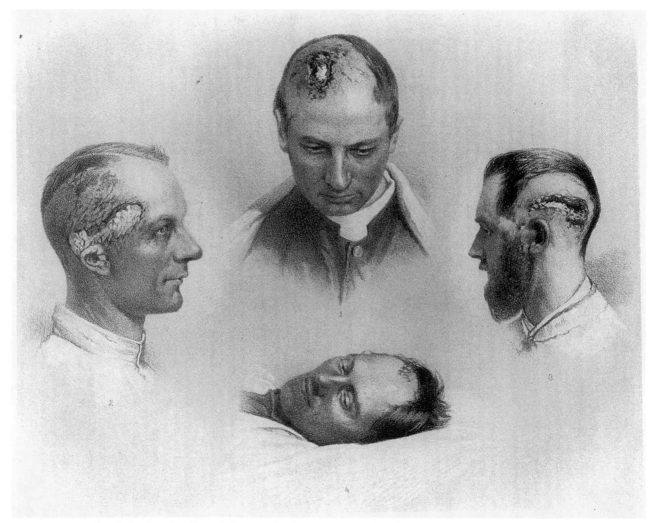

Gunshot wounds of the head inflicted during the last two months of the War. Clockwise starting at the left are Private Walter Wheeler, Corporal Ansell H. Beam, Private Pembroke Scott, and Private Denis Sullivan. Sullivan is lying quietly with the look of death on his face. MSH

Sergeant Winser was carried to a Fifth Corps hospital, taken by train to City Point, then by ship to Judiciary Square Hospital, Washington. He did well until 14 May 1865, when he suffered extreme inflammation at the site of the wound. He experienced massive swelling, redness, and pain in the shoulder and neck. This subsided in a few days. The wound filled in with granulation tissue over the next few weeks, and the patient was discharged from the hospital, and from the army, on 16 July 1865. When evaluated the next year for disability purposes, the examiner noted that the wound had not healed completely; it still occasionally produced a small amount of pus. Winser settled in Ottawa, Illinois, and was last seen in 1873, when measurements

showed that the right arm was two and one half inches shorter than the left.

The Army of the Potomac broke out of the siege and raced to cut off the rail connections to Richmond. Robert E. Lee informed President Davis that the city would have to be abandoned. The horrible night of the second of April of 1865 started with huge numbers of troops, government workers, and civilians streaming out of the city. The Confederate ironclads on the James River were set on fire to prevent them from falling into the hands of the Yankees. The ships were loaded with ordnance; one at a time each ship detonated with a frightening explosion. Government buildings and property in the city of Richmond were purposely set afire so they would be of no value to the Yankees. The surgeon general's office in the War Building was full of medicinal alcohol, assuring the total destruction of all that Samuel P. Moore had built up over three years.

The guards at the Chimborazo Hospital retreated with the rest of the army. Some of the chronic patients, people who had been there for many months, faking illness or disability to prevent their return to dangerous duty, saw an opportunity for a drunken debauch. They rushed to the alcohol storage area, but found it guarded by the very firm nurse Phoebe Pember. When they threatened forcefully to push her aside, she cocked her pistol. All night she stood guard over the alcohol supply.[2]

The nurses and some of the doctors were among the few Confederates on duty when the U.S. Army arrived. Phoebe Pember saw the first Yankee horseman riding down a deserted Richmond street just at dawn. She noted that his horse was a fine specimen and that all his harness and saddle straps matched. She had grown accustomed to the makeshift equipment and the poor horseflesh of the Confederate cavalry. She assumed this must be a high-ranking officer in such finery, but when he came closer, she saw that he was only a scout. When she suddenly realized that an ordinary Federal private was better equipped than Jefferson Davis or Robert E. Lee, she knew the Confederacy had been defeated.

More and more Yankee troops came into the city. Among them were black troops. One nurse was shocked when the black Yankees shouted to the Richmond slaves, "We have come to set you free." James B. McCaw stood in front of the Chimborazo Hospital to turn it over to Federal medical authorities. The U.S. Army doctor who arrived was the son of Valentine Mott; McCaw had known him as a boy when he apprenticed under Mott in New York. McCaw was offered a commission in the U.S. Army, to remain as commandant of Chimborazo, now a Union hospital. He turned down the offer, thinking that the retreating Lee might still pull off a miracle. He could not serve the damned Yankees while the Confederacy yet lived, however precariously. But he remained at Chimborazo to advise the Federal authorities.[3]

Lee and his Army of Northern Virginia retreated, hoping to forge a junction with the Army of Tennessee somewhere in North Caro-

lina. Federal cavalry raced ahead to cut off his retreat. The last battles in Virginia involved vicious cavalry clashes, with opposing horsemen slashing with their sabres.

Private Thomas K. Rogers, 5th Alabama, age forty-one, was wounded near Petersburg by Federal cavalry on 2 April 1865. A sabre struck the left side of his forehead, fracturing the frontal portion of the skull. He was taken to a Union field hospital, then to City Point, then by ship to Lincoln Hospital, Washington, arriving on 8 April. A photograph was taken. When on 20 April he began to experience symptoms and signs of brain swelling, Surgeon J. Cooper McKee performed trephination. He drilled a hole in the skull just above the forehead; he placed a tool into the hole in order to remove or elevate depressed skull fragments. After the operation, the patient recovered rapidly. The former Confederate took the oath of allegiance to the Union and returned to Alabama on 14 June 1865.

Private John A. Howard, 21st Pennsylvania Cavalry, was twenty-four years old when he was wounded on 5 April 1865 during the cavalry clash at Jettersville. He received two sabre cuts, one across his back and the other on the right side of his head. He was admitted to the field hospital of the Cavalry Corps on the day of injury. The cut on the back was dressed; it was not serious. However, the head wound was six inches in length and had fractured the parietal bone of the skull. The head was shaved and the two edges of the wound were bound together with adhesive tape. On 28 April he was evacuated to the base hospital at City Point. Two days later he was taken by hospital steamer to Harewood Hospital, Washington, where a photograph was taken. On 18 May he traveled by rail to Mower Hospital in Philadelphia. He received a partial pension for medical disability when discharged from the army on 18 July 1865. In 1867 Howard wrote from his home in Shippensville, Pennsylvania. He reported that he was doing well except that small pieces of bone kept working their way to the surface of his scalp and he had to pick them out of his hair.

Amos Shurey, a saddler with the 21st Pennsylvania Cavalry, was wounded at Jettersville on 5 April 1865. As Confederate cavalrymen slashed at him with their sabres, he raised his left arm to protect himself; a single blow fractured both bones of the forearm. More serious were the two slashes upon his head, both of which broke the skull. He was evacuated to City Point by rail and then to Annapolis by sea. He arrived at the Naval School Hospital on 15 April. He developed signs of brain hemorrhage and died on 12 May 1865.

Corporal Ansell H. Beam of the 26th Michigan was twenty-one years old when he was wounded in the head at Farmville on 6 April 1865. A minié ball made a ragged wound along the scalp, just to the right of the midline. He was taken first to the hospital of the 1st Division, Second Corps. On 15 April he was evacuated from City Point to Harewood Hospital, Washington, where a photograph was taken. On 18 May he was transferred to Satterlee Hospital, Philadelphia. The scalp wound healed, and he was discharged from the hospital and the army on 6 July 1865. He received no pension despite the fact that the last doctor to see him wrote in his record, "He has many symptoms of disturbance of the brain."

Private Robert A. Butcher, age twenty-one,

of the 82nd Pennsylvania was wounded on 6 April 1865 near Burke's Station. Confederate cavalrymen struck him on the top of his head with sabres as they tried to clear a way out for Lee's army. At the regimental hospital his head was shaved, the wounds were dressed, and the edges of the wounds were brought together and held with adhesive tape. The head was wrapped in bandages and he was evacuated by wagon to the Petersburg area, by rail to City Point, then by ship to Harewood Hospital, Washington, where he arrived on 16 April.

He was thought to be doing well until 29 May when he complained of a severe headache. He was extremely sensitive to light and noise. The doctor examined him and noted that the scalp near the wound was painful and bulging. When the edges of the wound were palpated, a large amount of pus flowed out. The wound was cleaned and allowed to heal by granulation, without any attempt to bring the wound edges together. On 8 June the patient requested discharge from the hospital

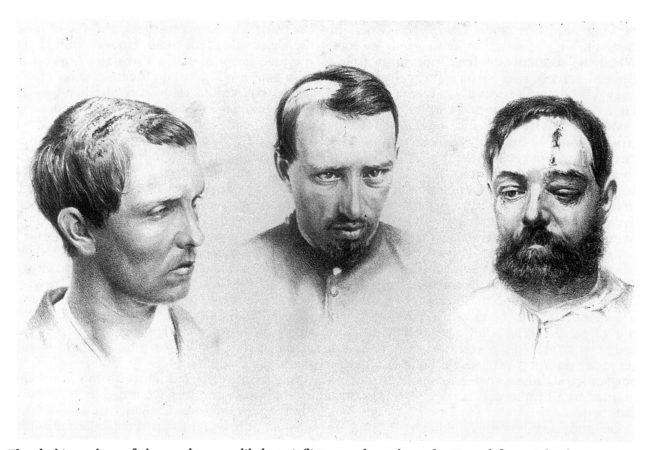

The slashing sabres of the cavalry were likely to inflict wounds to the scalp. From left to right these men are Private Robert A. Butcher, Private J. A. Howard, and Private T. K. Rogers. MSH

and from the army. Even though the wound was not completely healed, he was allowed to go home. He never applied for a pension.

Private Dennis Sullivan, 2nd Virginia Cavalry, was wounded at Harper's Farm near Appomattox Court House on 6 April 1865. He was struck in the head by a minié ball and knocked unconscious. He was picked up on the field by Federals and taken to a Union field hospital, where the portion of his hair around the wound was shaved and a wet dressing was applied. The next day the patient awoke and seemed rational. He was evacuated to City Point and then, by hospital steamer, to Harewood Hospital in Washington, arriving on 19 April. He experienced several chills and was given quinine, but he did not improve. On 24 April the patient slipped into coma. Surgeon R. B. Bontecou performed trephination, drilling a small hole in the skull. A depressed fracture of the skull was encountered during the operation and a second hole was drilled to allow removal of shards of bone. Pus exuded from these two holes. After the surgery, Sullivan never regained consciousness. He died on 16 April; autopsy examination showed a large abscess within the brain substance. Portions of the skull were sent to the Army Medical Museum.

Robert E. Lee surrendered the trapped Army of Northern Virginia on 14 April 1865. The War was just about over. Joseph Johnston surrendered the remains of the Army of Tennessee to General Sherman on 26 April. Former President Jefferson Davis was captured in Georgia on 10 May. The Confederacy still held much territory in Texas, Louisiana, and Arkansas, but the Confederate troops there just started walking home. General Kirby Smith surrendered this entire area on 2 June. The last Confederate general to surrender troops was Stand Watie on 23 June. The Confederate raider C.S.S. *Shenandoah* found out about these events and disarmed itself on 2 August; its captain surrendered the ship to British authorities on 6 November 1865.

The wounds of many soldiers, North and South, continued to discharge pus and pieces of bone for many years. For many, the War never ended.

21

Aftermath

THE SMALL ROUND BALL ENTERED THE BACK OF the neck and tore through the brain, blowing pieces of skull into the right orbit. Assistant Surgeon Charles Leale examined the victim. A bloody knife was lying on the floor, so Dr. Leale ripped the collar and shirt from the wounded man, expecting to discover a stab wound. He found none. When he saw blood on the shoulder and an enlarged pupil, he then suspected a brain wound. He ran his fingers around to the back of the neck and palpated the ball's entry wound. Dr. Leale concluded that the wound was mortal and he announced this fact.

Charles S. Taft, another army surgeon, performed a second examination. He noted that the left pupil was small and the right very large; neither reacted to the light of a candle. The right eye was discolored and protruded. Taft agreed with Leale that the patient had no hope for life. The victim was placed upon a bed and a sinapism was applied for its general stimulating effect. A small amount of brandy was placed in the victim's mouth and was swallowed.

Surgeon General Barnes arrived. He decided to search for the ball in the hope of removing it. A long metal probe was introduced into the wound and gently pushed forward. It came in contact with a firm object and Barnes withdrew it. The porcelain tip of the probe was not stained by lead, so Barnes decided that he had encountered a piece of bone, not a bullet. He decided to make no further search for the ball. Blood clots were removed from the wound and the victim breathed a bit more easily.

Just before midnight, the left side of the face twitched vigorously for twenty minutes. The wound continued to discharge blood and brain tissue onto the pillow. As the hours went by, the victim's respirations became loudly labored. His chest rose in amplitude and respirations were deep, then breathing became progressively more shallow and finally stopped. People in the room looked at their watches to note the time of death. But then respiration began again, slowly building in volume until the victim was again gasping. This cycle of rapid respiration alternating with periods of apnea occurred several times. Finally at twenty minutes past seven o'clock on the morning of 15 April 1865, respiration ceased. Surgeon General Barnes pronounced President Abraham Lincoln dead.

The body of the president was taken to the White House. Surgeon General Barnes supervised the post mortem examination, which was carried out by army physicians J. J. Woodward and Edward Curtis. Woodward determined the path of the fatal bullet. It had entered the back of the head, breaking the occipital bone just to the left of the midline. Dr. Woodward described the passage of the ball through the left cerebrum, lodging near the left corpus striatum. The ball was recovered.[1]

Despite the death of the president, a great parade, the Victory March, was held in Washington. Thousands of Union soldiers marched past the new chief executive, Andrew Johnson. Grant, Sherman, and their victorious troops marched down Pennsylvania Avenue. Some soldiers became exhausted and dropped out. Ministering to them at a tent erected at the corner of Pennsylvania and I Streets was Mrs.

Surgeon General Barnes holds the head of the dying president. Also present at the death bed is Charles H. Crane; he may be the person standing by the door. HW

Mary Bickerdyke. The leaders basked in the glory of a newly united nation; Mother Bickerdyke continued to nurse her sick and exhausted soldiers.

The prisoners came home. Stephen Payne was taken under guard from the horrible prison at Andersonville by train to Jackson, Mississippi, where he was turned over to Federal authorities. He could tell when he was nearing freedom; the rebel guards shifted from saying, "You damn Yankees move over there" to "Will you gentlemen please move over there."[2]

A special sorting center was set up near Vicksburg in order to hurry home the former prisoners. The civilian vessels that transported the prisoners were paid by the number of passengers that they carried; some became dangerously overloaded. Almost two thousand people, most of them emaciated and weak, crowded aboard the *Sultana*. It headed up the Mississippi, but on 27 April one of the boilers exploded and it rapidly sank. Most of the for-

mer prisoners were too weak to swim to shore; they survived the ordeal of the rebel prison camp but drowned on their way home.[3]

On 25 May 1865 the Union ammunition depot in Mobile detonated. At half past two in the afternoon the Ordnance Depot on the corner of Lipscomb and Commerce Streets suddenly exploded; sabotage by former Confederates was suspected. The huge explosion killed over two hundred people and completely demolished eight square blocks of the downtown area. Many Mobile physicians, some who had worn the Confederate uniform only a month before, treated the injured in local hospitals; many of the injured were black Union soldiers. Union army doctor J. C. Richards wrote a letter to the local newspaper thanking the Confederate physicians. He especially mentioned Dr. Josiah Nott, a leading racial theorist before the War who had claimed that the white and black races could not have descended from the same individual. Nott had strongly favored secession in 1861 and had

EXPLOSION OF THE STEAMER "SULTANA," APRIL 28, 1865.

An artist's representation of the sinking of the *Sultana* in the Mississippi River. Many crewmen were able to swim to shore, but almost all the weak and emaciated former prisoners drowned. HW

been the medical director of Confederate forces in Mobile. Now he mourned the loss of his two sons, both of whom had died in Confederate service.[4]

The huge Union army shrank in size. This was certainly fortunate, because the terrible cholera epidemic that hit the United States in 1866 decimated the army. In that year about 15 percent of black soldiers and 10 percent of white soldiers who remained in the U.S. Army died. A cholera epidemic two years earlier would have killed over one hundred thousand Union soldiers and brought the offensives of 1864 to a rapid halt.[5]

The wounded came home quickly, but the wounds healed very slowly. David Schively and Jacob Bieswanger, the two soldiers who had been wounded at Gettysburg and had been taken to Turner's Lane Hospital in Philadelphia, were still in that institution when the War ended. The terrible burning pain in their arms continued. Silas Weir Mitchell and his colleagues described these patients and de-

fined a new syndrome in their landmark book, *Gunshot Injuries of Nerves*. Mitchell called the disorder causalgia. Nothing relieved the pain except shots of morphine given directly into the painful arm. Many thousands of morphine injections were given at Turner's Lane Hospital before it closed. Mitchell continued to follow these patients in civilian life. After he retired from the active practice of medicine, his son, John K. Mitchell, continued to treat them.[6]

The senior Mitchell interviewed many patients who had undergone amputation. He wrote a fictional story about an army physician who lost, one at a time, all four limbs. The story, which came out in the *Atlantic Monthly* without indication of authorship, was so realistic that the physicians in charge of the Army Medical Museum checked their records to see if they could find the army physician described. They found that no individual in the Civil War had lost all four limbs.[7] This case was fictional, but many former soldiers spent

EXPLOSION OF THE UNITED STATES RECEIVING MAGAZINE AT MOBILE, May 25, 1865.—[Sketched by George Watters.]

CONFLAGRATION AT MOBILE, CAUSED BY THE EXPLOSION, May 25, 1865.—[Sketched by George Watters.]

The Union ammunition depot in the captured city of Mobile detonated without warning. Many Union soldiers, most of them black, were killed or injured. HW

A photograph shows the widespread destruction in the center of Mobile produced by the explosion. The cause of the detonation was never conclusively determined, but sabotage was suspected. USAMHI

For years after the War, hikers in many areas of the South were likely to find unburied bodies. These skeletons were photographed in the area of the Wilderness, where Grant's great bloodletting of 1864 began. Miller

A closer view of one of the cadavers seen in the figure above. The posture of the leg bones makes one wonder if this soldier had both legs crushed. Perhaps he crawled to this place and was burned to death by the fire that swept through the Wilderness that horrible night in May of 1864.

THE

ATLANTIC MONTHLY.

A Magazine of Literature, Science, Art, and Politics.

VOL. XVIII. — JULY, 1866. — NO. CV.

THE CASE OF GEORGE DEDLOW.

THE following notes of my own case have been declined on various pretexts by every medical journal to which I have offered them. There was, perhaps, some reason in this, because many of the medical facts which they record are not altogether new, and because the psychical deductions to which they have led me are not in themselves of medical interest. I ought to add, that a good deal of what is here related is not of any scientific value whatsoever; but as one or two people on whose judgment I rely have advised me to print my narrative with all the personal details, rather than in the dry shape in which, as a psychological statement, I shall publish it elsewhere, I have yielded to their views. I suspect, however, that the very character of my record will, in the eyes of some of my readers, tend to lessen the value of the metaphysical discoveries which it sets forth.

I am the son of a physician, still in large practice in the village of Ab— and 1860 attended lectures at the Jefferson Medical College in Philadelphia. My second course should have been in the following year, but the outbreak of the Rebellion so crippled my father's means that I was forced to abandon my intention. The demand for army surgeons at this time became very great; and although not a graduate, I found no difficulty in getting the place of Assistant-Surgeon to the Tenth Indiana Volunteers. In the subsequent Western campaigns this organization suffered so severely, that, before the term of its service was over, it was merged in the Twenty-First Indiana Volunteers; and I, as an extra surgeon, ranked by the medical officers of the latter regiment, was transferred to the Fifteenth Indiana Cavalry. Like many physicians, I had contracted a strong taste for army life, and, disliking cavalry service, sought and obtained the position of First-Lieutenant in the Seventy-Ninth Indiana Volunteers, — an infantry regiment of

A fictional story appeared in the *Atlantic Monthly* in 1866. The story concerned a Union army doctor who had had all four limbs amputated during the War. The author, not indicated in the magazine, was Silas Weir Mitchell.

the rest of their lives missing a limb. Throughout 1866 every issue of every medical journal carried advertisements for wooden legs.

In addition to the many thousands of amputees, other former soldiers had to learn to adapt to their war wounds. For many soldiers, such as Schively and Bieswanger, the pain of their wounds never left. For others, their wounds never completely healed; pus accumulated and drained at intervals; bone spicules made their way to the skin and the sufferers picked them out.

James C. Strong of the 38th New York had been wounded in the hip during the early phases of the Peninsula Campaign. In 1869 he was visiting in Washington, staying at the Willard Hotel, when he slipped and fell in a dark corridor. A doctor visiting the hotel examined him; the doctor turned out to be George Otis, still in the service of the U.S. Army. Otis recognized Strong as suffering from an unusual wound, one that had fractured the junction of the femur and the pelvic bone. Upon examination, the doctor noted that Strong's right leg was five inches shorter than his left. The right thigh had shrunk from loss of muscle tissue, being six inches smaller in circumference than the left thigh. The area of the fracture was fused, so that he was unable to bend his right leg at the hip. Dr. Otis thought that Strong was doing rather well and had adapted to his disability; he was receiving a small pension from the government. He arranged for a photograph and a drawing of Strong.

In 1877 Strong petitioned the government for an increase in his disability payment. He reported that as he got older, the weakness seemed greater; he even described an apparent associated weakness of the right arm. His petition for an increase in disability payment was denied.[8]

Private Milton E. Wallen had undergone an amputation of the arm while in a Confederate prison. While in the Naval School Hospital in Annapolis, he developed gangrene. His pitiful condition was illustrated by Hospital Steward Stauch. Wallen had failed to return from medical leave and was listed as a deserter. In 1873 former private Wallen, now 53, wrote from his home in Kentucky. He had survived the bout with hospital gangrene and was now asking for a pension. He enclosed two affidavits from former soldiers of his old unit, the 1st Kentucky Cavalry (Union). He was awarded his pension.

On the first day at Gettysburg, a minié ball slammed into the right thigh of Private T. W. Pease and fractured his femur. While still in Gettysburg hospitals, the patient underwent three operations: the first removed the minié ball (or so it was thought), the second removed bone spicules, and the third drained an abscess of the thigh. The young soldier was still at Camp Letterman at the time of President Lincoln's visit and he heard the Gettysburg Address. Pus discharge continued, requiring a fourth operation before his army discharge on 8 August 1864.

James C. Strong as he looked in 1869. He had been injured in the early phase of the Peninsula Campaign in 1862. MSH

J. Bien lith.

Private Pease returned to his home in Indianapolis, but pus continued to leak from three different sites in his thigh. Episodically he experienced generalized cellulitis of the upper leg with redness, swelling, and fever. In 1868 a civilian doctor performed another abscess drainage procedure. On 8 November 1871 Dr. J. K. Bigelow performed a sixth operation, removing under general anesthesia several more inches of the necrosed femur. Following this operation, measurement showed that the right leg was ten inches shorter than the left. A seventh operation was undertaken in September 1877; more diseased bone was removed; the tissue removed had parts of a minié ball embedded in it. The first operation, performed on 5 July 1864, some thirteen years earlier, had not removed the entire ball. Following this final operation, the patient was able to walk with a six–inch lift applied to his right boot. He obtained a position in Indianapolis as a Deputy United States Marshall.[9]

On 11 September 1865 Dorothea Dix received a brief note, telling her that the Women's Nursing Bureau was abolished and that all nurses were discharged. The women who had been matrons and nurses returned home, but few of them established any professional relationships to hospitals or medicine again. Mother Bickerdyke wound up running a boardinghouse in Salina, Kansas. Most of the upper-class women returned to their families and their prewar lives. Georgeanna Woolsey, who had fed the wounded soldiers while they waited for the train at Gettysburg, and her sisters helped establish a nursing school for women in New York.[10]

Mary Safford and Vesta Swarts had been nurses during the War. They were so stimulated by their wartime experiences that they attended medical school and became physicians. Safford was for many years on the faculty of Boston University School of Medicine. Swarts opened a general practice in Auburn, Indiana, and was still practicing in 1897 when she was asked to summarize her Civil War nursing experience. "The war for the preservation of our Union evidently did much to advance the best interests of women," concluded Dr. Swarts. "It created a necessity for her labor in new and untried ways. It gave her an opportunity to prove her ability, and also to cultivate that true courage without which the

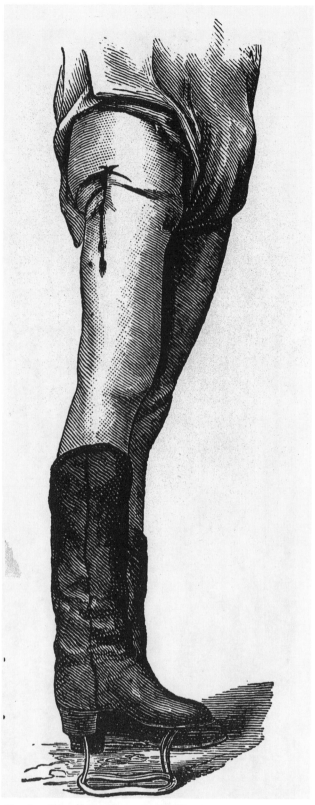

The leg lift of Deputy Marshall T. W. Pease, 1877. He had been wounded the first day at Gettysburg and had undergone several operations since. MSH

Vesta Swarts was stimulated to become a physician by her nursing experiences during the War. Holland

most capable person may utterly fail of success."[11]

The volunteer doctors went home. Some were exhausted by the War and died at a young age. Andrew J. Foard, the medical director of the Army of Tennessee, died of tuberculosis in 1868 at age forty-three. Jonathan Letterman, medical director of the Army of the Potomac, had gone to California as a railroad executive; he returned to medicine when he was elected coroner of San Francisco. But he became depressed after the death of his young wife, whom he had met after the Battle of Antietam; he died in 1870 at age forty-six. Lafayette Guild, medical director of the Army of Northern Virginia, found that he was too exhausted to practice medicine. He moved to California for his health and died there in 1870 at age forty-five. His body was shipped back to Tuscaloosa for burial.

Other physicians developed thriving practices and became leaders of American academic medicine: John H. Brinton, Samuel Stout, Silas Weir Mitchell, Joseph Jones, William Hammond, John Julian Chisolm, and Hunter Holmes McGuire among them. William W. Keen became the first American neurosurgeon.[12] Daniel B. Conrad, former fleet surgeon of the Confederate States Navy, captured aboard the C.S.S. *Tennessee* in Mobile Bay, served for many years as the superintendent of the Virginia state mental hospital. James B. McCaw returned to the faculty of the Medical College of Virginia, later becoming its dean. His son, Walter Drew McCaw, became a

doctor; he was the senior surgeon of the American Expeditionary Force in France at the end of World War I. Simon Baruch, captured at both Antietam and Gettysburg, became a hydropathic physician after the War; many years later his son Bernard presented the Baruch Plan for the control of atomic weapons.

Many of the regular army physicians went on to important careers in military medicine. J. J. Woodward performed the autopsy on John Wilkes Booth. He spent many years in service with the Surgeon's General Office, supervising the medical portion of the huge compendium, *The Medical and Surgical History of the War of the Rebellion.* George Otis wrote most of the surgical portion. John Shaw Billings expanded the library of the Surgeon General's Office into a major repository of medical knowledge and developed the international medical bibliography known as the *Index Medicus.* Surgeon General Joseph K. Barnes was in charge of the unsuccessful effort to save Presi-

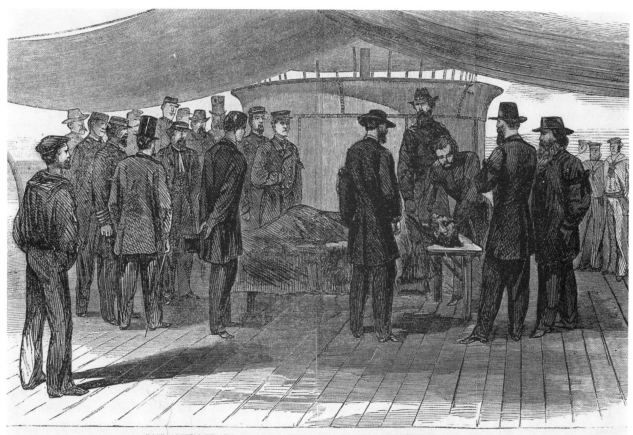

POST-MORTEM EXAMINATION OF BOOTH'S BODY ON BOARD THE MONITOR "MONTAUK."

J. J. Woodward performed the autopsy on the assassin John Wilkes Booth. HW

After the War, Union army doctor Mary Walker posed for a photograph while wearing her Medal of Honor. She was awarded the medal after being taken prisoner by Confederates while attending civilians near Chattanooga. A reevaluation of Medal of Honor recipients in 1917 withdrew the medal from persons who had not received it for heroism during combat. Dr. Walker, who was still living, refused to relinquish her medal. NA

dent James A. Garfield after his wounding by an assassin. Barnes remained the surgeon general until just a year before his death, when he was succeeded by Charles H. Crane. J. J. Woodward also helped treat Garfield, but then fell into a terrible depression. Prolonged sick leave allowed inpatient therapy at spas in Switzerland and Pennsylvania. In 1884 he committed suicide.

The leaders of the Confederate Surgeon General's Office entered civilian life. David C. DeLeon left the newly reunited nation with other former Confederates, trying to make a new life in Mexico. He later practiced medicine in New Mexico Territory but never again returned to his native South Carolina. Samuel Preston Moore retired in Richmond. He refused to discuss the War years, saying that he looked to the future, not the past. He was on the Richmond Board of Education and arranged for the testing of the eyesight of all school children.

Edwin S. Gaillard had been the inspector of Confederate hospitals. His career as a promising surgeon had been cut short, as had his arm. With his surgical career destroyed by a minié ball, Edwin S. Gaillard attempted to start a medical practice in postwar Richmond. He became editor of the *Richmond Medical Journal*. As he surveyed the effects of the War, he analyzed how the struggle had changed American medicine and surgery. He tried to define the medical and surgical lessons of the War.

Dangerous surgical operations were successfully performed by army surgeons of the North and the South. Trephination and disarticulation of the leg at the hip had both been performed by French and by British surgeons during the Crimean War, but the operations resulted in death every time. As a result, European medical authorities had concluded that these two procedures were impossible and should never be attempted. During the American Civil War, however, surgeons of both the Union and Confederate armies successfully completed these operations. While many of the unfortunate soldiers who underwent these dangerous procedures died, a significant number survived. Gaillard concluded that the Civil War had taught that both of these operations, contrary to the European experience, were possible. The War had raised surgical skill.

According to Gaillard, the most important medical discovery of the War was the unequivocal demonstration that quinine prevented malaria. Contrary to many opinions expressed during the War, most notably by Surgeon General Moore, experience had proven beyond doubt that quinine taken daily prevented the appearance of malaria. A second medical lesson concerned self-limited diseases. Certain diseases, such as measles, proceeded along a natural course regardless of intervention. The best treatment was simple supportive care; all heroic measures really only made the symptoms worse. The use of the lancet to induce bleeding was of no value in measles or, according to Gaillard, in any other disease.[13]

Gaillard thought that the epidemiological experiences of the War had shown much about the spread and prevention of yellow fever. Every epidemic in the United States began in a port city, transferred by ship from points further south. The Federal experience in New Orleans had shown, unequivocally according to Gaillard, that strict quarantine could prevent yellow fever.

With the press of commerce, however, quarantine regulations were relaxed. The most devastating epidemic of yellow fever in U.S. history spread up the Mississippi Valley in 1878. Among its victims was former Confederate John Bell Hood. He lost a leg at Chickamauga and the use of an arm at Gettysburg, but he lost his life to the failure of public health authorities to retain the War lesson of yellow fever. Yellow fever continued to be a public health problem in the American South until its cause and epidemiology were worked out early in the twentieth century.[14]

The great hospitals of the Civil War came down. Most of the wooden pavilion buildings were deteriorating even before the War was over. The churches resumed their role as places of worship; some still stand today. Still in use is the church in Fairfield, Pennsylvania, where Imboden deposited some of his wounded during the horrible retreat from Gettysburg. The warehouses again became places of storage; nearly all have seen the wrecking ball. Many historically minded people have worked very hard to save the structures that had housed the sick and the wounded. This opinion is not universal, however; some modern Americans think that the Civil War hospital is "no more than a romanti-

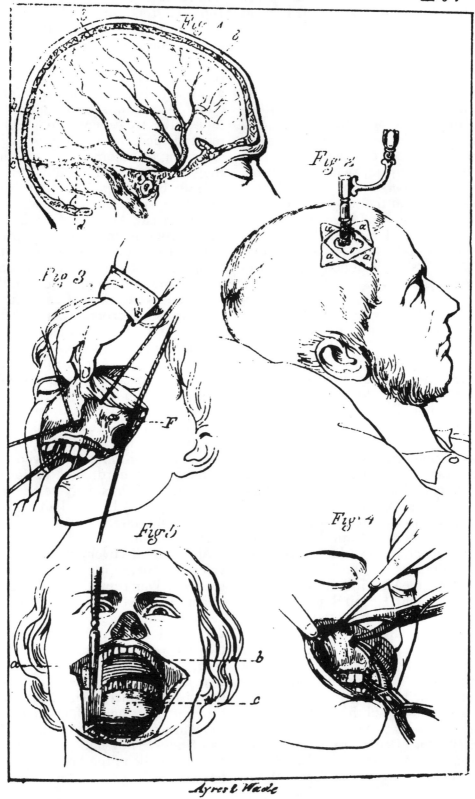

Ayres & Wade

Trephination, as pictured in the Confederate *Manual of Military Surgery*. This opera-tion was not always fatal during the American Civil War, as it had been during the Crimean War.

cized and dated war zone, a useless place where the stupidity of military violence was unleashed" and should be commemorated by a historical marker and replaced by a shopping mall.[15]

The Carnton House, where so much bloody surgery occurred after the Battle of Franklin, fell on hard times. In the 1970s a local historical group acquired the structure and undertook to restore it. They noted that a brown stain disfigured the floor of one of the rooms; this was the room, in fact, where tradition, handed down from person to person in the neighborhood, said that the surgery had taken place. Because the home had been occupied by many renters, the local historical group assumed the brown stain was spilled paint or shellac; they sent a sample of flooring for professional chemical analysis. The result came back: human blood. The stain is easily appreciated by anyone standing in the room today. If you are very quiet, you may still hear the echo of the surgeon's cry: "Next!"

Some hospitals turned into Old Soldiers' Homes. In 1930 the U.S. Congress formed the Veterans Administration to consolidate the complex series of soldiers' homes and hospitals for veterans. The motto of the V.A., as it was known, was taken from President Lincoln's Second Inaugural Address: "to serve him who has borne the battle." The V.A. medical system changed functions over the years, from providing care for the aged soldier to treating every form of acute and chronic illness. In 1991 the Veterans Administration became a cabinet-level agency, the Department of Veterans Affairs.

In July 1953 Walter W. Williams applied for treatment at the V.A. Hospital in Houston. Asked if he were a veteran of the American armed forces, he proudly identified himself as a former member of the 5th Texas Cavalry Regiment, Hood's Texas Brigade, Army of Northern Virginia. V.A. administrators informed him that their agency only served veterans of the armed forces of the United States; he was a veteran of the armed forces of another country, the Confederate States of America. At last, officials of the United States government recognized the existence of the

Confederate nation. If this had happened in 1861, all this gore and misery would never have occurred (but, on the other hand, the map of the North American continent would resemble Europe). After realizing the public relations debacle that would follow turning away a 110-year-old former Confederate soldier, V.A. administrators permitted Williams to receive treatment. Apparently the treatment helped; he lived another seven years, surviving to become the last living veteran of the War between the States.[16]

Physicians helped heal the wounds of national division. During its wartime meetings, the American Medical Association had listed in its program the missing representatives of the Southern states as though they were only temporarily absent. And so it proved; they returned and presented papers on their wartime experiences. A point of contention for the returning Southerners was the failure of the American Medical Association to take up Augustus Gardner's motion on the evil of holding medical supplies as contraband of war. In subsequent years several former Confederate doctors served the American Medical Association as its president; these included Henry F. Campbell, in charge of the Georgia division of the Winder Hospital, Hunter Holmes McGuire, Jackson's physician who arranged the Winchester Accord, A. Y. P. Garnett, personal physician to President Jefferson Davis, and David W. Yandell, who had arrived just a few minutes too late to save Albert Sydney Johnston at Shiloh.[17]

After the discovery of bacteria and the development of aseptic surgery, the physicians of the Civil War reinterpreted their experiences during the last great struggle without bacteriologic knowledge. In their memoirs, they vacillated from ironic humor at how they had treated wounds to unmitigated horror at the results. The Confederate physicians thought that they had done the best they could under the circumstances. The Northern physicians thought that their efforts had helped to win the War and maintain the Union of the American States. They had served what Silas Weir Mitchell called "the greatest cause the Earth has known."[18]

22

The American Civil War as a Biological Phenomenon

THIS WORK HAS EXAMINED THE EVENTS OF THE American Civil War from several different positions. We experienced the Battle of Gettysburg through the eyes of the wounded soldier. We studied the Vicksburg campaign from the so-called objective point of view. While appreciating the growth and improvement of medical care in the Union army, we saw the War through Northern eyes; the states in rebellion against the lawful government were the enemy. We alternated this with the view from the Confederate Surgeon General's Office in Richmond; the brutal Yankee invader was, in the words of Simon Baruch, "a drunken and infuriated foe."[1]

While great armies clashed on the North American continent, Louis Pasteur in France was developing the idea that disease could be caused by a living being so small that it was invisible. This chapter views the American Civil War from the viewpoint of that living infectious agent. For this invisible organism, the huge Civil War armies represented an opportunity for expansion, a gigantic petri dish.

DIARRHEA

Diarrhea was the soldier's companion during the Civil War. Diarrhea is not a specific disorder but a symptom of many diseases. Fecal contamination of the food and water supply was responsible for this syndrome in the vast majority of soldiers. Infectious agents that produced diarrhea during the Civil War included viruses, parasites, such as *Giardia* and *Entamoeba*, and bacteria, such as *Shigella*,

Salmonella, Campylobacter, and *E. coli*. These organisms developed in the gastrointestinal tract of one person and were discharged onto the ground, possibly in a latrine, but perhaps anywhere. They made their way into food or water and were ingested by other individuals. In the gastrointestinal tracts of these other people, the organisms multiplied. Acute diarrhea occurred. If the organism survived in the colon, the diarrhea became chronic. The fluid loss of chronic diarrhea led to dehydration, fatigue, and debilitation. The salivation produced by calomel worsened this dehydration.[2] Diarrhea occurred in civilian life, of course, but the congregation of large numbers of men increased the opportunity for infectious agents to disperse and multiply.

Outbreaks of diarrhea were also caused by food poisoning. Cooks fed soup or broth to the troops for lunch, then allowed the remaining food to sit until supper. This broth was a perfect medium for the multiplication of bacteria and parasites. The biological effect of bringing many hundreds of thousands of men together is an analogy to the warm broth: an opportunity for infectious agents to pass from one gastrointestinal tract to many, to multiply, and to flourish.

TYPHOID FEVER

The bacterium *Salmonella typhi* entered the soldier through contaminated food and water. It fastened to the lining of the gastrointestinal tract, producing diarrhea. In many soldiers, the disease ended with the expulsion of the bacteria. For some unfortunate patients, however, the salmonella organism entered the blood stream, producing a systemic illness characterized by chronic fever and pulmonary symptoms. This was typhoid fever.

In its early phase, typhoid fever is difficult to diagnose. The fever is chronic and was therefore called continuous fever by Civil War physicians, as opposed to the periodic paroxysmal rises of body temperature characteristic of malaria. Many patients develop a rash of rose spots and diagnosis becomes easy. It is likely that many milder cases of typhoid fever went undiagnosed during the Civil War. Patients with a severe infection developed fulminant pulmonary dysfunction progressing to cardiovascular collapse. About one in four Civil War soldiers who received the diagnosis of typhoid fever died.

TYPHUS

Epidemic typhus fever is caused by a rickettsial organism. The disorder can be hard to differentiate from typhoid fever; they were clinically separated only a few decades before the Civil War.[3] Very few cases of typhus occurred during the Civil War; most soldiers diagnosed with this condition probably really suffered from typhoid fever.

Typhus occurs only in certain populations because the causative organism spreads from person to person via body lice. There is no doubt that some Civil War soldiers had body lice. One sergeant described the clothes discarded by some of his troops: "they swarm with vermin like a live ant hill."[4] However, most soldiers bathed frequently in streams, at least during the summer. The Letterman system called for cleanliness: "The men should be required to wear their hair cut short, bathe twice a week, and put on clean underclothing."[5] The proportion of the soldiers in any one regiment who had body lice was not great enough to permit the spread of the typhus organism.

Typhus may have occurred among prisoners crowded into filthy stockades. Many contemporaries thought that typhus caused an outbreak of fever at the Confederate prison in Salisbury, North Carolina.

The distress aboard the captured slave ship described in the prologue may have represented typhus. African captives were chained in the hold of the ship for a prolonged period before its capture; they remained there as the ship was taken from the mouth of the Congo to Liberia, where a diminished number were freed. Body lice may have spread from the captives crowded into the ship's hold to the ship's company. The terrifying epidemic killed a large number of Africans, perhaps up to 130, as well as three crewmen. The remainder of the crew were so ill that the ship was in danger of foundering.

Although epidemic typhus swept through several European armies in the nineteenth century, it did not significantly affect either the Union or the Confederate army during the American Civil War.

MALARIA

Malaria is caused by a protozoa of the genus *Plasmodium*. This organism grows in the human body, in the liver and in the red blood cells. When the red cells are engorged by the multiplying parasites they burst. The organisms in the blood stream produce a fit of shaking chills. Different subtypes of the *Plasmodium* grow at different rates, so that some patients experience chills at varying times. It is thought that most of the malaria of the Civil War was caused by the subtype *Plasmodium vivax*. The disease debilitated but seldom killed, unlike malaria today, caused by the more virulent subtype, *Plasmodium falciparum*. Most malaria today is resistant to quinine.

Civil War era physicians tried to diagnose subtypes of malaria by the frequency of shaking chills. Quotidian, tertian, and quartan fevers were all separate diagnoses in the Farr system, but were recognized then and now as subtypes of malaria. When the shaking chills came intermittently, but not in a clear pattern, the physician diagnosed simple intermittent fever or remittent fever. Remittent fever may have included a few patients with other types of infection, but most patients with this diagnosis had malaria; we know this because remittent fever had the same seasonal and regional variations as malaria and because it responded to quinine. If the malaria was associated with pulmonary symptoms, a few physicians made another diagnosis: congestive

HARPER'S WEEKLY.

A JOURNAL OF CIVILIZATION.

VOL. VI.—No. 292.] NEW YORK, SATURDAY, AUGUST 2, 1862. [SINGLE COPIES SIX CENTS.
[$2.50 PER YEAR IN ADVANCE.

Entered according to Act of Congress, in the Year 1862, by Harper & Brothers, in the Clerk's Office of the District Court for the Southern District of New York.

CUTTING THE CANAL OPPOSITE VICKSBURG.—Sketched by Mr. Theodore R. Davis.—[See Next Page.]

Thousands of workers dig a canal near Vicksburg. The construction activities attendant to Civil War garrisons and campaigns led to stagnant water and an increased population of mosquitoes. HW

A photograph of soldiers swimming in a creek has biological significance. Soldiers of the American Civil War, unlike contemporary European soldiers, were not afflicted with a severe load of body lice. Thus, typhus, carried from person to person by lice, was not a problem for Civil War armies. Miller

intermittent fever. It does not seem likely that Civil War surgeons, as a group, could reliably differentiate malaria subtypes by clinical criteria; all the statistical material in this work sums all these subtypes into one diagnosis.[6]

Malaria is carried from an infected person to a healthy one by the mosquito. In the United States, mosquitoes disappear at the first frost, ending the "sickly season." No additional humans are infected. In the spring, the cycle starts again. Throughout the summer and fall, more and more humans are afflicted and a greater proportion of mosquitoes carry the parasite.

There are occasions in history when physical changes in the environment produced stagnant water, leading to an increased mosquito burden, leading in turn to a worsened problem of malaria. Erwin H. Ackerknecht hypothesizes that early settlement in the upper Mississippi Valley changed drainage patterns, producing more stagnant water and more mosquitoes; this led to a serious problem with malaria. The disease declined after more mature settlement patterns decreased the amount of standing water.[7] Mark Boyd identifies the completion of the Erie Canal and the switch from plantation agriculture to small farms in the Reconstruction South as two examples of the relationship between the physical environment and malaria.[8]

The Civil War involved the construction of a huge number of earthworks. The military science of the era devoted a great deal of intellectual energy to the proper construction of fortifications; no effort, however, was made to control drainage. In the Vicksburg region in late 1862 and early 1863 many thousands of workers dug canals. The increased standing water with these construction projects produced more mosquitoes. From the point of view of the malarial parasite, the Civil War was a period to multiply and to prosper.

YELLOW FEVER

Yellow fever is caused by a virus that, like the malarial parasite, is carried from person to person by mosquitoes. Unlike malaria, which remains endemic within the United States over the winter, the yellow fever virus must be imported from regions where mosquitoes live the year around.

During the Civil War, ships with feverish sailors were kept at a quarantine station. Lafayette Guild, the Confederate medical director of the Army of Northern Virginia, had experience with yellow fever before the War when he was the U.S. Army physician in New York harbor. He found that the disease could spread from the quarantine station to military posts and civilian establishments on the shore. Guild drew the conclusion that "morbific elements of the disease" were carried by the wind from ships at the quarantine station to the shore. These morbific elements were, unknown to Guild, mosquitoes.

Dr. Thomas T. Smiley's analysis of the Hilton Head epidemic was quite accurate. The soldiers aboard the U.S.S. *Delaware* were sick with yellow fever. Mosquitos carried the virus ashore and bit many people who lived and worked around the dock. There was a period of twenty-two days when no new cases occurred. Yellow fever had disappeared from those aboard the *Delaware;* they had either died or recovered. The virus was multiplying within unsuspecting soldiers, but was causing no symptoms. When the terrifying epidemic broke out among troops ashore, mosquitoes carried the virus so that it spread from person to person until the first frost. Smiley described the epidemiology of the Hilton Head yellow fever quite accurately, and he attributed the epidemic to building Union Square upon a swamp. But he never entertained the idea that the disease was carried from person to person by the ubiquitous mosquitoes.[9]

MENINGITIS

Spinal meningitis was diagnosed in many locations throughout the United States during the Civil War years. It afflicted civilians as well as military people. From the findings of postmortem examinations and the clear descriptions of the clinical presentation, including petechiae, there seems little doubt that these epidemics were caused by the organism *Neisseria meningitidis*, the meningococcus.[10]

A significant proportion of the general population harbors the meningococcus in the back of the throat. These individuals have immunity to the particular subtype of the organism that they carry. When a large group of people gather together, they share these organisms through their breath. When one subtype of this bacterium spreads to individuals without immunity to that specific subtype, the organism may enter the body and produce a fulminant infection.[11] Before the development of specific treatment, antisera and antibiotics, this affliction was almost always fatal. Today, the disease can be cured with antibiotics if they are given early enough. Even in the Vietnam era, recruits suffered outbreaks of meningococcal meningitis that came on so rapidly that fatalities occurred. Today, military recruits are immunized against most subtypes of the *Neisseria meningitidis*.[12] The Civil War physician was helpless against the meningococcus.

SMALLPOX

Before the twentieth century, smallpox virus spread from person to person via the breath. This disease has been eradicated, probably the greatest public health accomplishment in world history. During the Civil War era, medical and lay people knew that smallpox could be prevented by vaccination. Many soldiers were not vaccinated, however, and some who thought they were had received poorly prepared vaccine. Smallpox epidemics were frightening because no one could be absolutely certain that his vaccination against the disease had been done properly. Smallpox and chickenpox are hard to differentiate in the acutely ill person; it is possible that some smallpox scares during the Civil War were really due to chickenpox. Nevertheless, smallpox did occur and many soldiers died from this frightening illness.

An abnormal reaction of vaccine material occurred among some soldiers in the Confederate army. This may have been related to poor nutrition, but in most cases the vaccine material was probably contaminated by bacteria. One may note how the Confederacy reacted to the smallpox scare of late 1862. The medical authorities were slow to vaccinate and the troops took matters into their own hands. Unfortunately, some strains of the vaccine that they passed from person to person were adulterated. The lesson is that medical activity will occur even when medical personnel do nothing.

MEASLES

The occurrence of measles epidemics during the American Civil War tells us something about nineteenth-century America. Many people in rural America were immunologically isolated and, it may be presumed, isolated in other ways also. Black slaves were more isolated than white farmers, but both groups of people did not reach the mass needed for the ready transfer of measles virus.

Massive epidemics of measles afflicted the Union and Confederate armies as they were formed in summer 1861. A second major epidemic occurred in the Union army among the new black troops recruited throughout late 1863 and early 1864. Minor peaks in measles incidence occurred whenever new levies of troops entered military service.

While the full statistics from the Confederate army are not extant, the evaluation of admissions to one hospital identifies the nature of the Southern experience with measles. During the four years of its existence, a total of 1,137 soldiers were admitted to the Confederate States Army Hospital in Charlottesville, Virginia, because of measles. Of this total, 927 soldiers, or 82 percent, were admitted in the first three months of the war. Secondary peaks of measles cases followed the passage of Confederate conscription laws. The first call in April 1862 drafted all men aged eighteen to thirty-five (with significant exemptions). From April to June an increased number of soldiers were admitted to the Charlottesville Hospital. The final draft issued by the Confederate Con-

gress in February 1864 called for all men aged seventeen to fifty. A peak in measles incidence occurred during April through June 1864. These drafts either conscripted young men or induced them to enlist; they came out of their immunological isolation and went into training camp. Whenever measles virus was introduced, all the recruits who had never had measles came down with the disease simultaneously.

A regiment with a significant percentage of its soldiers sick with measles was not fit for military service. Robert E. Lee was stunned when recruits sent to reinforce the Army of Northern Virginia were afflicted by measles. "All the conscripts we have received are thus affected," he complained, "so that instead of being an advantage to us, they are an element of weakness, a burden. I think, therefore, that it would be better that the conscripts be assembled in camps of instruction so that they may pass through these inevitable diseases."[13]

The other childhood diseases, especially mumps but also chickenpox and diphtheria, were similar to measles in their epidemiology during the Civil War. A significant advance of medical thought early in the War was the appreciation by J. J. Woodward and Roberts Bartholow that these diseases occur only once in each individual. Heroic treatment with calomel and other toxic agents was not necessary to restore the patients to health. "Many cases of measles," said Bartholow, "if left to themselves, terminate favorably by the unassisted efforts of nature." But at the Nashville hospital where he was stationed, 42 of 209 measles patients died, perhaps due to excessive treatment.[14]

The Civil War was a time when great numbers of young men moved from isolated farms to the wider world in order to serve the national interest. The viruses of mumps, measles, and chickenpox multiplied in many thousands of people who might otherwise have remained immunologically isolated throughout their lives.[15]

WOUND INFECTION

Wounds during the Civil War always became infected. White pus formed and drained; this was the so-called laudable pus. Sometimes wounds became red and swollen. Civil

Table 28

Confederate Army Hospital, Charlottesville, Virginia

Date	Total admissions	Total deaths	Patients with: gunshot wounds	measles	diarrhea/ dysentery
1861:					
July	2608	147	300	656	178
August	329	87	6	116	16
September	571	32	9	104	43
October	556	33	15	51	31
November	448	31	0	22	31
December	329	12	7	7	19
1862:					
January	226	21	2	0	18
February	300	6	1	1	66
March	290	9	2	1	56
April	539	44	3	48	61
May	429	67	16	20	67
June	754	53	266	14	95
July	337	26	41	0	73
August	682	35	380	0	45
September	886	23	764	1	9
October	340	11	56	1	12
November	916	32	46	8	54
December	993	54	158	2	45
1863:					
January	601	41	42	1	42
February	312	26	24	2	35
March	198	17	31	0	27
April	124	14	14	0	21
May	572	11	66	1	115
June	417	8	77	2	100
July	821	7	444	0	49
August	449	11	93	2	51
September	271	10	47	0	67
October	397	7	176	0	34
November	301	10	68	0	44
December	469	27	84	3	72
1864:					
January	401	35	60	9	46
February	145	9	50	5	5
March	249	6	75	3	5
April	481	11	91	12	67
May	1152	68	738	7	51
June	1344	50	479	27	323
July	missing				
August	missing				
September	missing				
October	490	13	310	2	31
November	321	7	168	5	27
December	267	9	76	3	27
1865:					
January	148	1	57	0	12
February	137	2	69	1	2
March	missing				
April	taken over by Federal authorities				

Source: "Register of Patients, General Hospital, Charlottesville, Virginia," National Archives, group 109, chapter 6, volumes 214-16.

War physicians called this condition erysipelas. After the development of bacteriology, the term erysipelas took on a more specific meaning, an infection by streptococcus. Cellulitis would probably be diagnosed by a modern physician for the condition that the Civil War doctor called erysipelas.[16] This redness and swelling was due to bacterial growth. Natural human defenses could still overcome the infection and the wound could heal. Sometimes, however, the causative organism entered the blood stream. The sufferer became febrile and underwent circulatory collapse. This was called pyemia during the Civil War, meaning pus in the blood. The disorder was virtually always fatal.

Some wounds became complicated by a new type of infection called hospital gangrene. Tissue died and became black. This often occurred in specific hospitals, hence the term hospital gangrene. No modern physician fully understands what this horrible form of gangrene was. In the 1940s Frank Meleney hypothesized that two different organisms began growing in the same wound in symbiosis. These two were most likely some form of staphylococcus and some form of clostridia. They do not naturally grow together, but when they both colonized one wound, they were carried together from wound to wound. More recently, Alfred Jay Bollet has postulated a relationship between the unknown organism that caused hospital gangrene with the "new" strain of streptococcus that produces tissue necrosis, dubbed by the press "flesh-eating bacteria." In any event, the causative organisms were carried from one wound to the next. The element of contamination may have been the doctor's hands, as he dressed one wound after another, or the sponge, used to clean all wounds with only a rinsing between them.[17]

When the causative agent became established in a hospital, this horrible disease became rampant. A patient treated by Paul F. Eve demonstrates the relationship between hospital gangrene and the War. The noted Nashville surgeon had removed a bladder stone from a young man in 1849. When it recurred in 1855, he removed it again. When the stone recurred yet again in April 1863, the man searched out Dr. Eve, who was now a Confederate surgeon in charge of Gate City Hospital in Atlanta. The civilian was a patient in the military hospital, where he underwent a third successful bladder stone removal. Unfortunately he had, before admission, suffered a small injury to his wrist, a wound so slight that it had not been noticed before the operation. The civilian developed erysipelas at the site of the wrist wound, and this progressed to hospital gangrene. To prevent the spread of gangrene, Dr. Eve amputated the arm, but the gangrene recurred in the stump. This terrible course of events only ended with the civilian's death. He had survived two operations at his home in Nashville, but could not survive the unhealthy environment of a Confederate hospital.[18]

DIETARY DISEASES

The diets of many subgroups of citizens during the nineteenth century was marginal. The Commissary Department of both armies had difficulty bringing fresh vegetables to troops. A few cases of scurvy resulted from this diet deficient in vitamin C. For every patient diagnosed with scurvy, there existed many cases, hundreds or even thousands, of mild or subclinical vitamin C deficiency. Not severe enough to produce bleeding, and thereby to lead to the diagnosis of scurvy, the subclinical affliction produced lassitude and malaise. Many historians have been amazed at the stamina of the average Civil War soldier; the widespread occurrence of subclinical scurvy makes this stamina even more amazing.[19]

Another dietary deficiency that probably occurred during the Civil War was nutritional night blindness. This problem, due to vitamin A deficiency, especially afflicted Southern armies. Comparison of Northern and Southern versions of some night skirmishes shows that the Southerners considered the night to be pitch black, while the Northerners could see by the moon and the stars.[20]

Pellagra is a severe nutritional disorder caused by a dietary deficiency of niacin, a vitamin present in most foods, but not in corn. This nutritional deficiency appeared in Europe during this period but American physicians did not diagnose this condition in Civil War armies. Confederate physicians who survived to the turn of the century, when medical science realized that pellagra was common in the South, thought in retrospect that this disorder had occurred during the Civil War, especially among Yankee prisoners whose only sustenance was corn.[21]

SUMMARY

From the point of view of infectious organisms, the American Civil War was a gigantic culture broth. They multiplied and prospered because contemporary medical knowledge was completely ignorant of their existence. At the exact moment that infectious organisms were growing in the gastrointestinal tracts, the blood streams, and the wounds of many thousands of American soldiers, European scientists and doctors were coming to grips with the role of bacteria in infection. If the Civil War had occurred in the early 1870s instead of the early 1860s, the medical effort that went into ventilation would have been more rationally directed to prevent bacterial spread. The loss of human life would have been much less.[22]

23

Comparing Northern to Southern Medical Care

THE PREVIOUS CHAPTER REVIEWED THE BIOLOGI-cal changes produced by the American Civil War. This chapter analyzes the human efforts to counter these biological effects and evaluates the overall effectiveness of the medical departments of the Union and the Confederate armies.

A major function of the medical department involved the treatment of those soldiers wounded on the battlefield. Many soldiers bled to death before they could be evacuated; they never came under the control of the medical department and were classified as killed in battle. A few wounded patients died of hemorrhage days to weeks after wounding; their infected wounds slowly ate away surrounding tissue, including blood vessels. The majority of individuals who died from wounds, however, did not perish because of bleeding, but developed a direct infectious complication. Erysipelas or hospital gangrene worsened until it became pyemia and the patient, febrile, delirious, and prostrate, died.

Civil War era physicians knew that something, some "morbific principle," could spread from one wound to another. It is amazing how close some of them came to the basic principles of bacteriology. For example, Edmund Andrews, a graduate of the University of Michigan, surgeon of the 1st Illinois Light Artillery, submitted an official report on hospital gangrene. He recommended that "no probes or other instruments which have been used in a case of this disease should ever be used on another patient, until they have been thoroughly cleaned by washing, and then dipped in boiling water." He further argued that no

doctor should use a sponge on two different wounds.[1] As related in chapter 12, the Union physicians at DeCamp General Hospital on David's Island in New York harbor were able to stop an epidemic of hospital gangrene by restricting the use of sponges, one for each patient.

In his surgical manual, John H. Packard included a chapter entitled "Disinfectants." He argued that certain diseases, such as gangrene and dysentery, travel from person to person by infective particles that he called fomites. Heat could stop this transmission; Packard recommended that clothing and bedding should be heated or boiled in water before reuse. Wound-to-wound transmission could be stopped by painting certain chemicals upon either wound.[2] During the War, several different chemicals were recommended to stop the progression of hospital gangrene; the surgeon of the 11th Iowa had great success with iodine.[3] Many people still place iodine on a fresh abrasion today.[4]

To intercept the fomite or morbific principle that traveled from a sick person to a healthy one, medical authorities devoted most of their energy to the concept of ventilation. They hoped that the agent that transmitted the infection would be blown out the window. This desire for good ventilation in hospitals became a medical fetish. Hammond's directive of 24 November 1862 required twelve hundred cubic feet of space per hospital bed.[5] The special committee on military hygiene of the American Medical Association calculated that a hospital ward with fifty patients needed 1.175 million cubic feet of air each twenty-four

Table 29

Wound Mortality, Union Army

War Year	Wounded	Died of Wounds	Mortality
First	17,498	4,479	25.6%
Second	57,395	8,773	15.3
Third	96,970	9,238	9.5
Fourth	57,122	10,201	17.0

Mortality is the number of wounded who died of wounds during the year divided by the total number wounded that year (case fatality ratio). In the first year of the War, one in four wounded Union soldiers died from his wound. By the third year this had dropped to one in ten.

Source: <u>Medical and Surgical History</u>, Medical Volume, pt. 1, pp. 146, 296, 452, 604, 664, and 684, tables 24, 47, 71, 95, 104, and 107.

hours.[6] If the effort to obtain good ventilation had gone into cleanliness, much death and disability would have been avoided. Mother Bickerdyke's cyclone of cleaning was worth more than all the official medical insistence on ventilation.

Important in lessening the severity of wound infection was the rapid removal of the wounded from the battlefield to provide the prompt dressing of a minor wound or the prompt amputation of a limb damaged beyond repair. The modern treatment of combat wounds involves antibiotics and fluid replacement unavailable to Civil War physicians; however, early surgical intervention remains as important for the modern treatment of combat injuries as it was during the Civil War.[7]

Hammond, Letterman, and other Union medical authorities made an immense effort to evacuate the wounded rapidly. After the full development of the Letterman system, the percentage of wounded soldiers who died from their wounds dropped. In the last year of the War, under the pressure of the immense slaughter from Grant's campaign in Virginia, a slight rise in wound mortality occurred. As one can calculate from the statistics in table 29, if the mortality rate of the first year had continued throughout the War, an additional 25,928 Union soldiers would have died.[8]

Saving the lives of those who have been wounded is important, but the dominant military function of a medical department involves the maintenance of the strength of the army's combat arm. How many of the wounded were able to return to duty? This figure cannot be calculated from the information available in the *Medical and Surgical History of the War of the Rebellion*. We know from anecdotal information that some soldiers returned to duty after convalescence. Corporal Edson Bemis was wounded at Antietam, but returned to duty. Wounded at the Wilderness, he again returned to duty. Only his final head wound ended his military contribution to the Army of the Potomac.

John D. Brinton reviewed the statistical material in the Surgeon General's Office in 1862 to discover that most wounded Union soldiers did *not* return rapidly to their field commands. At the time of his report only 24.1 percent of wounded soldiers had returned to full duty.[9] Some less severely wounded Union soldiers served the war effort as guards or clerks; they were formally registered in the Invalid Corps or the Veteran Reserve Corps.[10]

The treatment of combat wounds was dramatic for the Civil War physician and nurse, but more important to the course of the War was the effort to prevent infectious diseases. "It is a popular delusion that the highest duties of medical officers are performed in prescribing a drug or amputating a limb," said Jonathan Letterman. The true function of the medical authorities of the army, he went on, "is to strengthen the hands of the Commanding General by keeping his army in the most

BEFORE PETERSBURG—ISSUING RATIONS OF WHISKY AND QUININE.—[Sketched by A. W. Warren.]

Union soldiers line up to drink quinine dissolved in whiskey; in a malarious region every soldier was required to consume this beverage every day. HW

vigorous health, thus rendering it in the highest degree efficient for enduring fatigue and privation, and for fighting."[11]

Medical knowledge existed to help keep the army healthy. Smallpox could be prevented by vaccination. Diarrhea could be lessened by proper handling of human waste. Malaria would not occur if all troops took enough quinine every day. Measles could not be prevented, but the effect of the disease on military function could be eliminated if troops were kept in training camps until everyone not previously exposed had experienced and recovered from the disease.

The Civil War physician could have no effect on the course of meningococcal meningitis or yellow fever. However, in one important instance a yellow fever epidemic was prevented. General Benjamin Butler, the commanding officer of the Union forces occupying New Orleans, undertook a two-pronged attack to prevent yellow fever from afflicting that important city. Both elements of his plan, quarantine and cleanup, were important. The quarantine prevented travelers from the Caribbean and Latin America who harbored the

yellow fever virus from entering the city. Drainage of puddles of dirty water associated with the cleansing of the city decreased the number of mosquitoes. We know the quarantine was not complete because several sailors with yellow fever were hospitalized in New Orleans during the War. But no mosquito carried the virus from these few sailors to the public. Yellow fever rampaged through New Orleans frequently in the 1850s; it would come back again after the War. The Union troops escaped an epidemic while the Southern rebellion was quelled.

The incidence of malaria may have been lessened in New Orleans during these years because of the cleanup. Nowhere else, however, did any action by individuals decrease the number of mosquitoes. In fact, as described in the previous chapter, the construction of fortifications and canals probably increased the mosquito burden. The appearance of malaria could be prevented, however, by quinine.[12]

In the Union army, the regimental physician, as urged by Hammond and other medical authorities, tried to force quinine down the throats of each and every soldier every day

This *Harper's Weekly* cartoon depicts President Lincoln greeting General Benjamin F. Butler after his cleanup of New Orleans. In the caption to the cartoon, Butler responds to the president: "Yes, Uncle Abe. Got through with that New Orleans Job. Cleaned them up and scrubbed them out. Any more scrubbing to give out?" Insofar as the cleanup involved draining of standing water, it lessened the number of mosquitoes in the city. This policy, combined with a quarantine, prevented a yellow fever epidemic from threatening the Federal occupation of New Orleans. HW

during malarial season. If the soldier was bitten by a mosquito carrying the malarial parasite, the parasite would be killed in the blood stream before it could multiply and cause symptoms. Of course, the effect of quinine upon malaria was a completely empirical ob-

Table 30

Deaths from Yellow Fever in New Orleans, 1852-1867

Year	Number of Deaths
1852	456
1853	8,400
1854	2,500
1855	2,670
1856	74
1857	199
1858	4,855
1859	92
1860	15
1861	0
1862	2
1863	2
1864	6
1865	1
1866	192
1867	3,320

The Butler clean-up and quarantine seemed to protect New Orleans from yellow fever. The quarantine was not completely successful, however, since two to six people died from yellow fever each year of the Federal occupation. Mosquitoes did not spread the infection from these few victims to the populace; perhaps drainage decreased the mosquito burden.

Source: Jo Ann Carrigan, The Saffron Scourge: A History of Yellow Fever in Louisana, 1796-1905 (Lafayette: University of Southwestern Louisana, 1994), 80, 95, 165.

servation; the underlying mechanism of quinine effectiveness was unknown.

How successful were the Northern medical authorities in forcing this bitter medicine upon the troops? The statistics of the overall health of the Union army reveal that malaria afflicted more soldiers as the War progressed. The incidence of malaria in the Union army rose from about 40 percent in the first year of the War to over 60 percent in the third and fourth years.[13] During the course of the War, a greater proportion of the Union army entered areas of the country where malaria was endemic, so one would expect some rise in malaria incidence. Union efforts to prevent malaria were not an unequivocal success; perhaps, however, it could have been worse.

The Confederate medical authorities were unable to use quinine as liberally as their Northern opponents. Unable to import enough quinine to give it prophylactically to all troops, they attempted to find a substitute indigenous to the Confederacy. Surgeon General Moore stated that because an adequate supply of medicines, particularly quinine, could not be imported, the medical officers should use such indigenous remedies "as may be found growing in proximity to every hospital and station."[14] Moore personally recommended the following cocktail as a substitute for quinine: dogwood bark, thirty parts, poplar bark, thirty parts, willow bark, forty parts; two pounds of dried bark to one gallon of whiskey, macerate fourteen days, then take one ounce three times a day.[15] Unfortunately, such local plants were probably of no benefit; we are unaware today of any plant material that grows anywhere in the United States that has any effect upon malaria.

Just as the symptoms of malaria could have been prevented by quinine prophylaxis, diarrhea and dysentery would have been much less of a problem if the Union army had maintained complete separation of human waste from the food and water supply. Medical science had no understanding of how contami-

Table 31

Malaria and Diarrhea, Union Army

War Year	Malaria Incidence	Mortality	Diarrhea Incidence	Mortality
First	40.4%	0.7%	77.0%	0.6%
Second	49.8	1.2	85.0	2.0
Third	62.2	1.1	66.4	2.9
Fourth	60.2	1.3	70.5	3.6

The incidence of disease in this table is the number of soldiers diagnosed with malaria (all forms) or diarrhea/dysentery (acute and chronic) divided by the average number of troops in the Union army during the year. Mortality is the number of soldiers who died of malaria (or diarrhea) during the year divided by the number of soldiers diagnosed with malaria (or diarrhea).

Source: Calculated from the Medical and Surgical History, Medical Volume, pt. 1, pp. 146, 296, 452, 604, 664, and 684, tables 24, 47, 71, 95, 104, and 107.

nated food and water produced disease, but the importance of cleanliness in hospitals and camps had been demonstrated empirically in the Crimean War.

How did Confederate medicine compare to Northern? Many observers both during and after the War thought that the medical department of the Union army was superior to its Confederate counterpart. Former Confederate physician Francis Peyre Porcher of Charleston claimed that the South "could not expect to compete with the highly organized and lavishly supplied medical and surgical departments of the United States of the North."[16]

But what is done with supplies is also important. The North had greater abundance of quinine; this was of great value in countering the symptoms of malaria. The North also had a greater supply of calomel than the South, but the overuse of this medication caused worsening of patients with diarrhea. Hammond was correct in his attempts to limit its use. Both sides used alcohol as a tonic and this is now known to be an error. Both sides had difficulty supplying nutritional foodstuffs to their troops and scurvy occasionally limited the effectiveness of troops in the field.

A careful reading of the previous twenty-two chapters of this work seem to demonstrate Northern medical superiority. Overall, the Union was superior to the South in the control of malaria by quinine, the rapid evacuation of the wounded, and the general organization of the medical department of the army. Both the North and the South were correct in their efforts to remove the wounded rapidly from the battlefield, but the Union Letterman system was superior to the similar but less organized Confederate evacuation attempts. Both sides were correct in efforts to vaccinate against smallpox, but only the South was afflicted by the problem of spurious vaccination.

Despite this apparent Union superiority in some aspects of its medical system, if one analyzes available statistics for the entire opposing forces, Northern superiority in medical care cannot be proven. The only national figures for rates of illness of the entire Confederate army are from an article in the *Confederate States Medical and Surgical Journal* based upon statistics kept in the Surgeon General's Office. In this report, all episodes of illness are divided into field cases and hospital admissions. Field cases are soldiers placed on the sick list and excused from some or all military duties. These numbers can be taken as the total number of occasions when soldiers became ill.[17]

The hospitalization statistics in this report are misleading. A soldier admitted to the Gordonsville R and D and then evacuated to Charlottesville would count as two admissions. Therefore, the number of hospitalizations can only be taken as an extreme maximum. One cannot calculate the incidence of various diseases without knowing the total strength of the Confederate army. In fact, accurate figures

Table 32

Confederate Soldiers Sick and Wounded
during the First Eighteen Months of the War

Diagnosis	Field		Hospital		Total
	Cases	Deaths	Cases	Deaths	Deaths
Continued fever	36,746	5,205	40,565	7,020	12,225
Malaria	115,415	848	49,311	486	1,334
Eruptive fevers	44,438	1,036	32,755	1,238	2,274
Diarrhea	226,828	1,696	86,506	1,658	3,354
Pulmonary	42,204	3,534	36,988	4,538	8,072
Rheumatism	29,334	–	30,438	–	–
Gunshot wounds	29,569	1,623	47,724	2,618	4,241
All others	324,321	2,278	123,402	1,802	4,080
Killed in action	–	8,087	–	–	8,087
Total	848,855	24,307	447,689	19,360	43,667

Confederate soldiers who died from enemy action numbered 12,328
(4,241 who died of wounds and 8,087 killed in action) or 28.2
percent of the total Confederate deaths during this period.

Source: "Grand Summary of the Sick and Wounded of the Confederate
States Army under Treatment during the Years 1861 and 1862,"
Confederate States Medical and Surgical Journal 1 (1864): 139–40.

would require knowledge of the strength of just those regiments who provided medical reports; some reports are undoubtedly missing. It appears quite obvious, however, that the Confederate army was significantly afflicted by illness. As with the Union forces, the major illnesses that kept soldiers from their military duties were diarrhea and malaria.[18]

The figure of total deaths from each illness is quite valuable. Since each of us dies but once, the number of deaths occurring in the field plus the number occurring in the hospital give the total number of deaths occurring from each illness. In the first one and one-half years of the War, a total of 43,666 men died in the service of the Confederacy. Of these 12,328 died from enemy action, 8,087 were killed in battle, and 4,241 died from wounds. The remainder of the deaths, or 71.8 percent, resulted from illness. This proportion of deaths due to illness is close to the Union figure of 66.5 percent.[19]

Although the comparison of medical care between North and South is difficult, one conclusion seems clear. No significant difference between Northern and Southern medical care can be proven from available statistics that compare the entire Union army with the entire Confederate army.

In some regions and in some campaigns, the Union forces were in poor health. Union troops along the Atlantic coast were very debilitated; almost everyone was afflicted with endemic malaria and quite a few soldiers died from epidemic yellow fever and meningitis. The Union troops in the Trans-Mississippi region were particularly sickly in 1864 because of a temporary shortage of quinine. The overall Union statistics average the results from these difficult situations with other campaigns where medical care might have been more successful. The last chapter examines the effect of medical care upon specific campaigns to see if medical care could have made a difference in the course of the War.

24

Did Medical Care Make a Difference?

MOST SOUTHERNERS IMMEDIATELY AFTER THE conflict and most historians since have claimed that the South stood no chance of victory in this great War Between the States. A leading history textbook states that "the North's military potential was so overwhelming that she should have been able to achieve a speedy victory."[1] The population of the Northern states produced a potential for a two-to-one superiority in troops, and the industrial differential superiority was many times greater.

A simple comparison of resources, however, fails to note the different national goals of the two antagonists. The South wanted to become an independent nation, not to subdue the federal government and occupy the Northern states. The Confederacy had merely to survive until the North tired of the conflict. To win the War, the North needed to crush its opponent completely. The North required all its superior resources and needed to apply them efficiently. Even with overwhelming advantages in material and organization, the North experienced several moments when the course of events could have proceeded down a different road.[2]

In his thorough review of the conflict, James McPherson provides the clearest analysis of this point. "Most attempts to explain southern defeat or northern victory," he argues, "lack the dimension of *contingency*—the recognition that at numerous critical points during the war, things might have gone altogether differently."[3] McPherson lists five special periods of contingency, when a different outcome on the battlefield might have changed the entire course of the War. Two of these are times when medical care was important: the campaigns in Vicksburg and in northern Georgia. The present work claims that Northern medical care was superior to Southern in these two campaigns, that this superiority made a difference in the outcome of each campaign, and that a reversal of either campaign could potentially have changed the outcome of the War.

Table 33 examines the health of Union field armies at several points during the War. The Army of the Potomac, as it huddled around Harrison's Landing after the failure of the Peninsula campaign, was greatly debilitated. Forty percent of its soldiers were unable to carry out their military duties. Only 4.2 percent of these were disabled because of wounds. The remainder were ill with a variety of diseases, especially malaria and diarrhea. The physical deterioration of the Army of the Potomac on the Peninsula was a major failure of the Union medical arm.

The Army of the Potomac never again had this great a proportion of its troops on the sick list. After Gettysburg, about a quarter of the troops of the Army of the Potomac were disabled, but 42 percent of these were in the hospital because of their wounds, not because of illness. After the great bloodletting of May 1864, 30 percent of the troops of the Army of the Potomac were disabled, but almost two out of three of these were wounded. There was not much the Union medical department could do to maintain the health of an army so chewed up by combat.

The Army of the Gulf invading Louisiana and Arkansas in 1864 had about a quarter of

Table 33

Health of Union Field Armies, Selected Times

	percentage of total troops sick and wounded	percentage of these wounded
Army of the Potomac		
July 1862, Peninsula	40.5%	4.2%
July 1863, Gettysburg	23.7	42.7
May 1864, Virginia	30.6	63.9
August 1864, Virginia	34.3	10.8
Army of the Tennessee		
June 1863, Vicksburg	25.5	1.7
Army of the Gulf		
April 1864, Louisiana	24.0	7.9
Sherman's Armies		
July 1864, Atlanta	23.8	16.3
November 1864, Georgia	10.8	2.7

The first column shows the percentage of troops in the indicated field army who were unable to perform their military duties because they were in hospitals or convalescent camps. This figure gives a general estimate of the health of the army. The second column states the percentage of these disabled soldiers who were wounded. A low number in this column indicates that the major medical problem of the field force was sickness.

Source: Calculated from data in MSH, Medical Volume, pt. 1, pp. 174, 240, 324, 384, 396, and 490, tables 28, 38, 51, 60, 62, and 77.

its troops disabled. Only 8 percent of these were wounded. The remainder were ill with malaria and with chronic diarrhea. The Army of the Gulf failed in its mission, and this failure was partly a result of medical mismanagement. This was the only campaign of the War where the Union suffered a shortage of quinine.

The Army of the Tennessee had up to a quarter of its troops disabled during the struggle for Vicksburg. This army appears sickly until one compares the opposing Southern force; up to one-half of the Confederate defenders were disabled even before Vicksburg was surrounded. The struggle for Atlanta is another important campaign. It immediately preceded the key moment of the War, the presidential election. As discussed below, these two campaigns deserve consideration as times when medical care made a difference.

Previous historical studies have compared Confederate and Union medical care in other battles. Gordon W. Jones evaluated medical activities at the Battle of Fredericksburg, fought in December 1862. He judged the Northern medical care at that particular battle to be superior to the Southern.[4] Horace H. Cunningham examined both battles fought at Manassas, or Bull Run. He concluded that at the first battle, in July 1861, the medical departments of both sides were equally unprepared. At the second encounter, just over one year later, Northern military medicine was definitely superior to Southern. During the intervening year, the Union had made major advances in the organization of its medical department while the Confederacy had not.[5]

While Northern medical care might have been superior to Southern in these battles, the degree of medical superiority could not overcome poor Union leadership, strategy, and organization. Both Second Manassas and Fredericksburg were decisive military defeats for the North. Superior care of the wounded did not influence the outcome of these battles, although, of course, lives may have been saved.

VICKSBURG

The Union Army of the Tennessee surrounding Vicksburg had about a quarter of its troops disabled, but only a few soldiers had been wounded. The great majority of the ill soldiers were sick with malaria. This army was successful in its siege of Vicksburg mainly because its opponents were even sicker.

The Vicksburg campaign was fought in one of the most unhealthy regions of the South. Confederate General Robert E. Lee thought that the Union forces would be devastated by the diseases subsumed under the heading of climate. When asked to send reinforcements to the Vicksburg defenders, he replied that "troops ordered from Virginia to the Mississippi at this season would be greatly endangered by the climate." Lee even predicted that Vicksburg would be safe because "the climate in June will force the enemy to retire."[6]

Lee was wrong. The Union army under Grant succeeded in surrounding and capturing Vicksburg and twenty-seven thousand Confederate defenders. Throughout the campaign, Grant's army was healthier than its Confederate counterpart. From late 1862 up until the fall of Vicksburg, the health of the Union army improved; the proportion of the troops who were sick diminished. On the other hand, the proportion of the Confederates who were disabled by sickness increased. At the time of the key battle of the campaign, at Champion's Hill, one-fourth of the Union soldiers were not with their commands because of illness. The corresponding figure for the Confederates was one-half. If the Southern proportion of sick had been the same as the Northern, several thousand additional Confederate soldiers would have been present and Champion's Hill might have had a different outcome.

The historical result of this key battle was the retreat of the Confederate troops into Vicksburg, where they were rapidly surrounded. If Confederate arms had shattered the Union force, the Northern troops would have been forced to make their way back to the Mississippi River. The disorganized remains of this force would then have been ferried to the other side of the river, Grant would have resigned in disgrace, and Vicksburg would have held out until the end of the sickly season. An entirely new effort to take Vicksburg would have been necessary and the great fortress of the Mississippi might have held out until 1864. In fact, it might never have fallen.

When discussing the Vicksburg campaign, one must mention one other medical aspect. General Grant was able to rely upon his Confederate opponents to take care of the wounded that he left behind. This story of medical care during the American Civil War is full of ironies. The South led the way in treating the wounded of both sides with great compassion. The Winchester Accord is one of the great events in all military medical history. Is compassion in war ever misplaced?

In the Vicksburg campaign, General Grant took advantage of the compassionate Confederate policy toward wounded Union soldiers. When he ordered his troops to leave their base of supply and move through Mississippi to envelop Vicksburg from the rear, he specifically ordered that the Union wounded should be left behind and treated by Union doctors within Confederate lines. If Grant had been unable to relieve himself of the burden of caring for his wounded in this manner, he would have been forced to maintain a connection with his base on the river; his ability to move freely through the countryside would have been lost. Grant undertook this policy against the advice of his medical director, Madison Mills. One can imagine the response if a U.S. officer in Vietnam had proposed an offensive that required leaving American wounded behind to be taken care of by the Viet Cong.

ATLANTA

The struggle in northern Georgia that ended with the fall of Atlanta was also an important campaign. The historical events are generally explained as a result of Sherman's brilliance, Joe Johnston's hesitation, and/or John Bell Hood's impetuosity. The number and quality of troops also made a difference, and this number and quality depended partly upon medical support.

The medical resources of the Southern defenders of Atlanta were strained to the utmost; only a small percentage of those Confederates who were wounded or disabled by sickness ever returned to defend Atlanta. If Stout and Foard had been able to stem the tide of sick soldiers transferred out of their control, the defenders of Atlanta would have been increased in number by at least a quarter. In just the last two months of the campaign, the Southern armies lost over thirty thousand soldiers because of medical transfer.[7]

Sherman's army in northern Georgia escaped a bout with scurvy to become the healthiest army in the War. As shown in table 33, about a quarter of Sherman's troops were disabled in spring 1864. This proportion dropped after the fall of Atlanta, so that only one in ten of Sherman's soldiers was on the disabled list during the March to the Sea.

The opposing Confederate army dwindled away from sickness and excessive medical furlough. Some might argue that the condition of each patient justified each medical furlough, but not all physicians could suppress their natural inclination to send a good man home for a rest, even if the army needed him. Not many doctors were able to handle furlough pleas as did Confederate general Nathan Bedford Forrest; he scribbled across a soldier's request, "I TOLD YOU TWICT GODDAMIT KNOW."[8] The regimental physician had a different relationship to the men than did the commanding officer; he had to work with them every day for years. John Thomas Graves was one of those sent home because he convinced the doctor he was about to die; he did die, but not until 1950 at age 108.[9]

If a significant proportion of the soldiers sent home or transferred for medical reasons had been retained by the Confederate Army of Tennessee, many thousands of additional defenders would have been available to resist the Northern investment of Atlanta. If the presidential election had taken place with Sherman stymied outside Atlanta, as Grant was stalemated outside Richmond, perhaps the voters would have called on McClellan to end the terrible war with negotiations.

LEADERSHIP

Why was Northern medical care superior to Southern during these two key campaigns?

For one thing, the North had supplies in abundance, including quinine to waste. It could afford to pile supplies where they might be needed under the theory that lost supplies could be replaced, while lives lost are gone forever. But in addition to supplies, the North organized efficiently. Leadership played a part in the Union success.

A major theme of this book has been the role of leadership in the medical departments of the opposing armies. A comparison of the policies and careers of the two key surgeon generals is revealing. Hammond moved heaven and earth to obtain supplies for the sick and the wounded. His orders to cut through red tape were cheered by all who heard them. But when his enemies wished to remove him, they convicted him of the crime of failing to use proper procedures to purchase supplies.

Hammond's counterpart, Samuel Preston Moore, tried to put through many of the same reforms in the South that Hammond had successfully championed in the North. He was unable to convince the quartermaster department to shift ambulance control to doctors. He was unable to obtain needed supplies from the commissary. He did not make enemies among the Confederate leaders; they rewarded him by placing his likeness on the Confederate thousand-dollar bond; he was one of the few individuals not in the cabinet so honored. After the War, doctors of the late Confederate army always treated Moore with the greatest deference and respect; Samuel H. Stout considered him the finest officer he had ever met.[10]

What happened to Surgeon General Hammond? In late 1864 he entered private medical practice in New York City. Because of his fame, Hammond developed a large referral network and was able to build a practice limited to diseases of the nervous system. He wrote the first American textbook on neurology and described the neurological condition known as athetosis. With his old friend Silas Weir Mitchell, Hammond founded the American Neurological Association.[11]

Despite his success in practice and in academic medicine, Hammond continued his efforts to obtain a reversal of his court-martial conviction. He initially attempted to show that the personal antagonism of Secretary of War Stanton had produced an improper trial. But when Stanton died in 1869, Hammond shifted strategy; he tried to prove that his ac-

MALARIA RATE

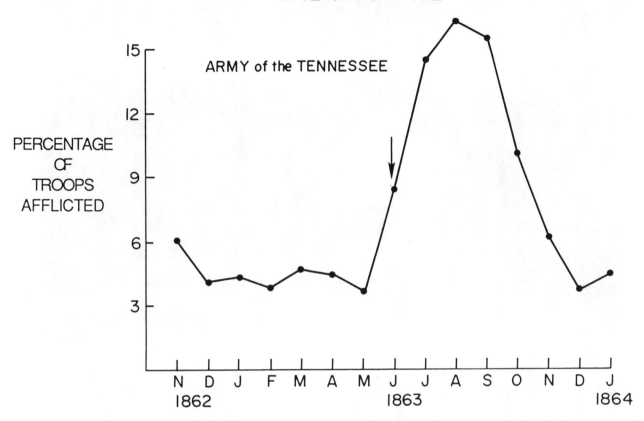

ARMY of the TENNESSEE

PERCENTAGE OF TROOPS AFFLICTED

Malaria in the Union army of Tennessee became a serious problem only **AFTER** the fall of Vicksburg on 4 July 1863. **By August, one in six Union soldiers was disabled by malaria.** The decline of malaria in September, before the first frost, partly resulted from a removal of major elements of the Army of Tennessee to healthier regions further North. The arrow indicates the last medical returns before the garrison surrender. If the Confederate defenders had been able to prevent this Union force from investing Vicksburg until later in the summer, they would have faced a debilitated opponent.

tions as surgeon general had helped benefit the Union armies. In 1878 Hammond moved to Washington to devote much of his time to lobbying Congress.

Senator George E. Spencer of Alabama read the court-martial transcript and became convinced of Hammond's innocence. "The period when the difficulties originated between Secretary Stanton and Surgeon General Hammond was one replete with perplexities and troubles," Senator Spencer reported to Congress.

A great civil war was in progress, large armies were arrayed in active hostilities, and the issue of events was uncertain and indeterminant. There were, of necessity, antagonisms, ambitions and jealousies without number, embarrassing and hampering the authorities. Chaos reigned supreme, and the untoward fate of a single person, just or unjust, merited or unmerited,

whether in exalted or humble station, weighed not a feather in the momentous balance. Success was the touchstone, and to the Moloch of its attributes, or what was conceived to be its necessities, victims were daily, nay hourly, sacrificed. Into this whirlpool of events, Dr. Hammond was drawn and carried down.

After an act of Congress, two presidential commissions, personal action by the vice president, a personal review of all the evidence by the secretary of war, and an order by President Rutherford B. Hayes, the guilty verdict was reversed and Hammond was restored to the retired list of the United States Army, with, however, the proviso that he could never obtain any financial retirement benefits. When he posed for a painting in his old age, he proudly wore the uniform of the surgeon general of the U.S. Army.[12]

Moore failed, but ended the War with honor

After the War, Samuel Preston Moore lived in Richmond as a distinguished gentleman. He never again practiced medicine. He refused to discuss the War years. NA

When William A. Hammond posed for a painting in the winter of his life, he wore the uniform of the Surgeon General, United States Army. From its style and fit, the uniform appears to have been made just for the painting. Courtesy of the Otis Historical Archives, National Museum of Health and Medicine.

and respect. Hammond maintained the health of the Union armies, but ended the War in disgrace. Hammond's actions to help the Union cause took great courage. In war, the type of courage that gains the greatest acclaim of contemporaries and historians is physical courage. The Northern cause was won by Chamberlain's bayonet charge at Gettysburg, by the Union flotilla pushing into Mobile Bay after the *Tecumseh* capsized, by thousands of men crossing open fields under fire. Glory. But in war and in peace, another type of courage is just as important. One must fight one's superiors if they are wrong. The Civil War medical experience teaches this lesson: if your mission is more important than your career, be prepared to sacrifice your career.

A minié ball had been present in the hand of an old soldier for 38 years when this X ray was taken. From Louis A. LaGarde, *Gunshot Injuries: How They are Inflicted, Their Complications and Treatment*, New York, William Wood, 1914.

Epilogue

In 1902 James M. Denn was living in the U.S. Soldiers' Home in Washington, D.C. He had been struck in the back of the hand by a minié ball at Spottsylvania during Grant's bloody advance through Virginia. He made his way to Fredericksburg, where his wound was dressed. One wonders if he is one of the soldiers lying on the ground in Figures 82 or 83.

Over the years, a cyst formed and the minié ball moved freely in it. When he entered the home for old soldiers, he found a new use for this apparently useless hand. He would ask young visitors if they had ever heard a minié ball. He held his damaged hand near their ears and shook it vigorously; the rattle of the ball within the cyst was distinctive. The old soldier laughed heartily at their amazement. He made the mistake of showing his hand to a radiologist, Dr. A. B. Herrick, who took an X-ray and showed it to the noted military surgeon, Dr. Louis A. LaGarde. Believing the old surgical maxim that no abnormal structure should be suffered to exist, Dr. LaGarde removed the ball later that same day.

This was the last surgical operation of the American Civil War.

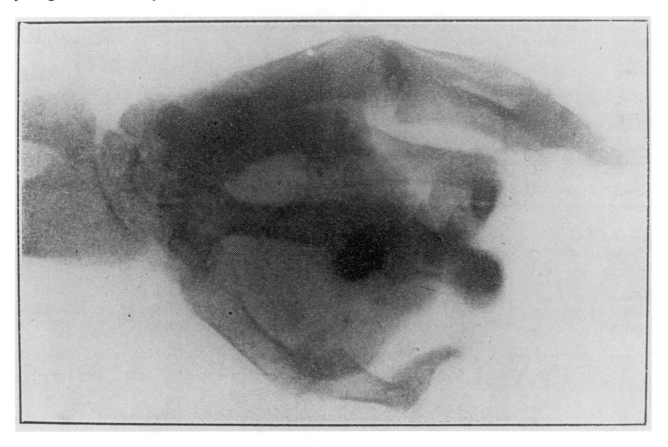

Glossary

ALLOPATH. A regular practitioner of traditional medicine, as differentiated from a homeopath, hydropath, or other practitioner of sectarian medicine.

AMBULANCE. A four-wheeled wagon (or, briefly at the beginning of the War, a two-wheeled buggy) for the removal of the sick and wounded.

AMPUTATION. The removal of a limb or a portion of a limb, such as a finger.

ANESTHESIA. Chloroform or ether was poured onto cotton or onto a cloth, and held over the patient's nose. After a few breaths, he became unconscious and went limp. The rapid surgery of the era was accomplished before he awoke. Anesthesia was the great blessing of the War.

APOPLEXY. Stroke.

BLUE MASS. A mercury compound given to induce a bowel movement.

BOIL. A pus-filled nodule in the skin. Also called furuncle. Now known to be produced by staphylococci bacteria.

BOTANIC PHYSICIAN. A type of irregular practitioner who emphasized the healthfulness of plant preparations.

BRIGADE. A military formation made up of a few, generally four, regiments and commanded by a brigadier general.

BRIGADE SURGEON. A high-ranking surgeon operating with field forces but not assigned to a particular regiment.

CALOMEL. Mercurous chloride given to induce a bowel movement. Too much, over a long period, produced severe side effects, such as tooth loss.

CATARRH. The common cold.

CATHARTIC. A medication that produces an emptying of the bowels, a purging.

CAUSALGIA. A clinical condition first described in Civil War soldiers who had experienced a gunshot wound of an arm or leg; the disorder is characterized by very severe, burning pain. Not related to neuralgia.

CHLOROFORM. A drug given to induce anesthesia, preferred by Confederate surgeons.

CHOLERA. A disorder caused by bacteria and characterized by massive watery diarrhea. Sometimes any disorder with diarrhea was loosely called cholera; the term Asiatic cholera was used to specify the epidemic disorder that began in India and spread all over the world, with major epidemics hitting the United States in 1832, 1849, and 1866.

CLIMATE. Certain diseases, such as malaria and yellow fever, occurred more frequently during particular seasons. The word climate therefore signified health conditions as well as weather. "We must conclude this campaign because of the climate" meant that the troops were too sick to continue.

CONGESTIVE INTERMITTENT FEVER. A type of malaria. When malaria became quite severe and the patient remained bedridden for several days, he might develop pulmonary congestion. This was called congestive intermittent fever and was more frequently fatal than other forms of malaria.

CONSUMPTION. A form of tuberculosis, referring to weight loss and debilitation.

CONTRACT SURGEON. A civilian who worked temporarily at a military hospital; also called an acting assistant surgeon.

CORRUPTION. A common term to signify inflammation

230

within the body; similar to mortification and putrefaction.

DEBILITAS. A diagnosis within the Farr system that generally referred to debilitation, probably caused by chronic exhaustion and poor diet.

DIARRHEA. Loose and frequent bowel movements. When used as a diagnosis, the term meant a nonspecific condition characterized by that symptom. The Farr system used four different conditions with diarrhea as the dominant system: acute diarrhea, chronic diarrhea, acute dysentery, and chronic dysentery.

DISARTICULATION. A surgical operation that removes a limb at a joint. This operation was more likely to be followed by serious complications than a simple amputation; therefore, when a joint was destroyed by a minié ball, the operation of choice was amputation by sawing the bone above the joint. Disarticulation at the hip, removal of the entire leg at the hip joint, was one of the most difficult operations attempted during the war.

DYSENTERY. Symptomatic diarrhea associated with the abdominal discomfort of tenesmus, or visible blood in the stools.

ECLECTIC. An irregular practitioner who practiced medicine using what he thought were the best parts of allopathy, botanism, homeopathy, and hydropathy.

EPILEPSY. A disease or group of diseases characterized by repetitive seizures. In the Union army, a single seizure disqualified a soldier from regular service with a combat unit; however, if he experienced less than one seizure per month, he could serve in the Invalid Corps, performing guard duty.

ERYSIPELAS. During the Civil War period, the term referred to a swelling of a wound, with redness and heat, now known to be caused by an infection with one or more forms of bacteria. The modern term for this condition would be cellulitis.

ERYTHEMA. Redness of the skin.

ETHER. A drug that induces anesthesia.

EXSECTION. A surgical operation involving the removal of tissue; also called excision. In Civil War parlance, the term referred to the removal of a portion of a limb bone destroyed by a gunshot wound; the resulting limb was shortened, but the only other operative choice was amputation.

FARR SYSTEM. The organized system of diagnoses developed by William Farr of England and used by both the Union and Confederate armies (but not navies).

FEMUR. The thigh bone.

FLEET SURGEON. In the U.S. Navy the term referred to a high ranking medical officer not assigned to a specific vessel but rather to the entire fleet. Reporting directly to the fleet commander, the fleet surgeon was analogous to the medical director of a field army.

FRACTURE. The breaking of a bone. Some limb fractures can be treated with splints. When pieces of the bone break through the skin, the lesion is called a compound fracture. During the Civil War, compound fractures always became infected; they were therefore often treated by amputation above the level of the fracture. Sometimes exsection, removal of the fracture site, was possible.

FURLOUGH. A soldier given permission to leave his unit and, usually, to return home to rest. A medical furlough was given when the soldier needed prolonged convalescence before returning to health.

HOMEOPATH. A practitioner of the medical sect that believed that very small doses of a medication could cure.

HOSPITAL GANGRENE. When infection of a wound progresses to the point where the edges of the wound become necrotic, the process is called gangrene. If unchecked, the gangrene will continue to spread until pyemia develops. The dead tissue exudes the horrible smell of mortification, similar to the smell of spoiled meat. The disorder developed in certain hospitals only, hence the name hospital gangrene.

HOSPITAL SHIP. A ship fitted out especially to carry sick and wounded soldiers. Also called hospital steamer or hospital transport.

HOSPITAL TRAIN. A train made up of cars especially constructed to convey sick and wounded soldiers.

HUMERUS. The long bone in the upper arm between elbow and shoulder.

HYDROPATH. A form of sectarian practitioner who emphasized the healing powers of water, especially warm baths.

INTERMITTENT FEVER. Malaria.

INVALID CORPS. Union soldiers too sick to remain with their combat units, but not sick enough to receive a medical discharge, were assigned to several companies that served as garrison troops. Late in the War the healthiest members of the Invalid Corps were transferred to the Veteran Reserve Corps; the most disabled members of the Invalid Corps were assigned directly to the Surgeon General for duty as hospital guards.

ITCH. An irritating sensation in the skin relieved by scratching. Also called pruritus. In the Farr system, this symptom was a separate diagnosis. Many soldiers suffered from itching; sometimes it seemed to come in epidemics.

LANCET. A small pointed knife used to lance boils or to induce bleeding for therapeutic purposes.

LETTERMAN SYSTEM. The name of the organizational system of medical care within the Union Army, developed by Jonathan Letterman when he was the medical director of the Army of the Potomac.

MALAISE. A general feeling of sickliness and fatigue.

MALARIA. A disease occurring in certain regions, characterized by intermittent bouts of high fever and shaking chills. It is most common in late summer and fall, called the sickly season. The disease is caused by a parasite, a protozoa of the genus *Plasmodium*, which is injected into the human blood stream by the bite of a mosquito.

MALINGERING. Feigning illness to escape military duty. Today, symptoms that result unconsciously from anxiety are not considered malingering. During the Civil War, no effort was made to determine motivation; any symptoms not due to destruction of bodily tissue were presumed to be due to malingering.

MEASLES. A viral disease acquired once in each person's life (until the recent development of measles immunization). A few days after exposure to the measles virus, the patient breaks out in a high fever, followed by spots in the mouth, and then by red papules over the body (the measles spots). The diagnosis is reasonably simple at this point, although lay people (and some Civil War nurses) could confuse measles spots with smallpox pustules. The high fever could cause prostration and be followed by bacterial pneumonia or other complications. Also called rubeola.

MEDICAL SERVICE. Each army had a medical organization that was officially called the Medical Department, but often referred to, even by its leaders, as the Medical Bureau or Medical Service. Doctors wore the initials M.S. on their uniforms to identify them as member of the Medical Service.

MENINGITIS. Inflammation of the covering of the brain and spinal cord. During the Civil War this was usually caused by infection with the meningococcus and was virtually always fatal.

MINIÉ BALL. A cone-shaped bullet made of lead. The major type of ordnance used during the Civil War, this bullet traveled much farther and faster than the round ball used previously. When the lead hit human flesh, it flattened and the bullet tumbled, producing terrible tissue damage. The minié ball inflicted more horrendous wounds than the subsequent steel metal-jacket bullet, which passes directly through the body, only destroying tissue directly in its path. The term derives from Captain Claude Etienne Minié of the French Army, who helped to develop the new bullet. It is variously spelled as Minié, minnié, or minié but is always pronounced "mini" as in miniskirt. Although Captain Minié placed an accent over the e in his name, contemporaries seldom used an accent when writing the words minie ball.

MORTIFICATION. Death of tissue.

MUMPS. A viral disease affecting the parotid glands, giving a characteristic facial swelling. This disorder has epidemiological features similar to measles; each person acquires the disorder once in life.

NEURALGIA. A separate diagnosis in the Farr system, the term neuralgia was used for any sort of pain. Pain in the abdomen was gastric neuralgia and pain in the face was called facial neuralgia (Jefferson Davis suffered greatly from what his doctor called facial neuralgia). This symptom, now known to be a number of different conditions, was treated symptomatically with various tonics and with morphine.

NIGHT BLINDNESS. A disorder within the Farr classification system characterized by normal vision in daylight but severely restricted vision in partial darkness. This disorder was not frequently diagnosed during the Civil War, but occasionally appeared in epidemic proportions, especially in the Confederate Army of Tennessee. it is now known to be due to dietary deficiency of vitamin A.

NOSTALGIA. Soldiers away from home for a long time might become homesick. This was called nostalgia and was a separate diagnosis in the Farr system.

NURSE. The term nurse was used for anyone who helped patients: those who fed them, wrote letters for them, bathed them, or changed their dressings. Most nurses were male enlisted men at the start of the War, but during its course these men were largely replaced by female volunteers.

OPIUM. Opium is an ancient drug used to treat pain and to slow the action of the bowel. The drug was available in many forms, including laudanum and morphine.

PELLAGRA. A disease characterized by mental changes, diarrhea, and darkening of the portions of the skin exposed to the sun. Caused by a deficiency of the vitamin niacin, the disease occurred in Europe in the two or three centuries before the Civil War, but was not thought to occur in America. In retrospect, the disorder was widespread, especially among Union prisoners. Since corn does not contain niacin, pellagra occurs among people subsisting on a diet of corn products.

PNEUMONIA. Inflammation of the lungs. This disease was most frequently seen as complication of a serious gunshot wound or a prolonged illness.

PURGATIVE. A medication to evacuate the bowels. "The first step in treatment involves complete purging."

PUS. A liquid inflammatory substance, now known to be made up of dead inflammatory cells. Creamy yellow pus without a bad odor coming from a wound was a good sign: laudable pus.

PUSTULE. A small collection of pus visible beneath the skin; generally smaller than a boil.

PUTREFACTION. Decomposition of dead tissue producing a rotten odor.

PYEMIA. A condition of fever, chills, sweating, and rapid pulse following an infectious illness such as erysipelas. It was almost always fatal. Later in the century this condition was called blood poisoning; a modern term is septicemia.

QUARTAN INTERMITTENT FEVER. A form of malaria, characterized by shaking chills coming about every third day (quartan means four, but the first chill occurred on day one, then two days without a shaking chill, then the next chill on the fourth day).

QUININE. A medication obtained from the South American cinchona tree. A person who took the drug every day would not develop the symptoms of malaria. If a patient with malaria took a higher dosage, his disease would soon remit. Quinine killed the circulating malarial protozoa of the Civil War era; modern *Plasmodia* have developed resistance to this agent. Usually given as the salt, quinine sulfate, dissolved in alcohol.

QUININE CALL. For some Union regiments in malarial areas, the bugle announcement of sick call required each and every soldier to line up and be administered quinine by the assistant surgeon or the hospital steward. The drug had to be given under supervision because of its bitter taste.

QUOTIDIAN INTERMITTENT FEVER. A form of malaria, characterized by shaking chills coming every day.

REGIMENT. The key organizational unit of both armies, the regiment generally contained, at the beginning of the War, about one thousand men. At Gettysburg the average regiment of each side contained just over three hundred soldiers. Two doctors were assigned to each infantry regiment.

REMITTENT FEVER. This disease was diagnosed in a patient with fever and shaking chills who rapidly improved. Most but not all patients who received this diagnosis had malaria. Remittent fever had a seasonal incidence identical to malaria.

RHEUMATISM. Aches and pains in the joints. A few patients diagnosed with rheumatism during the Civil War had what today would be called rheumatic fever or rheumatoid arthritis. Most probably had simple aches and pains from heavy physical activity.

SCORBUTIC TAINT. A term used for a soldier about to come down with scurvy or for a regiment in which some soldiers had clinical scurvy and others, eating the same diet, were expected to soon show scurvy symptoms. The major symptom of the taint was fatigue.

SCURVY. A disease characterized by fatigue, easy bruising, and hemorrhages into the skin, joints, or internal organs. The disorder could be prevented by a diet of fresh vegetables, even onions or potatoes. Civil War physicians knew that the disease was dietary in its origin; the disease is now known to be due to a vitamin C deficiency.

SCROFULA. Swelling of lymph nodes, especially in the neck, due to tuberculosis.

SICK CALL. At least once per day, one of the two doctors of each regiment, usually the assistant surgeon, would interview and examine each soldier who thought he might be ill.

SINAPISM. A paste made from ground mustard seed is rubbed upon the skin and covered with a bandage for several days. When the bandage is removed, material is visible that has the appearance and odor of putrefaction. Perhaps, went the theory, this putrefaction had been drawn from morbid processes within the body. Also called mustard plaster.

SMALLPOX. The first symptoms of this disease were chills and high fever; after a few days small pustules formed on the skin, giving the disease its name. Smallpox was highly contagious and often fatal; Civil War physicians knew that the disease could be prevented by proper vaccination. Also called variola. It no longer exists.

SPURIOUS VACCINATION. On several occasions during the short life of the Confederacy, vaccine material produced extensive inflammation at the site of its injection, followed by systemic symptoms such as fever. Did it produce immunity against smallpox? No one knew.

STEWARD. An enlisted man in each regiment assigned to medical duties. He held a rank equivalent to sergeant and was called the hospital steward. He was generally responsible for the administration of medications.

SUPPLY TABLE. The list of medication available to every physician. Doctors could obtain items not on the table, but with some difficulty. A modern synonym is formulary.

SURGEON. The term had two meanings during the Civil War: a medical practitioner who performed operations and a military medical officer who might or might not be called upon to perform surgery.

SYPHILIS. A venereal disease now known to be due to the spirochete *Treponema pallidum*. The chancre of primary syphilis and the systemic symptoms of secondary syphilis were recognized by Civil War physicians. Doctors of that era did not relate the series of conditions now called tertiary syphilis to the primary venereal disease. Civil War treatments were many, but none were effective.

TARTAR EMETIC. This medication, antimony potassium tartrate, was used to induce vomiting.

TENESMUS. Ineffectual efforts to evacuate the bowels. During the Civil War it also referred to a feeling of stomach cramping during diarrhea. The presence of tenesmus was the major symptom differentiating the diagnoses of diarrhea and dysentery.

TERTIAN INTERMITTENT FEVER. A type of malaria characterized by shaking chills about every other day.

TETANUS. A clinical condition, occasionally seen in wounded men, of stiffness of all skeletal muscles including those of the jaw (hence, its alternate name, lockjaw). Today it is known to be due to release of a toxin from the bacterium *Clostridium tetani* growing in the wound. During the Civil War the disease was usually fatal; today, when it occurs, it is still quite often fatal, but can be prevented by induced immunity against the toxin.

THOMSONIAN. An irregular medical practitioner who emphasized the use of botanical preparations. The original Thomsonians, as founded by Samuel Thomson, felt that most medical problems could be handled at home without the need of professional aid.

TREPHINATION. Drilling a hole in the skull. Generally used interchangeably with the term trepanation, although the trepan and the trephine are slightly different instruments.

TRISMUS. Tightening of the jaw muscles. If this symptom occurred in a wounded soldier, the doctor feared that the patient might be developing tetanus.

TUBERCULOSIS. A chronic disorder characterized by a slow wasting (consumption) or by swelling of lymph nodes, especially in the neck (scrofula). Now known to be an infection with *Mycobacterium*.

TYPHOID FEVER. The illness begins with headache and proceeds to a continuous fever, malaise, and constipation. Weight loss and chronic diarrhea produce a serious debilitation that can lead to death. The disease is caused by the bacterium *Salmonella typhi*, which passes from infected to healthy person by fecal contamination of food or water.

TYPHO-MALARIAL FEVER. A term suggested by J. J. Woodward to refer to patients who either had both malaria and typhoid fever or some sort of condition halfway between the two disorders. This diagnosis was added by Union medical authorities to the Farr list in 1862. The condition was infrequently diagnosed.

TYPHUS FEVER. A disease characterized by headache, continuous fever, and a skin rash. The causative rickettsia organism travels from person to person, or from rat to person, via fleas. This disease did not occur to any significant degree in Civil War armies; most soldiers diagnosed with typhus had typhoid fever.

VACCINATION. Vaccine material pushed into the skin with the head of a pin will, after the passage of several days, produce an eruption and a scab. The scab is removed and broken up to form new vaccine material. Today, we know that live vaccinia virus was present in the vaccine material. If the person-to-person chain was broken in some way and the vaccinia virus was lost, subsequent injections of the scab would not induce immunity against smallpox. Thus, Civil War soldiers were never completely certain that they were immune and a smallpox epidemic could be very frightening.

VETERAN RESERVE CORPS. Union army soldiers who were sick or injured or just exhausted (or who had completed their original three year enlistment) could be assigned to the Veteran Reserve Corps. Regiments of the Veteran Reserve Corps were assigned garrison duty but did not accompany field armies.

VULNUS SCLOPETICUM. Gunshot wound.

WAYSIDE HOSPITAL. A hospital alongside the railroad where the sick and wounded could stop and recuperate during an exhausting train evacuation. A Confederate institution.

YELLOW FEVER. A viral disease, endemic in many locations near the equator, brought to U.S. ports by infected sailors or ship passengers, and carried from a sick to a healthy person by mosquitoes. The disease produces liver failure and jaundice. Many patients infected by the yellow fever virus develop a mild disease, without jaundice. They are never diagnosed as having yellow fever, but they develop partial immunity. Therefore, an epidemic can be particularly devastating among new arrivals who are not, in contemporary parlance, "acclimated to the area."

Notes

Prologue

1. *ORN*, 1:13–14.

Introduction

1. This is the thesis of Richard H. Shryock, "A Medical Perspective on the Civil War," *American Quarterly* 14 (1962): 161–73. He argues that it is the duty of the medical historian to balance the celebratory aspects of military history with the agony of the sick and the wounded: "if medical aspects are omitted, the story is not only incomplete but is unrealistic."

2. Connelly judged Confederate generals only by information known to them. He disdained such false analyses as, "this was a terrible error, because Union forces had already been ordered to concentrate on that position." Thomas L. Connelly, *Army of the Heartland: The Army of Tennessee, 1861–1862* and *Autumn of Glory: The Army of Tennessee, 1862–1865* (Baton Rouge: Louisiana State University Press, 1967 and 1971).

3. George W. Adams, *Doctors in Blue: The Medical History of the Union Army in the Civil War* (New York: Henry Schuman, 1952; reprint, Dayton, Ohio, Morningside Press, 1985); Horace H. Cunningham, *Doctors in Gray: The Confederate Medical Service* (Baton Rouge: Louisiana State University Press, 1958).

4. Other major explanatory works covering medical care during the American Civil War are Stewart M. Brooks, *Civil War Medicine* (Springfield, Ill.: Charles C. Thomas, 1966); Louis Duncan, *Medical Department of the United States Army in the Civil War* [offprints] (Washington, D.C., 1910); reprint, Gaithersburg, Md.: Butternut Press, 1985); and Paul E. Steiner, *Disease in the Civil War: Natural Biological Warfare in 1861–1865*, Springfield, Ill.: Charles C. Thomas, 1968. The narrative by Mary C. Gillett, *The Army Medical Department, 1818–1865* (Washington, D.C.: Government Printing Office, 1987), includes an excellent narrative of the activities of the Union medical authorities during the Civil War. All primary and secondary sources published before 1992 are listed and discussed in Frank R. Freemon, *Microbes and Minie Balls: An Annotated Bibliography of Civil War Medicine* (Madison, N.J., Fairleigh Dickinson University Press, 1993). Important new works include Robert E. Denney, *Civil War Medicine: Care and Comfort of the Wounded* (New York: Sterling Publishing Co., 1994), a day-by-day summary of medical activities during the war, and Jack D. Welsh, *Medical Histories of Confederate Generals* (Kent, Ohio: Kent State University Press, 1995) (a companion volume on the health of Union generals has just appeared). A new periodical is devoted to this subject, the *Journal of Civil War Medicine*, edited by Peter J. D'Onofrio (539 Bristol Drive S.W., Reynoldsburg, Ohio 43068).

Chapter 1. American Medicine in the 1850s

1. Bernard J. D. Irwin, "The Apache Pass Fight," *Military Surgeon* 73 (1933): 197–203. Dr. Irwin's extended description of this action is in the National Library of Medicine. Some modern commentators think that the defenders at Apache Pass overestimated the number of Indian warriors with Cochise.

2. The best review of army physicians in this period is Mary C. Gillett, *The Army Medical Department, 1818–1865* (Washington, D.C.: Government Printing Office, 1987).

3. In this chapter, all quotations from the reports of U.S. Army officers are taken from Richard H. Coolidge, *Statistical Report on the Sickness and Mortality of the Army of the United States Compiled from the Records of the Surgeon General's Office; Embracing a Period of Five Years, from January, 1855 to January, 1860* (Washington, D.C.: George W. Bowman, 1860).

4. This problem would occur during the upcoming War. At several key moments, the Commissary Department of the U.S. Army was unable to provide troops with fresh vegetables. The present description shows the bureaucratic mentality: save government funds by doing no more than what is required by regulations. A civilian organization, the United States Sanitary Commission, was oriented more to mission than to regulatory requirements and provided what the official Commissary Department could not.

5. Bonnie Ellen Blustein, *Preserve Your Love for Science: Life of William A. Hammond, American Neurologist* (New York: Cambridge University Press, 1991), 38–50.

6. Joseph H. Bill, "Notes on Arrow Wounds," *American Journal of the Medical Sciences* 44 (1862): 365–87.

7. James O. Breeden, "States-Rights Medicine in the Old South," *New York Academy of Medicine Bulletin* 52 (1976): 348–72; John Harley Warner, "A Southern Medical Reform: The Meaning of the Antebellum Argument

for Southern Medical Education," *Bulletin of the History of Medicine* 57 (1983): 364–81.

8. The best review of the changes in medical thinking that occurred in the United States during the nineteenth century is Lester S. King, *Transformations in American Medicine: From Benjamin Rush to William Osler* (Baltimore: Johns Hopkins University Press, 1991).

9. Stanley B. Weld, ed., "A Connecticut Surgeon in the Civil War: The Reminiscences of Nathan Mayer," *Journal of the History of Medicine and Allied Sciences* 19 (1964): 272–86.

10. Leon S. Bryan, "Blood-letting in American Medicine, 1830–1892," *Bulletin of the History of Medicine* 38 (1964): 516–29.

11. Wayne Austerman, "Maynard: A Carbine Made in Massachusetts, the Favorite of Southern Soldiers," *Civil War Times Illustrated* 25 (April 1986): 42; G. Ward Hubbs, "John B. Read's Okra Paper," *Alabama Review* 43 (1990): 289–96.

12. Richard H. Shyrock, ed., *The Letters of Richard D. Arnold, M.D., 1808–1876.* (Durham, N.C.: Duke University Press, 1929).

CHAPTER 2. CREATING CONFEDERATE MEDICINE

1. The standard book-length work on Confederate medicine is Horace H. Cunningham, *Doctors in Gray: The Confederate Medical Service* (Baton Rouge: Louisiana State University Press, 1958). A number of excellent articles survey this topic. The two best are Cunningham, "The Confederate Medical Officer in the Field," *New York Academy of Medicine Bulletin* 34 (1958): 461–88; and Harris D. Riley, "Medicine in the Confederacy," *Military Medicine* 118 (1956): 495–501. Much of this chapter was presented at the Southern history seminar led by David L. Carlton at Vanderbilt University and later published as "Administration of the Medical Department of the Confederate States Army, 1861 to 1865." *Southern Medical Journal* 80 (1987): 630–37.

2. Thomas Cooper DeLeon [brother of the surgeon general], *Four Years in Rebel Capitals* (Mobile, Al.: Gossip Press, 1890), 28.

3. "Cases and Deaths from Typhoid Fever, Malarial Fever, Pneumonia, Measles, Diarrhea and Dysentery, and Gun Shot Wounds, General Hospital, Charlottesville, Va," Joseph Jones Papers, Howard-Tilton Memorial Library, Tulane University, New Orleans, La.

4. *Medical and Surgical History of the War of the Rebellion*, Surgical Volume, pt. 3, p. 143.

5. Warren D. Farr, "Samuel Preston Moore: Confederate Surgeon General," *Civil War History* 41 (1995): 41–56.

CHAPTER 3. LINCOLN FINDS A SURGEON GENERAL

1. *Medical and Surgical History of the War of the Rebellion*, Surgical Volume, pt. 1, p. 58. Needham, a citizen of Lawrence, Massachusetts, was the first soldier of the American Civil War to die of his wounds.

2. Thomas Lawson to Zachary Taylor, 1839. In Doro-

thy M. Schullian and Frank B. Rogers, "The National Library of Medicine," *Library Quarterly* 28 (1958): 4. See also James P. Phalen, "Thomas Lawson," *Army Medical Bulletin* 5 (1949): 30–35.

3. James P. Phalen. "Clement Alexander Finley," *Army Medical Bulletin* 5 (1940): 36–41.

4. Horace H. Cunningham. *Field Medical Services at the Battles of Manassas* (Athens: University of Georgia Press, 1968), 1–22.

5. *MSH*, Surgical Volume, pt. 1, p. 109.

6. "Red Tape," *American Medical Times*, 7 June 1862, 322–23.

7. The standard review of the U.S. Sanitary Commission is William Q. Maxwell, *Lincoln's Fifth Wheel: The Political History of the United States Sanitary Commission* (New York: Longmans Green, 1956), 372.

8. Hammond's prewar military experience is discussed most fully by Evelyn S. Drayton, "William Alexander Hammond, 1828–1900," *Military Surgeon* 109 (1951): 559–65.

9. This is Hammond's only specific criticism of his predecessor as surgeon general.

10. For more detailed discussion about Hammond's selection as surgeon general, including the possible role played by General George B. McClellan, see my article, "Lincoln Finds a Surgeon General: William A. Hammond and the Transformation of the Union Army Medical Bureau," *Civil War History* 33 (1987): 5–21.

11. Carl Sandburg, *Abraham Lincoln: The War Years*, 4 vols. (New York: Harcourt Brace, 1939), 3: 434–35.

CHAPTER 4. MAGGOTS AND MINIÉ BALLS

1. The development of this system is described by John M. Eylar, *Victorian Social Medicine: The Ideas and Methods of William Farr* (Baltimore: Johns Hopkins University Press, 1979).

2. John Julian Chisolm, *A Manual of Military Surgery for the Use of Surgeons in the Confederate Army with an Appendix of the Rules and Regulations of the Medical Department of the Confederate Army* (Richmond, Va.: West and Johnson, 1861), 405; William Grace, *The Army Surgeon's Manual for the Use of Medical Officers, Cadets, Chaplains, and Hospital Stewards* (New York: Bailliere Brothers, 1864), 139.

3. Ferdinand E. Daniel, *Recollections of a Rebel Surgeon* (Austin, Tex.: Von Boeckmann, Schutze, and Co., 1899).

4. Julius Augustus Leinbach, "Regiment Band of the 26th North Carolina," edited by Donald M. McCorkle, *Civil War History* 4 (1958): 225–36.

5. This is my conclusion based on interviews with World War II veterans. Of course, today medical department soldiers are identified long before battle and receive special training. But in the confusion generated by prolonged contact with an enemy army, such ideal organization is replaced by experience. The practical problem of what to do with the brave and resourceful soldier who will not or cannot fire his rifle at the enemy is solved by assignment to the ambulance corps.

6. Edward O. Hewitt, "A Letter from a British Military Observer of the American Civil War," Ed. R. A. Preston, *Military Affairs* 16 (1952): 49–60.

7. The younger doctors trained after the develop-

ment of anesthesia, of course, but their mentors still operated as fast as possible. Medicine and surgery change slowly.

8. Theodore Dimon, "A Federal Surgeon at Sharpsburg," edited by James I. Robertson Jr., *Civil War History* 6 (1960): 134–51.

9. *MSH*, Surgical Volume, pt. 2, p. 739.

10. Sam R. Watkins, *Co. Aytch, Maury Grays, First Tennessee Regiment; or, A Side Show of the Big Show* (Nashville, Tenn.: Cumberland Presbyterian Printing House, 1882).

CHAPTER 5. THE INTRODUCTION OF WOMEN NURSES

1. George Rosen, *The Structure of American Medical Practice, 1875–1914* (Philadelphia: University of Pennsylvania, 1983); Charles E. Rosenberg, *The Care of Strangers: The Rise of America's Hospital System* (New York: Basic Books, 1987); Paul Starr, *The Social Transformation of American Medicine* (New York: Basic Books, 1982).

2. The standard history of American nursing devotes four pages to the Civil War but does not mention male nurses. Susan M. Reverby, *Ordered to Care: The Dilemma of American Nursing, 1850–1945* (New York: Cambridge University Press, 1987). Most articles that review Civil War nursing restrict their view to female nurses, and mainly to the North. For example, see Julia C. Stimson and Ethel C. S. Thompson, "Women Nurses with the Union Forces during the Civil War," *Military Surgeon* 62 (January 1928): 1–17; Bonnie Bullough and Vern Bullough, "The Origins of Modern American Nursing: The Civil War Era," *Nursing Forum*, vol. 2, no. 2 (1963): 13–27; Ann Douglas Wood, "The War Within a War: Women Nurses in the Union Army," *Civil War History* (February 1972): 205; Marilyn Mayer Culpepper and Pauline Gordon Adams, "Nursing in the Civil War," *American Journal of Nursing* 88 (1988): 981–84.

3. Walter F. Atlee, "Review of Scrive's *Relation Medico-Chirugicale de la Campagne d'Orient*," *American Journal of the Medical Sciences* 42 (1861): 463–74. According to Sister Mary Denis Maher, a total of 617 Catholic nuns served as nurses during the Civil War with both the North and the South; *To Bind Up the Wounds of War: Catholic Sister Nurses in the U.S. Civil War* (Westport, Conn.: Greenwood Press, 1989), 69.

4. John H. Brinton, *Personal Memoirs of John H. Brinton: Major and Surgeon, U.S.V., 1861–1865* (New York: Neale Publishing Co., 1914).

5. Hannah A. Ropes, *Civil War Nurse* (Knoxville: University of Tennessee Press, 1980) 85.

6. An excellent biography of this dynamic nurse is Nina Brown Baker, *Cyclone in Calico: The Story of Mary Ann Bickerdyke* (Boston: Little, Brown, 1952).

7. John N. Beach, "Army Surgeons: Their Character and Duties," *Cincinnati Lancet and Observer* 6 (1863): 339–44.

8. Only late in the nineteenth century, when department stores began to cater to women shoppers, did the central section of the city lose its masculine character. See Gunther Barth, *City People: The Rise of Modern City Culture in Nineteenth-Century America* (New York: Oxford University Press, 1980).

9. Carroll Smith-Rosenberg, *Disorderly Conduct: Visions of Gender in Victorian America* (New York: Alfred A. Knopf, 1985).

10. This particular incident is not fictional. It was recorded by Mary Livermore, a very reliable and sober observer, in *My Story of the War: A Woman's Narrative of Four Years Personal Experience as a Nurse in the Union Army* (Williamstown, Mass.: Corner House, 1978), 505–6.

11. The original commission, signed by Secretary of War Leroy P. Walker, is on display at the Confederate Museum, Richmond. Captain Tompkins was the only woman to be officially accepted as a regular member of the Confederate army. See David B. Sabine, "Captain Sally Tompkins," *Civil War Times Illustrated* 4 (November 1965): 36–39.

12. John Levi Underwood, *The Women of the Confederacy* (New York: Neale Publishing, 1906).

13. Charles M. Snyder, *Dr. Mary Walker, the Little Lady in Pants* (New York: Vantage Press, 1962).

CHAPTER 6. UNION HOSPITAL SHIPS ALONG THE WESTERN RIVERS

1. *MSH*, Surgical Volume, pt. 3, pp. 977–81.

2. This battle and the evacuation of the wounded is described by Nathaniel C. Hughes Jr., *The Battle of Belmont: Grant Strikes South* (Chapel Hill: University of North Carolina Press, 1991). Brinton described his role in his *Personal Memoirs of John H. Brinton: Major and Surgeon, U.S.V., 1861–1865* (New York: Neale Publishing Co., 1914).

3. *MSH*, Surgical Volume, part 3, 971–86.

4. John Van R. Hoff, "Memoir of Alexander Henry Hoff," *Military Surgeon* 31 (1912): 47–51; Estelle Brodman and Elizabeth B. Carrick, "American Military Medicine in the Mid-Nineteenth Century: The Experience of Alexander H. Hoff, M.D.," *Bulletin of the History of Medicine* 64 (1990): 63–78. The letters of another doctor who served on a Union hospital vessel have been edited by Peter Josyph, *The Wounded River: The Civil War Letters of John Vance Lauderdale, M.D.* (East Lansing: Michigan State University Press, 1993).

5. Bruce Joel Hillman, "Their Floating Palace: The Union's Hospital Boat *Red Rover*." *Civil War Times Illustrated* 24 (October 1985): 20–25. See also *ORN*, especially volume 23, pp. 153–54.

6. Edward C. Kenney, "From the Log of the *Red Rover*, 1862–1865," *Missouri Historical Review* 60 (1965): 31–49.

7. Jacob G. Forman, *The Western Sanitary Commission.* (St. Louis, Mo.: R. P. Studley, 1864).

8. Emily Elizabeth Parsons, *Memoir of Elizabeth Parsons* (Boston: Little, Brown, 1880), 159. When Parsons' father wrote the introduction to this series of letters after she died, he was still amazed that a shy, retiring, disabled maiden could perform so well in such a demanding position; he attributed her success to her unremitting fearlessness and her belief in the Union cause.

9. A reviewer of this manuscript doubted the truth of this generalization, but I have found no evidence that any leader of any of these organizations even once attempted to coordinate the movements of their hospital ships with those of the other organizations.

10. James A. Rammage, "The Wounded at Shiloh." *Civil War: The Magazine of the Civil War Society* 9 (May 1991): 10–15.

11. In her biography of Yandell, Nancy Disher Baird claims that the tourniquet never left Johnston's pocket. *David Wendell Yandell: Physician of Old Louisville* (Lexington: University Press of Kentucky, 1978) 48.

12. Such minor matters as tourniquets and old dueling wounds determine the outcome of battles. Defective sensation in Johnston's right leg preventing proper therapy is the hypothesis of Jack D. Welsh, *Medical Histories of Confederate Generals* (Kent, Ohio: Kent State University Press, 1995), 118–19.

CHAPTER 7. THE BEGINNINGS OF THE LETTERMAN SYSTEM

1. *OR*, 11: 196–203.

2. William H. Page. "Letter," *Boston Medical and Surgical Journal* 66 (1862): 478–81.

3. Jane Turner Censer, ed., *The Papers of Frederick Law Olmsted, Vol. 4, Defending the Union* (Baltimore: Johns Hopkins University Press, 1986), 30–31.

4. Thomas T. Ellis, *Leaves from the Diary of an Army Surgeon; or Incidents of Field, Camp and Hospital Life* (New York: John Bradburn, 1863).

5. William H. Page, "I Shall Be a Prisoner," *Civil War Times Illustrated* 30 (September 1991): 42.

6. James Winchell, "Wounded and a Prisoner: A First-Person Account," *Civil War Times Illustrated* 4 (August 1965): 20–25.

7. General order 147, issued 2 August 1862.

8. These orders are given in full in Jonathan Letterman, *Medical Recollections of the Army of the Potomac* (New York: Appleton, 1866).

9. An excellent contemporary description of the Letterman system in operation is given by Richard Swanton Vickery, "On the Duties of the Surgeon in Action," *Civil War Times Illustrated* 17 (June 1978): 12–23. A detailed analysis that compares the Letterman system to modern evacuation of wounded is presented by David L. Nolan and David A. Pattillo, "The Army Medical Department and the Civil War: Historical Lessons for Current Medical Support," *Military Medicine* 154 (1989): 265–71.

10. A good overall description of the Peninsula Campaign is Stephen W. Sears, *To the Gates of Richmond: The Peninsula Campaign* (New York: Ticknor and Fields, 1992), 468. John J. Hennessy, *Return to Bull Run: The Campaign and Battle of Second Manassas* (New York: Simon and Schuster, 1993), 607, provides an excellent description of the strategy and tactics of the battle called Second Bull Run by the Union and Second Manassas by the South.

11. Hammond to Stanton, 7 September 1862, Secretary of War Correspondence, National Archives. Reproduced in *MSH*, Surgical Volume, pt. 3, p. 934.

CHAPTER 8. CONFEDERATE MEDICINE ORGANIZING

1. Edgar Erskine Hume, "Chimborazo Hospital, Confederate States Army, America's Largest Military Hospi-

tal," *Virginia Medical Monthly* 61 (1934): 189–95.

2. John R. Gildersleeve, "Chimborazo Hospital during 1861–1865," *Confederate Veteran* 12 (1904): 577–80.

3. Alexander G. Lane, "The Winder Hospital of Richmond, Va.," *Southern Practitioner* 26 (1904):35–41.

4. Edward A. Craighill, *Confederate Surgeon: The Personal Recollections of E. A. Craighill*, ed. Peter W. Houck (Lynchburg, Va.: H. E. Howard, 1989).

5. Jonathan O'Neal, "Gordonsville Receiving Hospital" (paper presented at the Second Annual Meeting of the Society of Civil War Surgeons, Nashville, Tenn. 6 November 1993). Old Joe probably had suffered measles earlier; he thought he had immunity to smallpox but he did not. Because no one could be sure who was immune to smallpox in this era, an epidemic could be terrifying.

6. An excellent survey of the medical center of Charlottesville is found in Ervin L. Jordan Jr., *Charlottesville and The University of Virginia in the Civil War* (Lynchburg, Va.: H. E. Howard, 1988).

7. Peter W. Houck, *A Prototype of a Confederate Hospital Center in Lynchburg, Virginia* (Lynchburg, Va.: Warwick House, 1986), 58–61.

8. L. Laszlo Schwartz, "James Bolton (1812–1869): Early Proponent of External Skeletal Fixation," *American Journal of Surgery* 66 (1944): 409–13.

9. A detailed discussion of this unusual inflammatory problem is Joseph Jones, *Researches upon Spurious Vaccination; or, The Abnormal Phenomena Accompanying and Following Vaccination in the Confederate Army during the Recent American Civil War, 1861–1865* (Nashville, Tenn.: University Medical Press, 1867).

10. John W. Schildt, *Hunter Holmes McGuire: Doctor in Gray*. Chewsville, Md.: privately printed, 1986), 3–20.

11. This has been called the Winchester Accord. See James O. Breeden, "The Winchester Accord: The Confederacy and the Humane Treatment of Captive Medical Officers," *Military Medicine* 158 (1993): 689–92.

12. "The Lieber Code, Washington, D.C., April 24, 1863: Instructions for the Government of the Armies of the United States in the Field by Order of the Secretary of War," in *The Law of War: A Documentary History*, ed. Leon Friedman (New York: Random House, 1972), 1: 168–69.

13. *Official Records*, vol. 11, pt. 3, pp. 633–34.

CHAPTER 9. NORTHERN MEDICINE ORGANIZED

1. Much of this chapter is taken from my publication "Lincoln Finds a Surgeon General: William A. Hammond and the Transformation of the Union Army Medical Bureau," *Civil War History* 33 (1987): 5–21.

2. John N. Beach, "Army Surgeons: Their Character and Duties," *Cincinnati Lancet and Observer* 6 (June 1863): 329–34.

3. "Red Tape," *American Medical Times*, 7 June 1862, 322–23.

4. Surgeon General William A. Hammond to Jonathan Letterman, 19 June 1862. In Jonathan Letterman, *Medical Recollections of the Army of the Potomac* (New York: Appleton, 1866), 14.

5. "Letter from the Surgeon General to Surgeon Letterman, Medical Director of the Army of the Potomac," *American Medical Times*, 28 June 1862, 360.

6. William A. Hammond, "Letter," *New York Times*, 29 January 1863, 6.

7. Abraham Lincoln to William A. Hammond and reply, in *Collected Works of Abraham Lincoln*, ed. Roy P. Basler (New Brunswick, N.J.: Rutgers University Press, 1953), 5: 467, 444.

8. Robert S. Henry. *The Armed Forces Institute of Pathology: Its First Century, 1862–1962* (Washington, D.C.: Government Printing Office, 1963), 9–32.

9. John H. Brinton, "Address: Closing Exercises of the Session 1895–96, Army Medical School" *Journal of the American Medical Association* 26 (1896): 599–605.

10. Hammond quoted this British compendium several times in a chapter for one of his books. See Hammond, "Scurvy," In *Military Medical and Surgical Essays*, ed. William A. Hammond (Philadelphia: Lippincott, 1863), 175–206.

11. William A. Hammond, "Medical and Surgical History of the Rebellion," circular Letter, 9 June 1862, printed in *American Medical Times*, 28 June 1862, 358–59.

12. *The Hospital Steward's Manual* (Philadelphia: J. B. Lippincott, 1862), 324; *Outline of the Chief Camp Diseases of the United States Armies as Observed during the Present War* (Philadelphia: J. B. Lippincott, 1863).

13. Henry I. Bowditch, "Remarks at the Boston Society for Medical Improvement," *Boston Medical and Surgical Journal* 64 (1862): 164–166; and "Abuse of Army Ambulances," *Boston Medical and Surgical Journal* 67 (1862): 204–7.

14. Henry I. Bowditch, *A Brief Plea for an Ambulance System for the Army of the United States* (Boston: Tichnor and Fields, 1863), 28. In this pamphlet, Bowditch tells about his son. The son had been shot in the abdomen, however, and probably would have died no matter what medical care he received.

15. Lawrence G. Blochman, *Doctor Squibb: Life and Times of a Rugged Idealist* (New York: Simon and Schuster, 1958).

16. Frank R. Freemon, "The First Neurological Research Center: Turner's Lane Hospital during the American Civil War," *Journal of the History of Neuroscience* 2 (1993): 135–142.

17. John H. Brinton, *Consolidated Statement of Gunshot Wounds* (Washington, D.C.: Government Printing Office, 1863).

CHAPTER 10. MEDICINE AT SEA

1. United States Navy Department, Bureau of Medicine and Surgery, *Instructions for the Government of Medical Officers of the Navy of the United States* (Washington, D.C.: A. O. P. Nicholson, 1857), 43.

2. *ORN*, 17:340.

3. Surgeon general, United States Navy became the title of this position in 1871.

4. Louis H. Roddis, "William Whelan: Third Chief of the Bureau of Medicine and Surgery (1853–1865)," *Military Surgeon* 90 (1942): 196–98.

5. Stephen Chaulker Bartlett, "The Letters of Stephen Chaulker Bartlett aboard the U.S.S. *Lenapee*, January to August, 1865," *North Carolina Historical Review* 33 (1956): 66–92.

6. Samuel Pellman Boyer, *Naval Surgeon: The Diary of Samuel Pellman Boyer* (Bloomington: Indiana University Press, 1963), 2 vols.

7. Some Confederate raiders powered only by sail remained at sea for many months. One may note that the during the Vietnam War the U.S. Navy maintained a fleet in the Gulf of Tonkin. Nuclear-powered aircraft carriers plus the replenishment of oil-powered ships while underway, along with scheduled rotation of ships and crews, allowed the maintenance for several years of a floating air base at a point in the ocean. This was an amazing logistical accomplishment. The descendants of Confederates served with pride at this floating naval air station despite the fact that the point in the ocean was called Yankee Station.

8. *ORN*, 1:491–92, 507–8, 546.

9. Samuel E. Lewis, "General T. J. Jackson and his Medical Director, Hunter McGuire, M.D., at Winchester, May, 1862," *Southern Historical Society Papers* 30 (1902): 226–36.

10. Daniel B. Conrad, "Capture and Burning of the Federal Gunboat *Underwriter*, in the Neuse, off New Bern, N.C., in February, 1864," *Southern Historical Society Papers* 19 (1891): 93–100.

11. John M. Browne, "Official Report," *ORN*, 3:69–71.

CHAPTER 11. STONEWALL JACKSON STRUCK BY FRIENDLY FIRE

1. Some have reasoned that no one could know if the Confederate pickets had shrunk back in horror, since these individuals have never been identified. The author believes that this description of the behavior of the pickets is justified by a study of other instances when soldiers discover they have inflicted wounds upon their own comrades. Death by friendly fire, sometimes called amicide, remains a problem in modern war as exemplified by the tragic deaths of Michael Mullin in the Vietnam War and of Lance Fielder in the Gulf War. See Courtland D. B. Bryan, *Friendly Fire* (New York: G. P. Putnam's Sons, 1976).

2. In 1866 McGuire described the death of Stonewall Jackson for the *Richmond Medical Journal*. This report has been recently reprinted in the April 1996 issue of *Civil War: The Magazine of the Civil War Society*. Many years later, McGuire reevaluated the entire case history and published his mature views in the book he wrote with George L. Christian, *The Confederate Cause and Conduct in the War Between the States* (Richmond, Va.: L. H. Jenkins, 1907). This chapter has paraphrased McGuire's report. All quotations are the words recalled by the doctor. McGuire stated that the servant Jim bore no responsibility for producing or worsening the lung inflammation. Unlike many surgeons before and since, McGuire never claimed that his amputation was successful, only spoiled by the death of the patient from another cause. The best book on the battle, with an excellent description of Jackson's wounding, is Stephen W. Sears, *Chancellorsville* (New York: Houghton Mifflin, 1996). The two biographies of McGuire emphasize his Civil War career: John Schildt, *Hunter Holmes McGuire: Doctor in Gray* (Chewsville Md.: privately printed, 1986); and Maurice Friedlander Shaw, *Stonewall Jackson's Surgeon, Hunter Holmes McGuire* (Lynchburg, Va.: H. E. Howard, 1993).

CHAPTER 12. "MINE EYES HAVE SEEN THE GLORY"

1. A detailed analysis of the hospitals at Gettysburg is Gregory A. Coco, *A Vast Sea of Misery: A History and Guide to the Union and Confederate Field Hospital at Gettysburg, July 1–November 20, 1863* (Gettysburg, Pa.: Thomas Publications, 1988). The burials at the National Cemetery are described in exhaustive detail by John W. Busey, *The Last Full Measure: Burials in the Soldiers' National Cemetery at Gettysburg* (Hightstown, N.J.: Longstreet House, 1988). The present chapter does not examine the battle itself, but only the sufferings of selected wounded soldiers. A good survey of the battle is Albert A. Nofi, *The Gettysburg Campaign, June to July 1863*, revised edition (Conshocken, Pa.: Combined Books, Inc., 1993).

2. Edward Marcus, ed., *A New Canaan Private in the Civil War: Letters of Justus M. Silliman, 17th Connecticut Volunteers* (New Canaan, Conn.: New Canaan Historical Society, 1984), 39–46.

3. Rhea Kuykendall, "Surgeons of the Confederacy: Arthur R. Barry," *Confederate Veteran* 34 (1926): 209–10.

4. These case reports are from the *MSH*, amplified by further details in Silas Weir Mitchell, George Read Morehouse, and William W. Keen, *Gunshot Wounds and Other Injuries of Nerves* (Philadelphia: J. B. Lippincott, 1864). Schively reported his cry, "I have been murdered," to the interviewing doctor at Turner's Lane Hospital.

5. Carl Schurz, *The Reminiscences of Carl Schurz* (New York: McClure, 1907), 3:39.

6. Mary A. Holland, *Our Army Nurses* (Boston: B. Wilkins and Co., 1895), 537.

7. Jonathan Letterman, "Report on the Operations of the Medical Department during the Battle of Gettysburg," *MSH*, Medical Volume, pt. 1, appendix, pp. 140–42. See Gerard A. Patterson, "Gettysburg's Abandoned Wounded," *Civil War: The Magazine of the Civil War Society* 54 (December 1995): 54–58.

8. George Barton, *Angels of the Battlefield: A History of the Labors of the Catholic Sisterhoods in the Late Civil War* (Philadelphia: Catholic Art Publishing Co., 1897).

9. Simon Baruch, "A Surgeon's Story of Battle and Capture," *Confederate Veteran* 22 (1914): 545–48.

10. DeWitt C. Peters, "Interesting Cases of Gunshot Wounds," *American Medical Times* 8 (1864): 3–4. See also *MSH*, Surgical Volume, pt. 2, pp. 266–67.

11. *The Sanitary Commission of the United States Army: A Succinct Narrative of its Works and Purposes* (New York: U.S. Sanitary Commission, 1864), 149–161.

12. W. C. Pryer, "Hospital Gangrene in the DeCamp General Hospital," *American Medical Times* 8 (1864): 4–6.

CHAPTER 13. NORTHERN VERSUS SOUTHERN MEDICINE AT VICKSBURG

1. For a more detailed analysis, the reader is referred to my article, "The Medical Challenge of Military Operations in the Mississippi Valley during the American Civil War," *Military Medicine* 157 (1992): 494–97. An older but excellent review of the medical aspects of this campaign, mainly using the official records and without statistical or disease analysis, is Joseph E. King, "Shoulder Straps for Aesculapius: Vicksburg Campaign in 1863," *Military Surgeon* 114 (1954): 216–26.

2. Jonathan E. Summers to William Hammond, 28 May 1863, *OR*, vol. 24, pt. 3, pp. 357–58.

3. Madison Mills, "Report of the Medical Director of the Army of the Tennessee, from May 1 to July 4, 1863," *MSH*, Medical Volume, pt. 1, appendix, pp. 331–32. In a complex procedure that even today is not fully understood, each wounded soldier who was repatriated had to agree not to fight again for the Union until he was officially exchanged (on paper) for a captured Confederate soldier returned to the Confederate forces. This theoretical exchange was widely disregarded by both sides.

4. The Union statistics are available through the *Medical and Surgical History of the War of the Rebellion*. The original Confederate returns were destroyed in the terrible fire that consumed part of Richmond on the night of 2–3 April 1865. But a young Confederate military officer, Joseph Jones, copied the returns of the Department of Mississippi and East Louisiana for his private files and they are now at Tulane University. It is interesting to think that these statistics were originally generated when the armies were only a few hundred yards apart, then went on their separate journeys in 1863, only to be brought back together again more than 125 years later. Some of the more complex aspects of the statistical analysis is covered in my article, "Medical Care at the Siege of Vicksburg." *New York Academy of Medicine Bulletin* 67 (1991): 429–38.

5. The present analysis conflates several diagnoses for clarity, as previously described.

6. John E. Summers, "Extract from a Report on the Inspection of Camp and Field Hospitals of General Grant's Army in the Field in the Rear of Vicksburg Mississippi, for the Month of June, 1863," *MSH*, Medical Volume, pt. 3, p. 95.

7. J. J. Woodward, *Outline of the Chief Camp Diseases of the United States Armies as Observed during the Present War* (Philadelphia: J. B. Lippincott, 1863).

8. These numbers can be deceiving since the same individual only occurs once in the numerator (one death) but can appear several times in the denominator (acute diarrhea, chronic diarrhea, etc.). In addition, very ill soldiers were sometimes transferred to other departments and their subsequent deaths do not appear in these statistics.

9. Actually, this sentence is slightly incorrect. The number who returned to duty was 97 percent of those who became sick and wounded during February; different soldiers were involved. In other words, a soldier could become ill in December and return to duty in February. The statistics are useful for comparison, however, and clearly indicated that the Confederate medical authorities were able to maintain the strength of the army in the early part of the campaign, but not in the spring.

CHAPTER 14. CONFEDERATE MEDICINE DETERIORATING

1. These cries were collected by interview with eyewitnesses by Jacob Hoke, *The Great Invasion of 1863, or General Lee in Pennsylvania* (Dayton, Ohio: W. J. Shuey, 1887), 485.

2. John D. Imboden, "The Confederate Retreat from Gettysburg," In *Battles and Leaders of the Civil War* (New York: Thomas Yoseloff, 1956), 3:420–29.

3. "Minutes of the 15th Annual Meeting of the American Medical Association, New York, June 7–9, 1864," *Transactions of the American Medical Association* 15 (1865): 39–40.

4. "Indigenous Remedies of the South," *Confederate States Medical Journal* 1 (1864): 106–8.

5. Stephen R. Wise, *Lifeline of the Confederacy: Blockade Running During the Civil War* (Columbia: University of South Carolina Press, 1988).

6. Spencer G. Welch, *A Confederate Surgeon's Letters to His Wife* (New York: Neale, 1911), 35.

7. The smuggling of medical supplies has been reviewed by James O. Breeden, "Medical Shortages and Confederate Medicine," *Southern Medical Journal* 86 (1993): 1040–48.

8. *OR*, ser. 4, vol. 2, p. 1021.

9. *OR*, ser. 4, vol. 2, pp. 1072–73.

10. Francis Peyre Porcher, *Resources of the Southern Fields and Forests: Medical, Economical, and Agricultural* (Charleston, S.C.: Evans and Cogswell, 1863).

11. Mary Elizabeth Massey, *Ersatz in the Confederacy* (Columbia: University of South Carolina Press, 1952), 119.

12. Joseph Jones, *Medical and Surgical Memoirs* (New Orleans, La.: Clark and Hofeline, 1890), vol. 3, pt. 2, p. 526–31. Quinine prevented the occurrence of malarial fever by killing the parasite. Quinine has no effect on the typhoid bacterium. Probably some patients were so debilitated with malaria that they were unable to obtain clean drinking water. This same experiment is described in another publication by Jones, *Quinine as a Prophylactic against Malarial Fever* (Nashville, Tenn.: University Medical Press, 1867).

13. L. Laszlo Schwartz, "The Development of the Treatment of Jaw Fractures," *Journal of Oral Surgery* 2 (1944): 193–221; L. Laszlo Schwartz, "James Bolton (1812–1869): Early Proponent of External Skeletal Fixation," *American Journal of Surgery* 66 (1944): 409–13.

14. C. W. P. Brock, "How the Confederate Army was Vaccinated," *Military Surgeon* 32 (1913): 114–15. But, as shown in table 6, a number of Confederate soldiers died from smallpox; probably the vaccination was not pursued with vigor in all military districts.

15. Louis Shaffner, "A Civil War Surgeon's Diary," *North Carolina Medical Journal* 27 (1966): 409–15.

16. The best review of the problem of medical furlough is Harris D. Riley Jr., "Medical Furloughs in the Confederate States Army," *Journal of Confederate History* 2 (1989): 115–31. Riley concludes that many soldiers who could have carried out their military duties received medical furloughs or discharges.

17. *OR*, ser. 4, vol. 2, p. 533.

18. A. A. Lyon, "Malingerers," *Southern Practitioner* 26 (1904): 558–62.

19. A controversy continues concerning who the editor of this journal of Confederate medicine was. In his introduction to a reprinting of the full journal, William D. Sharpe credits Surgeon General Moore as the "editor in fact if not in name" (*Confederate States Medical and Surgical Journal*, Metuchen, N.J.: Scarecrow Press, 1976). In the Norman edition of this collection, Ira Rutkow credits James B. McCaw. W. Middleton Michel told people after

the War that he had been the editor (see, for example, R. French Stone, *Biography of American Physicians and Surgeons* [Indianapolis, Ind.: Carlon and Hollenbeck, 1894], 324).

20. "Grand Summary of the Sick and Wounded of the Confederate States Army under Treatment during the Years 1861 and 1862," *Confederate States Medical and Surgical Journal* 1 (1864): 139–40. This article is discussed later.

21. *OR*, ser. 4, vol. 3, pp. 719–20.

CHAPTER 15. UNION ENCLAVES ALONG THE CONFEDERATE COAST

1. *MSH*, Surgical Volume, pt. 1, p. xxxi.

2. New Bern, North Carolina was usually spelled Newbern by the occupying Federals.

3. J. Baxter Upham, "Army Medical Intelligence: Hospital Notes and Memoranda," *Boston Medical and Surgical Journal* 68 (1863): 20–22.

4. J. Baxter Upham, "Further Observations in Regard to the Cerebrospinal Affection Occurring in and Around Newbern, N.C. *Boston Medical and Surgical Journal* 68 (1863): 311–7, 333–8.

5. Isaac F. Galloupe, "Army Medical Intelligence: Letter," *Boston Medical and Surgical Journal* 68 (1863): 203–6.

6. Nathan Mayer, "A Connecticut Surgeon in the Civil War: The Reminiscences of Dr. Nathan Mayer," ed. Stanley B. Weld *Journal of the History of Medicine and Allied Sciences* 19 (1964): 272–86.

7. Thomas F. Smiley, "The Yellow Fever at Port Royal, S.C.," *Boston Medical and Surgical Journal* 67 (1863): 449–68.

8. Isaac F. Galloupe, "Medical History of the Seventeenth Regiment Mass. Volunteers." *Boston Medical and Surgical Journal* 68 (1863): 136–41.

9. Beauregard's prediction to Davis was overheard by R. G. H. Kean, the head of the Confederate Bureau of War, and was noted in his diary on 17 May 1863. Edward Younger, ed. *Inside the Confederate Government: The Diary of Robert Garlick Hill Kean* (New York: Oxford University Press, 1957).

10. John Duffy, *Sword of Pestilence: The New Orleans Yellow Fever Epidemic of 1853* (Baton Rouge: Louisiana State University Press, 1966).

11. Jo Ann Carrigan, "Yankees versus Yellow Jack in New Orleans, 1862–1866," *Civil War History* 9 (1963): 248–60.

12. Benjamin F. Butler, "Some Experiences with Yellow Fever and its Prevention," *North American Review* 147 (1888): 525–41.

CHAPTER 16. THE TRIAL OF WILLIAM HAMMOND

1. Allan Nevins and Milton H. Thomas, ed. *Diary of George Templeton Strong* (New York: Macmillan, 1952), 3:314.

2. Alexander H. Hoff, "Hospital Steamer D.A. January, Quarter Ending September 30, 1862," *MSH*, Medical Volume, pt. 2, p. 91.

3. Estelle Brodman and Elizabeth B. Carrick, "American Military Medicine in the Mid-Nineteenth Century: The Experience of Alexander H. Hoff, M.D.," *Bulletin of the History of Medicine* 64 (1990): 63–78.

4. The injury and the examination are described by Silas Weir Mitchell, George Read Morehouse, and William W. Keen in *Gunshot Wounds and Other Injuries of Nerves* (Philadelphia: J. B. Lippincott, 1864), 116. Hammond is not identified by name, but from the context it is obvious that this case report refers to him. Robert J. T. Joy has suggested that Hammond's leg problem was due to a herniated nucleus pulposus (Hammond was overweight), but this does not explain why both legs were affected, nor does it address Hammond's strange sensory disturbance. While the diagnosis remains uncertain, hysterical paralysis seems most likely to me.

5. Henry Crecy Yarrow, "Personal Recollections of Some Old Medical Officers," *Military Surgeon* 60 (1927): 73–76, 171–75, 449–55, 588–93.

6. William A. Hammond, "Our Friends Who Have Passed Away," *Proceedings of the American Philosophical Society* 18 (1878–1880): 541–43.

7. Stanton had already ordered an old enemy of Hammond's from his days at Fort Riley to conduct such a review.

8. Alex Zeidenfelt, "The Embattled Surgeon-General, William A. Hammond," *Civil War Times Illustrated* 17 (October 1978): 24–32.

9. File 4743–ACP–1879, records of the Adjutant General's Office, "Pertaining to the Courts-martial Proceedings of William A. Hammond," National Archives, Washington, D.C.

10. John H. Brinton, *Personal Memoirs* (New York: Neale, 1914), 342.

11. A rumor existed in army circles for many years that Stanton had secretly ordered the court-martial board to find Hammond guilty when he feared that they were considering a verdict of innocent on all charges. See Louis C. Duncan, "The Strange Case of Surgeon General Hammond." *Military Surgeon* 64 (1929): 257; and Percy M. Ashburn, *A History of the Medical Department of the U.S. Army* (Boston: Houghton Mifflin, 1929), 84.

12. Richard J. Oglesby Papers, Illinois State Archives, Springfield, Illinois.

13. *OR*, ser. 3, vol. 4, p. 1035.

14. *New York Times*, 22 August 1864, 1; 24 August 1864, 4.

15. William A. Hammond, *Statement of the Causes Which Led to the Dismissal of Surgeon General Hammond from the Army with a Review of the Evidence Adduced before the Court* (Washington, D.C.: privately printed, 1864).

16. But today no copy is with the court-martial proceedings in the National Archives of the United States.

17. *American Medical Times*, 5 March 1864, 116; *Buffalo Medical and Surgical Journal* 4 (1865): 435.

18. "Statement of the Late Surgeon-General," *Boston Medical and Surgical Journal*, 1 December 1864, 360–68.

Chapter 17. Confederate Medical Support during the Atlanta Campaign

1. The best description of the military campaign from the Southern viewpoint is Thomas L. Connelly, *Autumn of Glory: The Army of Tennessee, 1862–1865* (Ba-

ton Rouge: Louisiana State University Press, 1971). An excellent general examination of the campaign is Albert Castel, *Decision in the West: The Atlanta Campaign of 1864* (Lawrence: University Press of Kansas, 1992).

2. The Confederate medical problems during this campaign have been reviewed in several important articles: James O. Breeden, "A Medical History of the Later Stages of the Atlanta Campaign," *Journal of Southern History* 35 (1969): 31–59; Bruce S. Eastwood, "Confederate Medical Problems in the Atlanta Campaign." *Georgia Historical Quarterly* 47 (1963): 276–92; Glenna R. Schroeder-Lein, "To Be Better Supplied than any Hotel in the Confederacy: The Establishment and Maintenance of the Army of Tennessee Hospitals in Georgia, 1863–1865," *Georgia Historical Quarterly* 76 (1992): 809–36; and Joseph E. King, "Shoulder Straps for Aesculapius: Atlanta Campaign," *Military Surgeon* 114 (1954): 296–306. An excellent book that summarizes the Confederate medical accomplishments is Glenna R. Schroeder-Lein, *Confederate Hospitals on the Move: Samuel H. Stout and the Army of Tennessee* (Columbia: University of South Carolina Press, 1994). My own publication on this campaign is "The Medical Support System for the Confederate Army of Tennessee during the Georgia Campaign, May to September 1864," *Tennessee Historical Quarterly* 52 (1993): 44–55.

3. Memorandum from George B. Douglas to Samuel H. Stout, 28 May 1864, Samuel H. Stout Papers, Southern History Collection, University of North Carolina, Chapel Hill, N.C.

4. Memorandum from Stout to Joseph P. Logan, 30 May 1864, Stout Papers, Chapel Hill.

5. George Pursley to Stout, 31 May 1864, Stout Papers, Chapel Hill.

6. Stout to Logan, no date, Stout Papers, Chapel Hill.

7. Samuel Stout Papers, Duke University Library, Durham N.C.

8. As an old man in his eighties, Dr. Stout wrote his memoirs in a series of twenty-two articles under the title, "Some Facts of the History of the Organization of the Medical Services of the Confederate Armies and Hospitals." They were published in volumes 22 through 25 of the *Southern Practitioner* (1900–1903).

9. Fannie A. Beers, *Memories: A Record of Personal Experience and Adventure during the Four Years of War* (Philadelphia: J. B. Lippincott, 1889), 109–11.

10. Joseph Jones Papers, folder 109, Howard-Tilton Memorial Library, Tulane University, New Orleans, La.

11. Kate Cumming, *A Journal of Hospital Life in the Confederate Army of Tennessee* (Louisville, Ky.: John P. Morton, 1866), 145.

12. Breeden, "Medical History."

13. *The Tennessee Civil War Veterans Questionnaires* (Easley, S.C.: Southern Historical Press, 1985), 2:510.

14. Carroll Henderson Clark papers, Tennessee State Archives, Nashville, Tenn.

15. Jonathan R. Buist, "Some Items of My Medical and Surgical Experience in the Confederate Army," *Southern Practitioner* 25 (1903): 574–81.

Chapter 18. Preparing for the Final Union Campaigns

1. The harassment that preceded the riot is carefully described by Robert D. Sampson in his excellent article,

"Pretty Damned Warm Times: The 1864 Charleston Riot and the Inalienable Right of Revolution," *Illinois Historical Journal* 89 (summer 1996): 99–116.

2. An analogy is the breakup of the Soviet Union into its constituent republics.

3. Walter DeBlois Briggs, *Charles Edward Briggs: Civil War Surgeon to a Colored Regiment* (Berkeley: University of California Press, 1960).

4. William A. Hammond, *A Treatise on Hygiene, with Special Reference to the Military Service* (Philadelphia: J. B. Lippincott, 1863), 76.

5. James Bryan, "Negro Regiments: Department of the Tennessee." *Boston Medical and Surgical Journal* 69 (1864): 43–44.

6. John Gardner Perry, *Letters from a Surgeon of the Civil War* (Boston: Little, Brown, 1906).

7. Isaac Smith Jr. "An Incident in Army Practice," *Boston Medical and Surgical Journal* 71 (1864): 340.

8. Peter Levine, "Draft Evasion in the North during the Civil War," *Journal of American History* 67 (1981): 816–34. For Mitchell's draft notice, see Ernest Earnest, *S. Weir Mitchell: Novelist and Physician* (Philadelphia: University of Pennsylvania Press, 1950), 54.

9. John David Smith, "Kentucky Civil War Recruits: A Medical Profile," *Medical History* 24 (1980): 185–96.

10. Roberts Bartholow, *A Manual of Instructions for Enlisting and Discharging Soldiers* (Philadelphia: J. B. Lippincott, 1863).

11. John Ordronaux, *Manual of Instructions for Military Surgeons on the Examination of Recruits and Discharge of Soldiers* (New York: D. Van Nostrand, 1863).

12. Petroleum V. Nasby [David Ross Locke], "Why I Should Not Be Drafted." In *Civil War Letters of Petroleum V. Nasby* (Columbus: Ohio State University Press, 1962).

13. This method for differentiating true from faked deafness is not recommended to the modern clinician.

14. William W. Keen, Silas Weir Mitchell, and George R. Morehouse, "On Malingering, Especially in Regard to Simulation of Diseases of the Nervous System," *American Journal of the Medical Sciences* 48 (1864): 367–94.

15. The concept of unconscious motivation was completely missing from the minds of Civil War physicians. Each patient either had symptoms from a physical illness or he was purposely feigning symptoms in order to escape exposure to shot and shell. See my article, "Detecting Feigned Illness during the American Civil War," *Journal of the History of Neuroscience* 2 (1993): 239–42.

Chapter 19. Union Medical Support for the Decisive Campaigns of 1864

1. David G. Farragut's official report of the battle is in the *ORN*, 21:405–6. Many other Union and Confederate reports, including medical material, are located in the remainder of volume 21.

2. *ORN*, 21:492.

3. As reported by Palmer in his autobiographical statement in William B. Atkisson, *The Physicians and Surgeons of the United States* (Philadelphia: Charles Robson, 1878), 212–13.

4. The best description of these trains is by Ralph Gordon, "Hospital Trains of the Army of the Cumberland," *Tennessee Historical Quarterly* 51 (1992): 147–56.

5. Gordon, "Hospital Trains."

6. The best summary of the military aspects of this campaign is Noah Andre Trudeau, *Bloody Roads South: Wilderness to Cold Harbor, May to June 1864* (Boston: Little, Brown, 1989).

7. William T. G. Morton, "The First Use of Ether as an Anesthetic at the Battle of the Wilderness in the Civil War," *Journal of the American Medical Association* 42 (1904): 1068–73.

8. *MSH*, Surgical Volume, pt. 1, p. 75.

9. Walter R. Steiner, "A Physician's Experience in the United States Sanitary Commission during the Civil War." *Charaka Club Proceedings* 10 (1941): 172–91.

10. *MSH*, Medical Volume, pt. 1, p. 566, table 89.

11. He thought that he did not fully recover his health until 1871. Charles B. Johnson, *Muskets and Medicine, or Army Life in the Sixties* (Philadelphia: Davis, 1917), 167–83.

12. Paul E. Steiner, *Disease in the Civil War: Natural Biological Warfare in 1861–1865.* Springfield, Ill.: Charles C. Thomas, 1968), 218.

13. Joseph R. Smith, "Sanitary Report, Department of Arkansas, from its Organization to 31 December 1864," manuscript C126, Surgeon General's Office, Manuscript Collections, National Library of Medicine, Bethesda, Md., 10.

14. Samuel K. Towle, "Notes of Practice in the U.S.A. General Hospital, Baton Rouge, La., during the Year 1863," *Boston Medical and Surgical Journal* 70 (1864): 60.

Chapter 20. The Last Full Measure of Devotion

1. All of the patients described in this chapter are abstracted from the Surgical Volume of the *MSH*.

2. Phoebe Yates Pember, *A Southern Woman's Story: Life in Confederate Richmond* (New York: G. W. Carleton, 1879).

3. Edgar E. Hume, "Chimborazo Hospital, Confederate States Army, America's Largest Military Hospital," *Virginia Medical Monthly* 61 (1934): 189–95.

Chapter 21. Aftermath

1. The most detailed description of the medical aspects of Lincoln's death is by John K. Lattimer, *Kennedy and Lincoln: Medical and Ballistic Comparisons of Their Assassinations* (New York: Harcourt Brace Jovanovich, 1980), 21–38. From his review of the clinical descriptions, Dr. Lattimer thinks that Dr. Woodward meant to say that he recovered the bullet from the right cerebral hemisphere, not the left. This author agrees. Leale, Taft, and others all recorded their actions during and reactions to that horrible night; these descriptions are discussed by Milton H. Shutes, *Lincoln and the Doctors: A Medical Narrative of the Life of Abraham Lincoln* (New York: Pioneer Press, 1933). A modern neurosurgeon has argued that excessive search for the ball may have hastened death; see Richard A. R. Fraser, "How Did Lincoln Die?" *American Heritage* 46 (Feb./March 1995), 63–70. Most physicians, including this author, who have compared the arguments of Lattimer and Fraser, think that nothing could have been done to save Lincoln once the lead ball entered his brain. More conservative therapy, without searching for the missile, would at best have prolonged his life a few hours. If Hammond had been

present instead of Barnes, the outcome would have been no different.

2. Stephen E. Payne Diary, Illinois State Historical Library, Springfield, 10.

3. Salecker, Gene Eric *Disaster on the Mississippi: The Sultana Explosion, April 27, 1865* (Annapolis Md.: Naval Institute Press, 1996).

4. Reginald Horsman, *Josiah Nott of Mobile: Southerner, Physician, and Racial Theorist* (Baton Rouge: Louisiana State University Press, 1987).

5. J. J. Woodward, *Report on Epidemic Cholera in the Army of the United States During the Year 1866,* (Circular Number 5, Surgeon General's Office, 4 May 1867, Washington, D.C.: Government Printing Office, 1867). The 1866 epidemic occurring in 1864 would also have afflicted the Confederate army, but two armies crippled by illness most often sink into a stalemate. One medical historian thinks that a cholera epidemic "at any time during the war could have ended hostilities in a matter of weeks." Gordon W. Jones, "Sanitation in the Civil War," *Civil War Times Illustrated* 5 (November 1966): 12–18.

6. David T. Courtwright has advanced the hypothesis that the difficulty in America with narcotic addiction that has continued to this day began with the excessive use of morphine during the Civil War, particularly with the injection of morphine at Turner's Lane Hospital. See "Opiate Addiction as a Consequence of the Civil War," *Civil War History* 24 (1978): 101–11; and "The Hidden Epidemic: Opiate Addiction and Cocaine Use in the South, 1860–1920," *Journal of Southern History* 49 (1983): 57–72.

7. "The Case of George Dedlow," *The Atlantic Monthly* 28 (July 1866): 1–11.

8. *MSH*, Surgical Volume, pt. 3, p. 68.

9. *MSH*, Surgical Volume, pt. 3, p. 115.

10. Anne L. Austin, *The Woolsey Sisters of New York: A Family's Involvement in the Civil War and a New Profession, 1860–1900* (Philadelphia: American Philosophical Society, 1917).

11. Vesta M. W. Swarts, in Mary A. Gardner Holland, *Our Army Nurses* (Boston: Lounsbery, Nichols, and Worth, 1897).

12. James L. Stone, "W. W. Keen: America's Pioneer Neurological Surgeon," *Neurosurgery* 17 (1985): 997–1010.

13. Edwin S. Gaillard, *The Medical and Surgical Lessons of the Late War* (Louisville Ky.: Louisville Journal Job Print, 1868). Other medical and surgical advances were not apparent for many years. Bonnie Blustein thought the major new development was the authority of a medical elite over medical practice, including the concept of judging physicians by giving them a test: "To Increase the Efficiency of the Medical Department," *Civil War History* 33 (1987): 22–41. F. William Blaisdell pointed to the system for handling mass casualties, the pavilion style of hospital construction which continued through World War II, and the introduction and acceptance of female nurses: "Medical Advances during the Civil War," *Archives of Surgery* 123 (1988): 1045–50. The discoveries at Turner's Lane Hospital were a key development in modern neuroscience; for a discussion of this issue see Frank R. Freemon, "The First Neurological Research Center: Turner's Lane Hospital during the American Civil War," *Journal of the History of the Neurosciences* 2 (1993): 135–42.

14. Khaled J. Bloom, *The Mississippi Valley's Great Yellow Fever Epidemic of 1878* (Baton Rouge: Louisiana State University Press, 1993). See also Margaret Humphreys, *Yellow Fever and the South* (New Brunswick, N.J.: Rutgers University Press, 1992).

15. Colman McCarthy, "Manassas Battlefield is Not Worth Protecting." *Washington Post*, 24 July 1988, sec. C, p. 8.

16. Suzanne V. McIntosh, "Competitive to the Last, Aged Union and Confederate Veterans Vied to See Who Would Live the Longest," *America's Civil War* 4 (September 1991), 61.

17. Morris Fishbein, *A History of the American Medical Association, 1847 to 1947* (Philadelphia: W. B. Saunders, 1947), appendix.

18. Silas Weir Mitchell, "The Medical Department in the Civil War." *Journal of the American Medical Association* 62 (1914): 1445–50.

Chapter 22. The American Civil War as a Biological Phenomenon

1. Simon Baruch, "Two Cases of Penetrating Bayonet Wounds of the Chest." *Confederate States Medical and Surgical Journal* 1 (1864): 133–34.

2. The best description of the microbiological aspects of diarrhea in the Civil War soldier is Alfred Jay Bollet, "To Care for Him That Has Borne the Battle: A Medical History of the Civil War," *Medical Times* 117 (April 1989): 121–26, (May 1989):101–8; and (October 1989): 74–80. Diarrhea remains a problem for modern armies; see Buhari A. Oyofo, Atef El-Gendy, Momtaz O. Wasfy, et al., "A Survey of Enteropathogens among United States Military Personnel during Operation Bright Star '94, in Cairo, Egypt," *Military Medicine* 160 (1995): 331–34.

3. William W. Gerhard, "On the Typhus Fever, Which Occurred at Philadelphia in the Spring and Summer of 1836," *American Journal of Medical Science* 19 (1837): 289–92.

4. James I. Robertson Jr., *Soldiers Blue and Gray* (Columbia: University of South Carolina Press, 1988), 157.

5. Jonathan Letterman, *Medical Recollections of the Army of the Potomac* (New York, D. Appleton, 1866), 148.

6. An additional diagnosis, typhomalarial fever, was introduced by J. J. Woodward in his book, *Outline of the Chief Camp Diseases of the United States Armies*. This was an apparent hybrid of typhoid fever and malaria, but analysis of the condition late in the century showed that most patients had only typhoid fever. This was an infrequent diagnosis and for statistical analysis this work discarded these few patients. For the ups and downs of this diagnosis, see Mary C. Gillett, "A Tale of Two Surgeons," *Medical Heritage* 1 (1985): 404–13.

7. Erwin H. Ackerknecht, *Malaria in the Upper Mississippi Valley, 1790–1900* (Baltimore: Johns Hopkins University Press, 1945).

8. Mark F. Boyd, "An Historical Sketch of the Prevalence of Malaria in North America," *American Journal of Tropical Medicine* 21 (1941): 223–44.

9. Yellow fever in the Southern United States during the nineteenth century has been reviewed by Margaret Humphreys, *Yellow Fever and the South* (New Brunswick, N.J.: Rutgers University Press, 1992).

10. A review written in 1867 makes reference to over forty publications in American journals that seem to represent at least ten separate outbreaks of meningococcal

meningitis. See Alfred Stillé, *Epidemic Meningitis, or Cerebro-spinal Meningitis* (Philadelphia: Lindsay and Blakiston, 1867).

11. How immunity to subtypes of the meningococcus relates to the epidemics that occur when large numbers of people congregate is discussed by Patrick S. Moore, "Meningococcal Meningitis in Sub-Saharan Africa: A Model for the Epidemic Process," *Clinical Infectious Disease* 14 (1992): 515–25.

12. The development of immunization against the organism that causes meningococcal meningitis is described by Harry A. Feldman, "The Meningococcus: A Twenty-Year Perspective," *Reviews of Infectious Disease* 8 (1986): 288–94.

13. *OR*, vol. 19, pt. 2, p. 657.

14. Roberts Bartholow, "Synopsis of a Report upon Camp Measles, Based upon an Analysis of One Hundred Cases, Made to the Surgeon-General," *American Medical Times* 8 (1864): 231–32, 242–44.

15. A personal experience shows that immunological isolation could still occur in the United States many decades after the Civil War. At age six, I developed mumps. When I was getting over it, my father, A. Lyle Freemon, who had spent his childhood in rural Illinois, developed parotid swelling. The doctor diagnosed mumps with humorous comments how a man had contracted the disease from his son. My father spent the next two weeks in bed listening to funeral music; President Roosevelt had just died.

16. Ann G. Carmichael, "Erysipelas," in *The Cambridge History of Human Disease*, ed. Kenneth F. Kiple (New York: Cambridge University Press, 1993), 720–721.

17. Frank L. Meleney, *Treatise on Surgical Infections* (New York: Oxford University Press, 1948), 12–17 and 437–69; Alfred Jay Bollet, "Flesh-Eating Bacteria: A Major Civil War Disease Returns," *Resident and Staff Physician* 8 (July 1994): 11–13.

18. Paul F. Eve, "Report of Eight Cases of Lithotomy Performed during the War," *Nashville Journal of Medicine and Surgery* 1 (1866): 136.

19. Alfred Jay Bollet, "Scurvy, Sprue, and Starvation: Major Nutritional Syndromes During the Civil War," *Medical Times* 117 (November 1989): 69–74, and 118 (June 1990), 39–44.

20. John K. Stevens, "Hostages to Hunger: Nutritional Night Blindness in Confederate Armies," *Tennessee Historical Quarterly* 48 (1989): 131–43.

21. "The symptoms of pellagra as known now are identically those of a large number of cases that occurred at Andersonville," writes the surgeon who had been in charge of the Andersonville prison hospital. W. J. W. Kerr, "Pellagra and Hookworm at Andersonville," *Confederate Veteran* 18 (1910): 69.

22. "The Civil War was fought too soon," concludes a modern expert on infection, "only 10 years later, the death toll from disease might have been a mere fraction of what it was." Jeffery S. Sartin, "Infectious Disease During the Civil War: The Triumph of the Third Army," *Clinical Infectious Diseases* 16 (1993): 580–84.

CHAPTER 23. COMPARING NORTHERN TO SOUTHERN MEDICAL CARE

1. Edmund Andrews, "Hospital Gangrene." *Chicago Medical Examiner* 2 (1861): 515–16.

2. John Hooker Packard, *A Manual of Minor Surgery* (Philadelphia: J. B. Lippincott, 1863).

3. John G. Miller, "Application of Iodine for Arresting the Spread of Hospital Gangrene," *American Journal of the Medical Sciences* 62 (1871): 573.

4. My childhood is punctuated by the pain of iodine liberally applied by my mother upon each of my minor cuts and abrasions.

5. See the discussion by Samuel L. Abbot, "Air-space in Hospitals," *Boston Medical and Surgical Journal* 67 (1873): 403.

6. Edmund Andrews, G. H. Hubbard, and Rufus H. Gilbert, "Report of the Committee on Military Hygiene," *American Medical Association Transactions* 15 (1864): 167–81.

7. The modern treatment of combat wounds is reviewed by Dan Michaeli, "Medicine on the Battlefield: A Review," *Journal of the Royal Society of Medicine* 72 (1979): 370–73; and Richard D. Forrest, "Development of Wound Therapy from the Dark Ages to the Present," *Journal of the Royal Society of Medicine* 75 (1982): 268–73.

8. Wound mortality is, in epidemiological terms, the case fatality ratio. The savings in lives by the decrease in this number is easily calculated. The total number of wounded during the War is multiplied by the wound mortality during the first year of the War. This gives the number of soldiers who would have died from wounds if that first year rate had remained constant. From this one subtracts the number who actually died from wounds. The difference is the number who would have died from wounds if the first year mortality had continued. This type of counterfactual thinking is sometimes difficult for people in the humanities. A history journal editor forced the insertion of the word probably in a sentence that claims that this calculation gives "an overall savings of 25,928 men who survived the war after being wounded but who *probably* would have died if the mortality rate had remained at its first year level." This is the same logic as in the famous syllogism:

> All men are mortal.
> Socrates is a man.
> Therefore, Socrates is probably mortal.

9. John H. Brinton, *Consolidated Statement of Gunshot Wounds* (Washington, D.C.: Government Printing Office, 1863).

10. For the military use of the partially disabled, see Gary L. Todd, "An Invalid Corps: Will the Wounded Serve?" *Civil War Times Illustrated* 24 (December 1985): 10–19.

11. Jonathan Letterman, *Medical Recollections of the Army of the Potomac* (New York, Appleton, 1866), 99–100.

12. An anonymous reviewer pointed out that quinine does not actually prevent malaria, but kills the circulating parasite after the infection has occurred; quinine, technically, is a curative rather than a preventative agent. Nevertheless, quinine prophylaxis, when done correctly, prevented the symptoms of malaria and kept the army fit to fight.

13. This does not really mean that forty out of every one hundred soldiers had malaria. The ratio of the sick (with malaria) during the year to the total number of soldiers in the army was not forty to one hundred. Rather, some people had malaria more than once. The actual ratio is the number of instances when malaria was diagnosed to the total strength of the army during

the year. Nevertheless, this calculation permits a year to year comparison.

14. *OR*, ser. 4, vol. 3, p. 402.

15. *OR*, ser. 4, vol. 2, p. 1024.

16. Francis Peyre Porcher, "Confederate Surgeons," *Southern Historical Society Papers* 17 (1889): 12–21.

17. However, some wounded soldiers went directly from the battlefield to the hospital, without registering with the regimental authorities, so that they appear in the hospital admission numbers but not the list of sick persons in the field.

18. "Grand Summary of the Sick and Wounded of the Confederate States Army under Treatment during the Years 1861 and 1862." *Confederate States Medical and Surgical Journal* 1 (1864): 139–40.

19. The most careful analysis of deaths within the Union army was performed by Frederick Phisterer, *Statistical Record of the Armies of the United States* (New York: Charles Scribner's Sons, 1883). For the entire War, he calculated these fatalities:

Killed in action	44,238
Died of wounds	49,205
Died of disease	186,216
Died, unknown cause	24,184
Other (execution, homicide, suicide)	526
Total deaths, Union army	304,369

A total of 280,185 men died of known cause; of these 186,216 or 66.5 percent died of disease.

Chapter 24. Did Medical Care Make a Difference?

1. Hugh Brogan, *Longman's History of the United States of America* (London: Longman, 1985), 331.

2. The best reviews of the military balance between North and South are by Herman Hattaway and Archer Jones, *How the North Won: A Military History of the Civil War* (Urbana, University of Illinois Press, 1983); and by Richard E. Beringer, H. Hattaway, A. Jones, and William N. Still Jr., *Why the South Lost the Civil War* (Athens: University of Georgia Press, 1986).

3. James M. McPherson, *The Battle Cry of Freedom: The Civil War Era* (New York: Oxford University Press, 1988), 857–58.

4. Gordon W. Jones, "The Medical History of the Fredericksburg Campaign: Course and Significance." *Journal of the History of Medicine and Allied Sciences* 18 (1963): 241–56.

5. Horace H. Cunningham, *Field Medical Services at the Battles of Manassas (Bull Run)* (Athens: University of Georgia Press, 1962).

6. *OR*, vol. 25, pt. 2, p. 790. One may note that Lee's medical observations were made from his own experience without consultation with medical authorities.

7. James O. Breeden was the first to argue that better Confederate medical care might have saved Atlanta: "A Medical History of the Later Stages of the Atlanta Campaign," *Journal of Southern History* 35 (1969): 31–59.

8. J. H. Mathes, *General Forrest* (New York: D. Appleton, 1902), 383.

9. Harris D. Riley Jr. "Medical Furloughs in the Confederate States Army," *Journal of Confederate History* 2 (1989): 115–31.

10. Walter D. Farr, "Samuel Preston Moore: Confederate Surgeon General," *Civil War History* 41 (1995): 41–56. The other noncabinet faces on Confederate bonds were John H. Winder, after whom Winder hospital was named, and P. G. T. Beauregard.

11. Bonnie Ellen Blustein, *Preserve Your Love for Science: Life of William A. Hammond, American Neurologist* (New York, Cambridge University Press, 1991). See also my article, "The First Career of William Alexander Hammond," *Journal of the History of the Neurosciences* 5 (1996):282–7.

12. Hammond had asked that he receive no retirement benefits in order to improve the likelihood that his reputation would be rehabilitated. Late in life, he suffered financial misfortune and asked for benefits, but he died before any action was taken. The complex events that led to the reversal of the court martial verdict are well described by Mark D. Miller, "William A. Hammond: Restoring the Reputation of a Surgeon General," *Military Medicine* 152 (1987): 452–57.

Index of Names

Subject Index